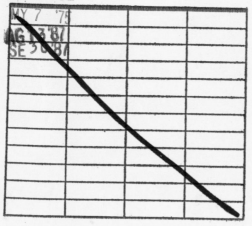

Books by Shirley Hazzard

Cliffs of Fall
The Evening of the Holiday
People in Glass Houses
The Bay of Noon
Defeat of an Ideal

DEFEAT OF AN IDEAL

DEFEAT OF AN IDEAL

A Study of the Self-Destruction
of the United Nations

BY *SHIRLEY HAZZARD*

AN ATLANTIC MONTHLY PRESS BOOK
Little, Brown and Company—Boston—Toronto

FIRST EDITION

T 03/73

The author wishes to thank the following for permission to reprint material:

The Macmillan Company, New York. *In the Cause of Peace: Seven Years with the United Nations* by Trygve Lie, 1954. Copyright, 1954, by Trygve Lie.

Alfred A. Knopf, Inc., and Faber & Faber, Ltd. *Markings* by Dag Hammarskjöld, translated by W. H. Auden and Leif Sjöberg. Translation copyright © 1964 by Alfred A. Knopf, Inc., and Faber and Faber, Ltd. Foreword copyright © 1964 by W. H. Auden.

Doubleday & Company, Inc., and Cassell & Company, Ltd. *Dag Hammarskjold: Custodian of the Brushfire Peace* by Joseph P. Lash, copyright © 1961 by Joseph P. Lash.

Saturday Review. "What's Wrong at the United Nations" by Hugh L. Keenleyside. June 19, 1971. Copyright © 1971 by Saturday Review, Inc.

ATLANTIC—LITTLE, BROWN BOOKS
ARE PUBLISHED BY
LITTLE, BROWN AND COMPANY
IN ASSOCIATION WITH
THE ATLANTIC MONTHLY PRESS

Library of Congress Cataloging in Publication Data

Hazzard, Shirley, 1931–
  Defeat of an ideal.

"An Atlantic Monthly Press book."
Includes bibliographical references.
  1. United Nations. I. Title.
JX1977.H38   341.23   72-3783
ISBN 0-316-35266-7

Published simultaneously in Canada by Little, Brown & Company (Canada) Limited

PRINTED IN THE UNITED STATES OF AMERICA

". . . only on a scrutiny of truth can a future of peace be built."

—Dag Hammarskjöld to the
United Nations General Assembly,
3 October 1960

Contents

CONTENTS

Preface

The United Nations concept is often said to be new: rather, it is as ancient as human reason, and as primitive as the instincts of conciliation and self-preservation. The United Nations Organization, on the other hand, as realized in the present body, is almost thirty years old. In the history of the universe, that span is as nothing; in the story of nations it is much; in government, as in individual life, it may be everything. Two or three decades can encompass the rise and fall of a Napoleon or a Hitler, the lifework of a Raphael or Schubert, the lifetime of a Keats. Much is now known, or at least is discernible, about the evolution of the present United Nations body: that is to say that there is evidence of both the extent to which it has departed from the United Nations concept, and the manner of its failure.

Less apparent, and commonly speculated upon in abstractions, are the causes of the United Nations' deterioration. Yet no such decline merely springs into independent being; nor can there be reversal of it without full knowledge, and acknowledgment, of cause. This book has been undertaken because formative and self-destructive experiences, of which an understanding is imperative to any assessment or reform of the present organization, have been largely excluded or suppressed from the many siftings, public and private, of United Nations affairs; and, with the passage of a generation, seem to be in danger of obliteration from any contemporary record of cause, although their consequences lie at the heart of United Nations incapacity.

What is publicly called "the United Nations" is formed, on the one hand, by the national delegations of over one hundred thirty member nations, seasonally augmented for the General Assembly and analogous UN conventions, meeting to present their respective official views and recommendations for action on political, economic, and social questions; and on the other by the international staff of the United Nations Secretariat, a civil service that numbers thirty-five thousand in UN agencies around the world and employs tens of thousands of temporary personnel in advisory capacities

The first of these categories, the governmental, comprises the public life of the Organization — a political expression that would manifest itself, even if the present United Nations did not exist, in the world events which are the object of our obsessive attention, and in some forms of intergovernmental negotiation. It is frequently said that the United Nations is nothing more than the governments represented in it. Nevertheless, despite many disillusionments, the peoples of the world have never fully renounced the expectation that deliberations in United Nations councils would render, as was implicit in the Organization's founding, something more than an airing of national intransigencies, and provide a more potent and positive form of mediation than could otherwise be achieved.

The second category, the institutional, is, so to speak, the private life of the United Nations Organization. The distinction, and relation, between the two seem scarcely to be made in the public mind; and are defined empirically, according to the issue, by United Nations officials themselves. There is, too, a fusion in the public mind between the constitutional principles and professed goals of the United Nations, and the Organization's actual practices. This fusion, and confusion, has precluded the application of serious — and, in some cases, even minimal — standards to United Nations operations and procedures. There can be no question as to the necessity and worth of stated United Nations objectives, just as there can be no doubt as to the indispensability of some form of realization of the United Nations concept; there can, equally, be no doubt that these objectives are being defeated by the manner in which the present body executes, or claims to execute, them.

It is not my purpose here, in dwelling on the interior nature and experience of the United Nations, to minimize or overlook the vast political forces at work or in abeyance there; but rather to trace a more intricate relation between the two than has yet been suggested, and to depict a set of reciprocal, and mutually destructive, repercussions. Nor is it the intention, in accounting for aspects of the failure of the current United Nations, to catalogue a series of isolated deficiencies, or pretend to expert or detailed knowledge of the Organization's many undertakings; but instead to show how the present body — and the *basis* on which it conducts all its operations — has been to a large extent shaped by a continuity of events and attitudes which, unlike the much-chronicled political developments, has not so far as I know been drawn to public attention.

Had there been a show of authentic corrective impulse, or even of accessibility, in the ranks of United Nations authority, there would have been no need for this book. Nothing here, however, is directed to any response, hostile or favorable, from those quarters: *all is addressed to the public that brought the United Nations into being, and on whom alone the Organization's immense potential depends for fulfillment.* Certain crucial issues are dealt with at length; other, contingent ones are summarized or merely touched upon. It is to be hoped that full exploration of all avenues leading to the United Nations' present condition will be undertaken eventually, not in a spirit of retribution or piety but from the need to salvage invaluable knowledge from an historic and complex human experience, towards the reconstitution of the United Nations in an active body. The multiplicity of factors leading to the Organization's present extremity has been one of the deterrents to an understanding of it: yet even these can be seen as an interaction of consequences, ultimately attributable to specific and dramatic human causes.

It is precisely the predicament of the present body that produces, for the first time, an opportunity for a revitalized and radically different United Nations. Anyone who makes, as does the present author, the assertion that this must come about through the insistence of the peoples of the world, and that the current organization, through severe and often self-inflicted internal injuries, has made itself inaccessible to reform, will be accused — by those he holds responsible — of disrespect to the United Nations idea. He might bear in mind the response of Igor Stravinsky to persons who, long ago, accused him, in his *Pulcinella* transposition, of disrespect to the genius of Pergolesi: *"You respect. I love."*

No separate bibliography is appended to the reference notes that conclude this volume. While reference is made, in the text and in the notes, to many books and papers that have been specifically cited, it will be seen that a vast body of documentation figures, as it were, as a leading character in the narrative. It is my hope that any reader wishing to study in full the documentary evidence supporting the events chronicled here, and my conclusions regarding them, will find all sources clearly indicated.

During a twenty years' interest in the fortunes of the United Nations, including ten years' employment at its headquarters, I have read tens of thousands of United Nations documents, both perforce and by choice: of these, some have contributed directly, some indirectly, still others inadvertently, to the present work; and all may be said to have made their collective, and cumulative, impression. As this work is an account of human affairs, however, many papers and books other than the "official" have had a bearing on it; and many sources other than the documentary have been drawn upon, the first of these being experience.

Similarly, in expressing gratitude to persons who have helped me, I prefer to offer this general tribute. Invaluable assistance was given me by dedicated members in contrasting positions on the United Nations staff who have never lost their grasp of, or belief in, the United Nations concept; and these should be foremost in any list of my acknowledgments. The reader of these pages will discover why such an enumeration is impossible.

DEFEAT OF AN IDEAL

One.

The Tunnel of Love

The United States' role in the inception and shaping of the United Nations is, in capsule, the story of America. The attitudes of the United States government and people towards the United Nations enterprise have been successively, and even simultaneously, touching and maddening, positive and destructive, superficial and profound. It should be said at once that there might well have been no United Nations Organization but for the American people. While the United States authorities were leaders in the UN's formulation, any great embarkation — whether it be a marriage or the inauguration of a nation or an idea — requires more than proponents: it requires passion. And the heartfelt enthusiasm of the American public for the United Nations venture launched in the opera house at San Francisco in June 1945, far from being misplaced, was in a sense what made its creation possible. No such undertaking could conceivably have got under way without an impetus of public approval, and that approval was provided by the people of the United States.

Other continents were battlefields on which the carnage of the Second World War had barely ceased, or still continued,

3

and where enthusiasm had been, to say the least, depleted; if in some instances human ideals had been heroically upheld, for the most part they had received a battering which, coming on that of the First World War, was to send them into what now seems chronic invalidism. Of the other great powers, only Britain — where the first United Nations General Assembly convened, in London, in January 1946 — showed widespread public interest in the new body. Postwar Russia, in the terminal stage of Stalinism, seemed scarcely to know what to make of its membership in the United Nations — a situation which in many ways persists today. In France there was apathy and detachment, along with intelligent exceptions; and even some antipathy — as later, when de Gaulle was largely to ignore the Organization, referring to it as *"ce machin."* In general, the United Nations idea was taken seriously in other countries; but postwar emergencies of starvation and of economic and political collapse were uppermost. It was in the United States that the United Nations was floated, and on warm waves of emotion.

The entertainment of high hopes is essential to human life. Human beings must believe their species capable of disinterested goodness, even if they look for the proof of this in others. Those who flatter themselves that they are showing tolerance by claiming that, given the circumstances, they — and by implication the rest of us — would act just as an Eichmann or a Calley has done, refuse for themselves and others even the possibility of a being that is not either bestial or psychotic: what they are in effect saying is, "We're only inhuman." Civilized history gives us repeated examples of natures that did not avail themselves of this false indulgence; in fact, they form the favorable part of it. If one cannot attain to that high standard, the least one can do is to be disappointed in oneself. For the United Nations to come into existence, it was necessary for a large body of persons to believe in the human capacity for good, and to feel that their hopes might be justified.

Maturity might be said to be an understanding of the conditions in which hope can be sustained and fulfilled. With reference to the United Nations it must be said that the American public, in this respect, has — with private exceptions — shown no signs of maturity whatever. And that the people of the world in general have done no better, though distance and detachment have rendered their omission both less noticeable and less influential. In the fairground of public attitudes, the United Nations has traveled the wheels and slippery-dips and switchbacks, has been embraced in the tunnel of love and buffeted on the dodgems. Very little of this treatment, whether hostile or sympathetic, has had authentic relation to the reality of the United Nations either as it might have been or as it has developed. A deep, intelligent understanding of what the UN would face, and what kinds of support it must have if it were to be effectual was at no time inculcated upon the public either by UN dignitaries or by world leaders in America or elsewhere. This is not to suggest that governments themselves possessed such an understanding: evidence points to the contrary. Senator J. W. Fulbright has written that "Franklin Roosevelt's project was consigned to the care of unsympathetic men of his own country. . . . Among these, so far as I know, none was a strong supporter of the plan for a world organization."

When congressional approval was requied for American acceptance of the United Nations Charter as a treaty, the presentation was made with a mingling of cynicism and sentimentality. Dean Acheson, then the Under Secretary of State assigned to lobby for the Charter's passage, later asserted: "I did my duty faithfully and successfully, but always believed the Charter was impractical." On the other hand, the United Nations had been so thoroughly acknowledged as unexceptionable "good works" that there was a danger of its scarcely being discussed in the Senate; at the last moment Senator Tom Connally was seen walking round the Senate floor imploring senators to speak on behalf of the United Nations lest an impression of congressional indifference be created. At that moment the United Nations was regarded in official circles at

5

worst as — in Acheson's still later designation of it — "bunk"; and at best as an uncontroversial philanthropic specter (to which the immediate postwar relief efforts of UNRRA lent substance), enjoying public goodwill and, in the political mind, a rating of the "motherhood" variety.

One generation only had passed since the United States had spurned the League of Nations; and an informed international outlook, or even the lip service to international outlook we now have in high places, was rare among America's elected representatives of the 1940's. Undoubtedly there were those who without success urged more profound contemplation of the UN's future; and certainly there were those who recognized the United Nations' potential well enough to wish to limit or incapacitate it, both in outright and in covert ways. These last should not, for their cognizance, be accorded even pejorative stature as Machiavellian manipulators of our destiny (though the provincial rulers exhorted in *De principatibus* were possibly as limited in their thinking): theirs was the most parochial and shortsighted approach of all, and ultimately the most self-defeating.

The reader of these pages will find that the expression "self-defeating" recurs.

The report of the 1946 United Nations Headquarters Commission is a touching, if embarrassing, testimony to postwar dreams of a utopian United Nations community embodying spiritual leadership and disseminating harmony throughout the family of man. The offer of an American site had been — predictably — contested; and — predictably — accepted; and the United States, being by far the major provider of funds, energy, and goodwill, dominated the United Nations' infancy, acting as both good and bad fairy at the christening. A nursery was laid out, toys were provided; siblings were spawned, in the form of affiliated UN agencies in specialized fields (of health, of culture, of agriculture, and so on), and in due course a resemblance to the parents was discerned. The great nation that had refused to join the League of Nations became host to the United Nations. Fifty-one national delegations arrived in New York to represent their governments at the new body. "We don't want this to go the way of the League" was the cry, and insufficient attempt was made to study, *humanly rather than legalistically*, the brief career of that doomed antecedent;* a pity, as there are no lessons like those of failure.

What was withheld, of course, was authority. The seventeenth-century French monk Eméric Crucé, in his work *Le Nouveau Cynée* proposing a world assembly analogous to the present United Nations, makes its success contingent upon its "powers of compulsion." Powers of compulsion were not invested in the United Nations Organization, except in so far as they might reside in the very members most likely to need compelling.† And a more subtle, though closely related and equally important, denial of authority was the — largely intentional, in part inadvertent — withholding of quality. Evidence and effect of the first of these deprivations, that of authority, is charted every day in the world's newspapers and has already been the subject of countless articles, studies, and books. It is the second — less readily traced, generally minimized or ignored, and publicly apparent only in its cumulative manifestations — that is the central theme of this book.

Had the world's great postwar powers intended that the new United Nations should make independent, moral judgments in

* It will be said that the incorporation of the League's experience into the legal being of the United Nations is of prime importance. However, no provision was made against a situation — which almost instantly arose, and for which the League's history provided tragic precedent — where the legal safeguards guaranteed by the Charter and by other United Nations statutes, would be openly violated as the result of a conspiracy between the Secretary-General and the Organization's most powerful member state, while the other member nations impotently looked on.

† In 1919, John Maynard Keynes accurately forecast, in his *Economic Consequences of the Peace*, that the similar denial of authority to the League of Nations by the great powers would reduce the League to "a body merely for wasting time . . . an unequalled instrument for obstruction and delay . . . an unwieldy polyglot debating society . . . with an almost fatal bias towards the *status quo*."

accordance with its Charter and take forceful action on them, they would, in nominating nationals to hold high international office there, have proposed men with commensurate abilities. Their negligence in this respect, on the contrary, did much to ensure that *the Organization itself* would never unpleasantly surprise them by a show of character, tenacity and principle that would bind them to their own public declarations.

The international United Nations Secretariat (as distinct from the fifty-one original national delegations) was overstaffed at the outset; and its leading positions filled, with a few exceptions, by persons of average endowments not practiced in wielding strong influence or even necessarily widely experienced in administration and public life. To have determined it should be otherwise would have involved an act of faith that member governments had little inclination for. In devastated Europe — or for example in India, which was preparing for partition and independence — outstanding abilities were at a premium, to be hoarded at home rather than exported to an untried institution of no immediate value. The United States was disinclined to provide the unknown quantity with high brainpower; and the first Secretary-General of the United Nations was later to complain loudly of the lack of American cooperation in this respect.

The appointment of Trygve Lie as first Secretary-General gives the impression of having been picked out of a hat. (That in itself, given the customary results of more elaborate rituals of official appointment, was not necessarily a bad thing.) He himself declared that the possibility "had not entered my head. . . . I had been nothing less than catapulted into the Secretary-Generalship. . . . Why had this awesome task fallen to a labour lawyer from Norway?"* The task had fallen, and the choice was made — as so many United Nations appointments were to

* Of his previous, far less significant, candidacy for presidency of the first UN General Assembly, Lie stated: "It seemed to me that presiding over the General Assembly of the United Nations would demand a profound experience in international relations and an expertness in the languages of diplomacy — qualifications I could not claim."

be made — according to paper requirements, with little regard to the living person.

What was wanted was a national of a country that had suffered in the war and had conducted itself well in its tribulation; a country with high standards of tolerance and justice, and advanced domestic policies. It was too soon for a Swede, Sweden having been neutral in the war, and a Swiss was out of the question for reasons of that country's permanent neutrality (Switzerland has never become a member of the United Nations, since membership would involve her in political commitments to world issues; but a number of UN agencies have their headquarters in Swiss cities, and Switzerland continually gives hospitality to UN conferences). But some measure of detachment, however nominal, from big-power blocs must at least be implied in order to gain the acceptance of the Soviet member nations.

Lie had been a member of the Norwegian cabinet since the 1930's and Norway's Foreign Minister-in-exile during the war. He was a weak man, but his weakness was of the kind accompanied by bombast, truculence, and self-dramatization. His own memoirs, *In the Cause of Peace*, are the best index to the temperament and capacities of this disappointing figure: boastful, mawkish, vulgar, and essentially trivial, their most important emanation as regards the United Nations is the inability of their author to grasp the international nature of the organization he headed for eight years. Here is Mr. Lie on the subject of Communism: "I had fought the Communists all my life in the Norwegian trade unions and labour movement and fought them successfully." It may be imagined what confidence the Soviet member states — or for that matter any other country — might retrospectively feel, on reading those words, in the objectivity of their Secretary-General.

Just as the United States concept of the "international" was — as it continues to be — at best a sort of benign unilateralism through which American policies would work uncontested for everybody's benefit (a parochial concept inherent in the very expression "town meeting of the world" coined by the late Senator Vandenberg and invoked by every United States ambassador to the UN since), Trygve Lie's was limited to what the word had meant in his national vocabulary.

Appealed to for recruits to this new legion, governments seldom sent their best (and sometimes sent their worst — just as the United Nations itself was later, on occasion, to send its own incompetents out on field missions to be rid of them). There was calculation in this, even by default — and governments were in fact quite right in sensing that a high-caliber UN Secretariat might influence world events in unlooked-for ways, as was later to be demonstrated in the case of Dag Hammarskjöld. Within this general restriction, muddle prevailed.

Applications were also made independently by persons of many nationalities who wished, often from altruism, to work in the new organization. Of these applicants, those without governmental associations were mostly recruited at the junior levels and of course were of infinitely varied character and qualifications — many of them neither equipped with governmental training nor inhibited by bureaucratic conditioning. Some who might have been recruited as minor officials arrived in time to fill a geographical need (to help provide, that is, a diversity of nationalities in the upper grades) and were whizzed to the top — where, it need hardly be said, they clung on for dear life. The residual staff of the postwar international relief operations found its way to the throng that was gradually established, first at Hunter College, then at Lake Success, before settling, throughout 1951, into the new headquarters on the East River.

It may be said therefore that the United Nations Secretariat was formed under a Secretary-General of significant limitations, and with little regard beyond lip service to the quality of its personnel or to the suitability of launching a new organization with a complement of several thousand staff of largely unsifted possibilities who were to perform largely unspecified functions. Within five years of its inauguration, the UN Secretariat had a New York staff of 3,300, of whom only 1,000 were said to have responsible professional duties. (By comparison, although UN staff in affiliated offices overseas has burgeoned enormously, the New York Headquarters total was approximately 8,200 in 1972,* and generally agreed to be heavily overstaffed; about thirty per cent of the present "Professional" staff were recruited during the first five years of the United Nations' existence.)

Stranger things have, however, happened than that such an unpromising situation might still have turned itself to good. The outcome of human affairs cannot always be ordained by politicians, and even the road to heaven may contain a few slabs of bad intention. In all categories of the United Nations Secretariat, many had joined from idealism, and there is something to be said for a mixed bag. The *ranks* of the Secretariat staff in the early years included a number of gifted and distinguished persons, most of whom were to be deliberately driven out of the Organization by 1953, by means and for motives that will be seen.

By far the predominant element, numerically, authoritatively, and psychologically, in the Secretariat was that of the United States, many American employees having come from government careers in Washington or elsewhere, many others being known as "local recruits" — that is, staff in the lower grades who had not been recruited on an international basis but had simply turned up at United Nations Headquarters asking for employment. The Assistant Secretary-General (as Under-Secretaries-General were then called) for Administrative and Financial Services, Mr. Byron Price, an American, had been Director of the United States Office of Censorship during the war, having had a previous incarnation as an executive of the Associated Press: in coming to the United Nations he — as

* Official figures for United Nations Headquarters staff greatly vary according to the activities and departments included. The above is a comprehensive figure that excludes, however, approximately 1,200 Headquarters personnel temporarily on duty in UN field missions.

Trygve Lie tells us — "left a much higher salary with the Association of Motion Picture Producers." These are unexpected qualifications for the most senior administrative post in the United Nations international secretariat short of the Secretary-Generalship itself. (Price was subsequently, in Lie's absence abroad, designated Acting Secretary-General.) The United Nations "Chief Security Officer," also an American, had trained with the FBI.

The official terms and concepts of United Nations employment, for the junior — and major — portion of the staff, to a large extent followed the basic tenets of municipal employment in New York itself.* The Bureau of Personnel was heavily staffed with United States citizens, many of them women; and the national hand was felt, if at first confusedly, throughout the United Nations administration. The possibility that opponents of internationalism might be installed in high positions in the new Secretariat probably occurred to few of the staff, however, in the early days.

That governments had denied to the Organization any powers of intervention beyond their own, however, was unconsciously recognized by the staff. The utopian dreams lyrically expressed in preparatory documents necessarily gave place to a quotidian exercise of converting idealism into practical energy. When the first emotions waned, it grew apparent that, for the United Nations to develop as an instrument for the reconciliation of nations, deep traditions of nationalism would have to be won over to this new concept; and that, given the limitations of member states' intentions, these would yield, gradually and ultimately, only to a sustained show of quality and usefulness on the part of the Organization itself. On the other hand, within the Secretariat, vision, authority, and a grasp of events did not show themselves as unhesitatingly as

---

* When I applied to the United Nations in 1951, the intelligence test incorporated baffling (I had been in the United States less than one month) references to "Queens" and "Great Neck," and was in general phrased for the attention of a New York native, though not necessarily an intelligent one.

the Charter had implied they would. Lofty intentions had not in every case produced lofty responses; human failings ignominiously made themselves felt; and it was seen that, even within the walls of the United Nations, internationalism was a discipline as yet in its infancy.

Recruits from overseas began to sense unexpected difficulties in the United Nations' having been sited in the United States. Large numbers of aliens, many of them in modestly paid positions, tended to be lumped together in the public mind as immigrants who should be glad to immerse themselves in American customs and attitudes and grateful to be far from their less fortunate places of origin. The existence of this tendency outside the Organization would alone have made an unwelcome discovery; but that it should be exhibited inside the United Nations itself, and in areas concerned with staff administration, brought twinges of foreboding, not only among staff members from abroad but among intelligent Americans.

Americans were not — and have never been — "internationalized" in the United Nations Secretariat. Living on their own ground, speaking their own idiom, and existing within their own culture, they have been required to make far less adaptation to other ways of thought, speech, and life than would have been the case had the United Nations been established in Oslo or Geneva, as was originally suggested. On the other hand, the non-American, international contingent of the staff has tended, to a greater or less degree, to become "Americanized," living under the immense, unchallenged pressure of the American way of life. A certain fraction of the international staff takes out United States citizenship; others will stay on in America for years after retirement from the United Nations.

Nevertheless, in the earliest years and through the Lake Success era, a form of true internationalism was created by the initial impetus of the United Nations idea: there was considerable *esprit de corps*, little discrimination between ranks — except at the top — and of course a pervading sensation that this was a beginning from which "things" must presumably go forward. Nostalgia for Lake Success was to set in early.

Two.

"The Purgatory of the Investigations"

"Administration" at the United Nations Secretariat may be said to reside in the Secretary-General's office, in the group of most senior officers having divisional and departmental control, in the bureaus concerned with personnel, with finance, with the Organization's legal affairs; and in the sections charged with what might be called the logistics of the United Nations operation — purchasing, maintenance, transport, and so on, both at Headquarters and in the field. (This last category is one in which inappropriately high positions are notoriously held, and disproportionate power dispensed.) In the first years of the United Nations, the uppermost levels of administration had secretly and critically alienated themselves from the rest of the staff — that is, from those in the majority departments dealing with economic and social matters, and with the multiplicity of all other United Nations business except political negotiation. The staff remained unaware of this until 1952.

In June 1949, the administrative chief of the United Nations, Mr. Byron Price, secretly approached the United States Federal Bureau of Investigation, with Trygve Lie's blessing, to inquire — as Lie tells us in his memoirs — whether "it would be possible for the FBI to give us any derogatory information on American applicants for Secretariat positions." The inclusion of the quite unnecessary adjective says everything about the spirit in which this inquiry was made, and in which its results were to be applied. In September and October of that year, the United Nations Secretary-General contracted a secret agreement with the United States Department of State whereby United States citizens who were candidates for, or incumbents in, Secretariat positions were screened, without their knowledge, by official American security agents as a check on their opinions, political sentiments, and private lives.

This latter event is not commemorated in Trygve Lie's memoirs: indeed, it is the least-mentioned official transaction in all the United Nations' history. Most members of the present United Nations staff, should they read these pages, will learn of it here for the first time.

United States citizens — together with a number of Secretariat employees who had applied for resident status in the United States — then comprised approximately two-thirds of the United Nations Headquarters staff. (This proportion was confirmed by Hammarskjöld to the General Assembly as prevailing late in 1953.) The *majority* of the "international" United Nations Secretariat work force had thus — with the concurrence of the Secretary-General — become subject, by 1949, to secret screening, and to approval or rejection, by the government of the United States.

The 1949 secret agreement, a landmark in United Nations affairs and the ascertainable point at which the international Secretariat delivered itself conclusively, in its earliest years, into the hands of national interest, had been made and implemented in direct violation of the United Nations Charter, which binds the Secretary-General and the Secretariat, under oath, to a scrupulous independence from national pressures. Its corrupt and clandestine provisions were exposed in exhaustive detail during the interrogation of State Department representatives before the McCarran Internal Security Subcommittee in the autumn of 1952. The intent of the subcommittee was of course to demonstrate that the illicit connivance between the United Nations hierarchy and the State Department did not go far enough in establishing United States control over the interior of the United Nations. One State Department representative, Mr. Carlisle Humelsine,* arguing that "I knew there was a secret arrangement that involved the United Nations, and I was under the impression it was proceeding along quite satisfactorily," was at pains to describe what was called the "cover plan" by which a show of propriety was maintained in the routine exchange of documents while "highly confidential" dealings were conducted "orally" with a United Nations official whose name, it had been agreed, would not be revealed. (It was Byron Price.) Due to the eagerness of the McCarthy-McCarran movement to embarrass the State Department (no very difficult task in the circumstances), a series of papers defining the secret agreement and illuminating the conduct of it appear as appendices to the printed volume of the McCarran Subcommittee's hearings for the autumn of 1952. The text of the provisions for secrecy summarized above will be found in the notes that conclude the present book.

The records of the McCarran Subcommittee hearings for 1952 and 1953 are essential to any history of the United Nations, and to a full understanding of the Organization's development and present condition. The revelations contained in them of collusion between the United Nations administration and the United States authorities were never reported in the press or otherwise drawn, before now, to public attention; nor have their full implications ever been explored.

Also in 1949, a board of inquiry conducted an investigation into charges of anti-Semitism against certain supervisory personnel in the United Nations Secretariat. Mr. Lie then issued a statement, at the beginning of 1950, to the following effect:

* Humelsine, who was Deputy Under Secretary of State in Charge of Security, had inherited his role in the secret agreement from his predecessor at the State Department, John Peurifoy.

"On the basis of the report of the Special Board of Enquiry I have found no evidence establishing an overt act of anti-semitism. . . . There were, however, administrative actions of an irregular character which had the appearance of unfair discrimination against the complainants and certainly caused them to suffer unjustly." Five dismissed employees were reinstated, and others were reassured as to their standing.

In March 1950, a few weeks after Lie's statement was issued, three of these persons were again dismissed, this time on the grounds that their function (that of English and French verbatim reporters, one of the essential conference services of the United Nations) was no longer required by the Secretariat.

Another significant wedge to be driven among the staff was one of "class." By 1951 the staff had been arbitrarily and inflexibly divided into two categories, "Professional" and "General Service" — although many in the lower, General Service category were doing the identical work of their Professional counterparts. The General Service was intended to absorb those "local recruits" in junior positions, without rights of repatriation or home leave, and without privileged standing in the eyes of their countries' delegations. (The majority of these were United States citizens, but many non-Americans were included.) These people were to be frozen, so to speak, at their posts (of secretary, clerk, or "administrative assistant") like Pompeiian relics, with virtually no possibility of promotion into the Professional grades and little advance within their own. This category formed, as it still forms, the larger part of the Secretariat staff.* Aside from obvious repercussions in morale and productivity — which in the event have been such as to erode the entire United Nations system and which will be examined in their place — the fact that many of the posts styled "clerk" or "administrative assistant" precisely corresponded to the more highly paid and supposedly prestigious jobs on the other side of the fence made the arrangement to-

* Of the 1972 Headquarters total of approximately 8,200, the General Service constitutes almost two-thirds.

tally absurd. Its overt injustice and implicit snobbery were in any case thoroughly inappropriate at the United Nations or anywhere else. No member of the hierarchy stepped in to protest this segregation — the purpose of which was to reserve advancement for "geographically" favored candidates.

The next abrogation of rights was the suspension of assigning contractual guarantees — although at first few of the staff fully grasped the intention and implications of this. Personnel, particularly senior personnel, had at first been recruited, sometimes after brief probation, on "Permanent" contracts (theoretically subject to five-yearly review, but incorporating contractual commitments and indemnities); or increasingly on "Temporary-Indefinite" contracts, which were probationary and intended to lead to the lustral "Permanence" at the end of two years. By 1950, almost all employees who had served two years, or three, or four, on Temporary contracts found themselves extended on that basis, and wondered why. They did not have long to wonder.

The great currents of world power which were to shape the United Nations as instrument and as entity had begun to make themselves felt internally at the Organization. The Cold War, and its concomitant, the Korean War, and nearer at hand a wave of isolationist hysteria sweeping the United States were causing the official hosts of the United Nations to look with wild surmise on the professedly supranational child they were rearing within their borders. Endorsement of the Korean operation by the UN, and the equivocal role of "the United Nations" in that conflict, emphasized the weaknesses of the new organization rather than showing its strength, as was claimed. It appeared that "United Nations action" could only take place on any scale if initiated, manned, and equipped directly by one or more of the great powers, in all probability against the aggression, and interests, of another power bloc: in short, something all too like what had hitherto been known as war — war of the kind the United Nations had been created to prevent. Despite strenuous efforts on the part of Trygve Lie and the

United States government to present the Korean enterprise as an international crusade commanded by General Douglas Mac-Arthur, it could not be felt to be authentically so, nor was there spontaneous public confidence that this was the form that an international action ought to take. The United Nations thus gained little credit in the United States as a promulgator of the Truman Doctrine; while within the Organization's membership political divisions were sharply declared, and the Soviet bloc withdrew its recognition of the Secretary-General.

Into this scene, there advanced, through 1949 and 1950, in the United Nations Secretariat the personalities and events that were to destroy the premises on which most United Nations employees had enlisted and worked; and which, over the next few years, were to dictate in a negative sense the nature of the present Secretariat and much of United Nations operations. By the winter of 1950, the United States was entering the high summer of what has since, despite its innumerable participants and partisans of the time, come to be called McCarthyism. The public outline of this movement followed a design by then growing familiar, through thousands of publicized cases, to every citizen of the United States: the denunciation of a "security threat," who was called before one of the several Congressional inquisitions (committees and subcommittees headed by Joseph McCarthy and his fellow senators McCarran, Wiley, Jenner, Eastland, Ferguson, O'Conor, and company) or before a loyalty review board or federal grand jury, to testify about past affiliations with groups or associations designated "subversive" by the inquisitors; testimony, or refusal to testify accompanied by invocation of citizen's rights under the Fifth Amendment to the United States Constitution; publicized dismissal from employment, with consequent loss of reputation, passport, and professional standing; followed by a vacuum into which indictment or other legal process rarely entered.

The oath administered to the Secretary-General of the United Nations binds the holder of that office to the following principle embodied in Article 100 of the United Nations Charter:

19

In the performance of their duties the Secretary-General and the staff shall not seek or receive instructions from any government or from any other authority external to the Organization. They shall refrain from any action which might reflect on their position as international officials responsible only to the Organization.

To say that the policy of persecutions and dismissals now embarked on by Trygve Lie and his administration at the behest of the McCarthyite movement in the United States was a breach of the United Nations Charter hardly meets the case. In allowing themselves to become the implements of precisely those oppressive forces the United Nations had been created to contend with, and in contravening the very liberties held to be basic in the UN Universal Declaration of Human Rights, the Secretary-General and his associates made a mockery of the Organization itself and of everything that took place there. Even Trygve Lie did not seriously attempt to make moral coherence of his actions over the next two years; and his legal justification seems to have rested on a belated claim of special conditions for "the host country." Even outraged and perverted legalities were not the full significance of an episode in which elementary standards of justice and humanity were violated. In a time of monumental personal, national and international cowardice, the United Nations administration, far from standing firm, was pliant to the most evil prevailing forces and bowed to the ground.

In 1951 a group of dismissed staff members, supported by the elected representatives of the Staff Association of the United Nations and by a petition backed by hundreds of their colleagues asking Lie for their reinstatement, took their case to the United Nations Administrative Tribunal — an international body of jurists meeting periodically to consider claims brought by UN employees for legal redress. In this case the claim rested on dismissal without stated cause. In his deposition, drawn up in consultation with the UN's chief legal officer, Mr. Abraham Feller, an American, and other counsel, Trygve Lie declared: "It must therefore be stated emphatically that under the Staff Regulations and Staff Rules in force, the Secretary-General is under no obligation whatsoever to specify his reasons for termination of staff members."* The case of the employees was upheld by the Tribunal in an important judgment dealing with the basic principles at issue. The Secretary-General refused to reinstate the persons concerned; and indemnities were substituted.

A Secretary-General who categorically states that he finds himself under no obligation to account for administrative actions against his staff may be thought a questionable leader for the United Nations. The briefs for this and other cases successfully brought against the Secretary-General by United Nations personnel in the early 1950's make grim reading: the Lie–Feller presentations being obsessively concerned with the devising of legalistic formulae for circumventing principle, seeking every latitude for the Secretary-General to take despotic action and insisting on his right to withhold his reasons for doing so; while the Tribunal itself and the cases for the claimants — presented by, among other distinguished jurists, Mr. Telford Taylor — repeatedly revert to the fundamental issues of human rights involved, citing "the most elementary attributes of due process of law universally prevailing in democratic governments and firmly fixed in the Charter of the United Nations."

As one of the briefs points out: "The civilized legal order does not exist which does not insist upon the right to defend an appeal against specific charges and facts, to be assured that actions taken against an individual are based on proved, substantial facts, and to be protected against indictment and trial by pillory and slander. Not only did the Secretary-General cloak the true *reasons* for the actions, but he acted on the basis of charges and conclusions *wholly unsupported by facts*."

All these briefs deserve the attention of those who would

---

* Lie's assertion that the issue had never been discussed in drawing up the UN statutes and that "nowhere in the vast mass of General Assembly records" was there a statement obliging him to justify terminations, drew from the Administrative Tribunal, in its judgment in favor of the group of 1951 claimants, the Gertrude Stein-like comment: "If there was no discussion of the problem, there could not possibly have been a statement on the matter."

trace the history and fully comprehend the failure of the present United Nations. One of them — that presented in 1953 by a group of New York law firms on behalf of nineteen applicants to the United Nations Administrative Tribunal — provides, in three hundred pages, a monumental, engrossing, and impressively documented account of this extraordinary episode; and serves to mark the high ground on which members of the staff made their stand, against the Organization's leaders, on behalf of the principles of the United Nations Charter.

The judgments of the Administrative Tribunal are passed over in two sentences in Trygve Lie's memoirs.

From the outset it was apparent that Lie and his administration would seek to appease the McCarthyist pressures being brought to bear on the Secretariat, and would throw to these wolves any United Nations employee whose blood was demanded. The elected representatives of the staff responded to the first visible intimations of this with an organized defense, both through legal action and by expressed — and sometimes vociferous — opposition to these policies of the Secretary-General. It is probable that at that stage neither they, nor Lie himself,* grasped the utter recklessness of the evil confronting them — or the lengths to which that evil would go, carrying the Secretary-General and the Organization along with it.

The reports and circulars drawn up by the staff leaders at this time have a unique place in the documentation of the United Nations. They are the last statements by United Nations personnel that reflect a rational, democratic attitude towards the Secretary-General. In them, the Secretary-General is, for the last time, solemnly held by his staff to his undertakings under the Charter and to the moral obligations of his office, and

* In December 1952, Mr. Carlisle H. Humelsine told the McCarran Subcommittee: "I am a little inclined to believe that the individuals who entered into this on the part of the United Nations Secretariat did not realise what they were committing themselves to when they entered into it." In his memoirs, Trygve Lie tells us: "I was dismayed and horrified as I saw the American concern for security go far beyond the reasonable precautions against subversion that any government should take."

called to account for "impairment of the international character of the staff" by his departures from those standards. He is addressed, though formally, as a fallible being in need of courage and tenacity for the proper execution of his huge responsibilities — rather than as a sacred monster requiring protection from unwelcome truths and from any shade of criticism, as was thereafter to be the role of each Secretary-General vis-à-vis his staff. One of the first such documents closes on an optimistic note, expressing confidence that the impasse between staff and administration will be resolved, and reverting to less controversial matters with the heading, *"Farewell to Lake Success" Dance and Human Rights Concert.*

Farewell indeed, both to Lake Success and to human rights. Defense of their colleagues by the Staff Association brought a series of flagrant and savage reprisals. Staff representatives who had spoken out against Trygve Lie's collaboration with the FBI and the United States State Department were among the earliest and least ceremonious departures. The dismissals were accompanied by intimidating and abusive statements from the administration to those remaining. Byron Price accused the Staff Association of "disloyalty and self-seeking" and of "doing an immense amount of harm to the interests of the staff." Trygve Lie harangued them: "If you are really sincere in asking for the re-establishment of a satisfactory relationship you can give tangible evidence by marshalling your Committee and Council in support of the position I have taken."*

Administration circulars addressed to the staff at the time demand loyalty and respect as if these were due to Trygve Lie personally, whatever his conduct, rather than to the founding principles of the United Nations; and call, by implication, for

* Of the seven members, of diverse nationalities, who comprised the Committee of the Staff Association at this time, six were terminated in the following weeks and months. At a press conference on 16 February 1951, Byron Price stated: "If some of these [recent terminations] happened to be members of the Staff Committee I suppose it was a coincidence. I do not know . . . and, of course, any charge that this is an attempt to break the Staff Association is reckless and absurd."

an unquestioning reverence for the holder of the office of Secretary-General. An attempt, in the autumn of 1950, on the part of the staff to bring their concern to the attention of the General Assembly brought an open threat from Lie: "I would strongly advise the Staff Committee to withdraw the statement." On the same day Mr. Byron Price distributed a circular throughout the Secretariat, stating that "if any specific cases of disloyalty to the Secretary-General appear, there will be no choice but to call them to his attention."

Staff representation stood firm,* and its leaders became particular objects for the vindictiveness of the Secretary-General. In 1951, Mr. Lie laid the issue on the line: "If the staff in New York want to make trouble, the issue will be a simple one; it will be a question of either loyalty to [the Vice-Chairman of the Staff Committee] or loyalty to me." This particular official, a young Canadian whose professional distinction had moved the administration to *invite* him to join the Secretariat only two years before, was terminated shortly after that statement was made, the Secretary-General again declining to give a reason for the termination. When the case was brought before the United Nations Administrative Tribunal, on a claim of improper motive for nonrenewal of contract, the Secretary-General argued that the terms of the contract did not require an explanation for its nonrenewal, saying: "The question of the motive for a failure to give a new contract is legally immaterial, even if there were in fact an improper motive." This disgraceful statement again illustrates the departure from principle freely expounded by the Secretary-General and his legal advisers at the time. It need only be recalled, for example, that motives of anti-Semitism had recently been charged against officials of the United Nations administration, to see some of the dangers inherent in such a position.

In awarding substantial damages to this claimant (who do-

---

* "The Staff Council cannot accept the charges made in the statements [quoted above] which, in its view, cast an unjustified reflection on itself and the Association as a whole. The Staff Council and the Staff Committee, as one, stand on their record."

nated a considerable part of them towards the legal costs of appeals being brought by other Secretariat members), the Administrative Tribunal reported that the sum might have been still larger had it not been for "the high qualities possessed by the Applicant, and the shortage of persons of his knowledge and experience," which guaranteed his immediate reemployment on his return to his own country. Thus the United Nations lost the services of one of the most highly qualified officials ever to join its ranks.

Lie made no bones about his lack of preoccupation with the rights and wrongs of the matter, or with its humanitarian aspects. In his memoirs, having acknowledged that every Secretariat member is entitled to full freedom for his personal political and religious convictions, he goes on to say: "If there was even one American Communist in the Secretariat I wished to get rid of him.* I would do it quietly and in accordance with the Staff Regulations, in the ways to which I had been accustomed in Norway." What should now be added here is that, at the end of 1951, following the upholding of that year's crop of appellant cases by the United Nations Administrative Tribunal, Mr. Lie — far from interpreting the Tribunal's judgments as reproof or guidance — requested and obtained from the General Assembly a set of *Amendments* to the Staff Regulations (which, having been themselves provisional, were now made permanent) permitting the Secretary-General to terminate staff in temporary status with no other reason than that, "in his opinion, such action would be in the interests of the United Nations." The "temporary" designation had by then come to refer to the majority of UN staff, and was now declared by Lie to be capable of extension "up to nine years or more."

Seldom can expediency have been so forthrightly, and self-

---

* Asked, however, at a press conference in June 1952 whether it was his policy to terminate American "Communists" in the Secretariat, Lie replied: "There is no such policy at all . . . I do not know any more about these things than you."

righteously, espoused by a world leader. Whatever the ways to which, in Mr. Lie's sinister little phrase, he "had been accustomed in Norway," they cannot have included adapting the constitution to suit his own convenience.

Lie's only moral stand, predictably enough, is made against the demand of the Soviet authorities for a show of "equal treatment" — which would have involved dismissal of White Russians employed in the Secretariat as translators and interpreters — and similar pressure from the Communist regime in Prague for the removal of emigré Czechs and Slovaks from the United Nations staff. Mr. Lie informs us that, on this question, Gromyko "submitted no facts which indicated that these people had done anything amiss, and so I declined to discharge them." Nevertheless, a few paragraphs later, he tells us: "On the one hand, the sweeping attacks upon the standing and integrity of the Secretariat were vicious and distorted and out of all proportion to the facts. On the other hand, there was no question in my mind that the cases involving the Fifth Amendment ought to go, as a matter of sound policy entirely divorced from the public hue and cry."

Here we have the Secretary-General of the United Nations declaring that those who have claimed their constitutional rights during a national witch-hunt "ought to go" without question (and why should there be "no question in my mind" on so momentous an issue?), with no reference to the gross injustice and human suffering involved,* or to the absence of any opportunity for self-defense or self-vindication; and deluding himself that this attitude is in some way detached from the hysterical excesses of the times, or from the McCarthyist strategy itself, which was the adoption of totalitarian methods under the claim of combating them.

The expansion from "American Communist" to "Fifth

* "I decided, however, to give them the normal indemnities and severance pay to which summary dismissal did not entitle them, in order to help them over the difficult time they faced in finding other employment, after all the publicity."

Amendment cases" — in itself a McCarthyist device — will be noted. It would be interesting to know whether "even one American Communist" was expelled from the United Nations Secretariat as a result of Trygve Lie's purges. It is exceedingly unlikely that Senator McCarthy and Senator McCarran believed American Communists to be active within the staff;* and Lie in his memoirs tells us that he himself did not:

I did not want them there for good policy reasons; but I was not afraid that any who remained would overthrow the US Government and subvert its constitution. . . . There was nothing to spy on in the United Nations. . . . Had there been meaningful evidence of illegal subversive activity against any member of the Secretariat [the federal grand jury] would have returned indictments in accordance with its duty. *It did not return even one.* [My italics]

In 1952, Mr. John D. Hickerson, Assistant Secretary of State for United Nations Affairs, informed the McCarran Internal Security Subcommittee, in response to a question as to whether the State Department's rating of "adverse" in respect to a United Nations official meant that the "person was a member of the Communist Party, or was subject to the discipline of the Communists," that "it doesn't go quite that far. In some cases it indicated that there was a strong suspicion, or a likelihood. . . . Or likely to become so [sic]. Or that we suspected. Of course, we did not have the facilities for making a full investigation."

In 1953 Byron Price confirmed to the General Assembly that "it must be borne in mind that adverse evaluations, when re-

---

* In 1948, in response to an assertion by Robert C. Alexander, assistant chief of the State Department Visa Division, that "hundreds of foreign agents" were using UN employment as a cover for subversive activity, the Secretary of State, George Marshall, replied that the United States did not have knowledge of a single individual associated with the United Nations who was engaged in anti-American activity. An investigating committee upheld this assertion. Alexander was reprimanded, but — as Trygve Lie reflects in his memoirs — "it is doubtful that the repudiation ever caught up with the charge — as is so frequently the case."

ceived, have been wholly unaccompanied by security evidence or information on which the evaluations were based."

Nor should Trygve Lie be allowed to leave, as he intends, the impression that his sole basis for dismissal in these cases rested on invocation by a staff member of constitutional protection. We have already seen that several terminations resulted from the activities of staff members in defense of their colleagues, and that non-Americans were also victimized. (A number of Western European nationals were eventually fired by Lie in pursuance of these political reprisals against the staff.) The invocation of the Fifth Amendment by United Nations personnel did not become an issue until 1952, when scores of UN employees were called before the grand jury and McCarran inquisitions; Lie's political dismissals began, as far as is known, in 1949, included persons who denied Communist affiliations under oath, and were in a number of cases feebly disguised as "redundancies" although the vacancies were simultaneously advertised in the New York *Times*.

Several of the United States citizens interrogated by the McCarran Subcommittee in 1952 testified to having belonged to leftist groups during the 1920's or 1930's (the allegation, by Whittaker Chambers, against one staff member rested on his having once shown enthusiasm, while at college in 1923, on behalf of a Communist-led mutiny in the German fleet). Others denied leftist affiliations under oath. No distinction was made in favor of these cases.

It was, furthermore, well known that many persons interrogated by McCarthyist bodies were legally advised to invoke constitutional privilege as protection against the possibility of contrived charges of perjury, or to avoid implicating others in the witch-hunt; and a number of UN employees gave these reasons for doing so. The few exceptions made to termination by the UN administration were mostly in favor of persons who acceded to every demand of the investigators and gave lists of others who might be interrogated: of these few, more than one stayed on and prospered.

One of the first United Nations casualties was Professor

Owen Lattimore, who will be remembered as having fallen into official disgrace for urging United States recognition of mainland China. Lattimore returned from a UN consultant mission to Afghanistan in 1950 to refute McCarthy's charges of subversion; his association with the United Nations was never resumed.

The ignorance of world affairs, and other gross limitations displayed by the senators who tormented a group of thirty UN employees called before the McCarran Internal Security Subcommittee in the autumn of 1952 provide, in the official records, a dismal reflection of this level of government life and thought at the time. American citizens born in other countries are literally invited to "go back where you came from"; suspicion is attached to the fact that employment at the United Nations brings the witnesses into contact with nationals from Communist countries; one witness is attacked for pointing out that the UN Charter provides for representation of all nations in the world organization. Many of the questions are inane, and some of them illiterate.

With these records too, as with the respective briefs presented to the UN Administrative Tribunal by the Secretary-General and appellants against his decisions, one is forcibly struck by the contrasting quality of "Power" on the one hand, and its victims on the other. The Southern Democrat and Middle Western Republican senators of whom the subcommittee is mainly composed, and their cohorts, make what can only be called a barbarous showing in the name of "Democracy"; while democratic principles, and the claims of liberty and reason, are bravely and often nobly spoken for by the defendants.

Aside from the limited possibilities for "spies and saboteurs" in an organization staffed, as it was then, from sixty countries, with persons of all nationalities sharing access to documents and deliberations* — and where policy, as in the case of the Korean War, then in progress, was dictated from without by

* The alleged potentialities for "espionage" in international organizations were dismissed as an incongruity by a committee of American jurists who considered the question in the 1950's.

the postwar powers — the American inquisitions of the early 1950's were even then recognized throughout the world as an unscrupulous right-wing campaign to discredit democratic thought and practice, led by cynical demagogues and supported by a variety of reactionary groups in which the yahoo, the segregationist and the anti-Semite were by no means unrepresented.

Trygve Lie himself wrote — subsequently — of the "awful pressure of the hysterical assault upon the United Nations that reactionaries were promoting and using for their own ends. . . . The situation lent itself to demagogic exploitation by politicians and publicists not encumbered with principles or a sense of responsibility."* It is to Trygve Lie's ungovernable desire to put himself on the right side of every issue, in no matter how self-contradictory a manner, that we owe the most significant revelations of his memoirs.

Mr. Lie was also later to declare that "an American Communist is not a representative American." Aside from the central question of definition, the spectacle of a United Nations Secretary-General taking it upon himself to decide what constitutes a representative national in the case of all his member states suggests, for obvious reasons, a highly dangerous precedent.

It would also be interesting to know which clauses of even

---

* Roy Cohn, in his biography of his friend and mentor Joseph McCarthy, describes how McCarthy "bought the package" of the political issue of "subversion," after an interested group had unsuccessfully "peddled the package around the Senate Office Building," as follows: "Joe McCarthy bought Communism in much the same way as other people purchase a new automobile. The salesman showed him the model; he looked at it with interest, examined it more closely, kicked at the tires, sat at the wheel, squiggled in the seat, asked some questions, and bought. It was just as cold as that."

In a later book, *A Fool for a Client*, Cohn states that "some of my most rewarding work was done with grand juries. . . . One grand jury filed a presentment documenting heavy infiltration by American Communists in the United Nations over the specific objection of some of my superiors in the Justice Department. I supported the grand jury." This is the same grand jury which, as Trygve Lie reports, did not return a single indictment.

the "revised" Staff Regulations Lie had in mind. Substantial damages (to the extent in one case of forty thousand dollars — a large sum twenty years ago) were eventually awarded by the United Nations Administrative Tribunal to those of the dismissed whose contracts afforded them career protection under the Staff Regulations. The single brief reference to the Administrative Tribunal in Lie's memoirs does not include this fact — indeed, the entire episode of the McCarthyist investigations is dispatched in twenty pages. Again, one must comment on the absence of almost any indication that the misery of the victims was taken into account by their Secretary-General: "Mr. Feller and I . . . with Byron Price — carried the main load of the 'subversive' issue." There were doubtless those who felt that the load was quite otherwise deployed.

By the year 1952 madness had set in. With the ironic exception of Iron Curtain nationals — who were, so to speak, above suspicion — virtually every non-administration member of the staff was now viewed as a potential "security threat." What initially had been thought to be directed at a handful of American citizens, and at staff representatives aroused on their behalf, now involved every one of the two thousand Americans in the United Nations Secretariat and was to spill over on to citizens from other countries, and to UN agencies abroad, such as UNESCO and FAO. Officials who were known to deplore Trygve Lie's policies found themselves eased out, or assigned to UN field missions overseas; former members of Resistance groups, Spaniards who had opposed Franco, Australians who had demonstrated in their student days were flown to UN outposts where their unfortunate pasts might be redeemed in a Foreign Legionesque oblivion. Terminations and resignations multiplied at this time. A last distress signal from the sinking Staff Association (soon to be, under massive administration pressure, remolded nearer to the heart's desire) regrets "the unceremonious nature of the terminations. . . . Persons who had served for from four to seven years were informed

31

of their dismissals — of which in some cases they had had no previous warning — by a memorandum which expressed no regret and which was delivered in an envelope not even marked 'Personal' or 'Confidential.' In some instances, immediate supervisors were not even aware of what was happening until shortly before the event."

While ignoring the indications of the Administrative Tribunal, Lie set up an international committee of three jurists to advise him on his rights in the matter; the panel was composed of a former Attorney General under Herbert Hoover, a British businessman, and a Belgian professor from the Catholic University at Louvain. It was they who came up with the jesuitical "host country" formula already referred to. Their deliberations were concluded in two weeks, to the satisfaction of the Secretary-General. Eminent jurists in America and elsewhere, and UN delegations such as that of India, and of Norway itself, objected to the findings of this panel, without effect.

Mr. Lie publicly promised his cooperation to the inquisitors. And his staff learned that, in his office on the thirty-eighth floor of the United Nations building, their Secretary-General was conferring with Roy Cohn. The Secretary-General and his associates on several occasions also received the Special Counsel to the McCarran Subcommittee, Robert Morris. The inclusion, in the secret agreement with the State Department, of a face-saving clause to the effect that the ultimate decision on dismissals would rest with the Secretary-General can, in these circumstances, only be regarded as farcical.

The extent of cooperation between the McCarthyist forces and the United Nations leadership at this time, while manifest in the events and formalized in the secret agreement, may be illustrated by the following examples. When an officer of the State Department informed the McCarran Subcommittee that the United Nations Secretariat had approached him "asking that the State Department agree in a promotion" for a specific UN official, even the subcommittee members seemed surprised and the following dialogue ensued:

Mr. Sourwine [counsel for the McCarran Subcommittee]: Why should the United Nations ask the State Department to agree to the promotion of an individual if both were zealous in the principle that what the United Nations did with its personnel was not to be influenced by the member nations?

Mr. Humelsine [of the State Department]: I cannot answer that question.*

(Permission to promote this United Nations staff member was refused to the Secretariat by the State Department — the Secretary-General of course complying with the decision.)

Similarly, the interrogations to which staff members under the McCarthyist cloud were subjected by UN administration officials precisely corresponded to those inflicted on them by the American investigating committees and demonstrate the degree of coincidence between the two. The brief for one applicant to the Administrative Tribunal informs us that "when he objected to this political inquisition, he was dismissed summarily on the pretext of 'serious misconduct.' " Another applicant to the Tribunal was subjected, by a leading Secretariat official, to a series of interrogations "about the identical political matters which the Federal Grand Jury had raised. In fact, the only specific factual questions put to the Applicant by Mr. Vaughan precisely duplicated those which had been asked by the grand jury."

---

* It is interesting to contrast the relations between the State Department and the United Nations administration described by State Department officials at the McCarran hearings with the account given by Dean Acheson, who was Secretary of State from 1949 to 1953. Excluding all reference to the secret agreement, Acheson has written in his memoirs: "Under the stimulus of Senators Joseph McCarthy of Wisconsin and Patrick McCarran of Nevada, then at the height of their power, the charge [against UN employees] kicked up quite a row and soon had both the State Department and the Secretary-General taking embarrassing positions inconsistent with those they had previously maintained. From the outset we had urged that the United Nations should build a staff truly international in outlook, responsible and loyal to the organization and not nominated or directed by any national states. Secretary-General Trygve Lie took the same view. . . . I did not want to claim a right to police his appointments and appointees."

The squalor of these conditions, punctuated by announcements of summary dismissals, acted on the staff with a combination of attrition, confusion, and violence. Indignation, anguish, apprehension, self-dramatization, and — not infrequently — nobility were now ranged against fear, resentment, incomprehension, prejudice, and the wish to survive. Each department had its informers, and its victims.

Those who had truly sought internationalism in the United Nations Secretariat thus found themselves, as in some grotesque fable, betrayed into the keeping of the very forces of darkness against which they had enlisted to serve.

The total of United Nations employees affected by the McCarthyite pressures of the late 1940's and early 1950's undoubtedly runs in the hundreds. The total of those actually dismissed is difficult, if not impossible, to arrive at. (The toll for the year 1952 was estimated at a minimum of 45 by the New York *Times*; the majority of these were "Professionals" — Americans in the United Nations Professional Category at the time numbered 345.) Figures which can be calculated from cases of appeal and from newspaper reports, while in any case incomplete, cannot account for what is possibly an equal number of enforced resignations — since employees were permitted to resign with extra indemnities, "in exchange for their silence" as one of the Tribunal briefs puts it, and with at least a possibility of escaping wide publicity. Nor can such estimates account for political terminations disguised as "economies," or for the deportations to the field, or the careers shunted into sidings from which they were never to emerge; nor for a secret blacklisting of those who had expressed disapproval of Lie's performance on this issue and who were thenceforth to find their careers, even in UN terms, inexplicably retarded, at Headquarters and in the United Nations agencies.

No calculation can of course give us the toll in human quality — in qualified applicants who were turned away at this period because of "adverse" ratings from the State Department and the FBI; and in the drifting away, throughout the early 1950's, of able persons of various nationalities who could not bring themselves to accept such a situation, even though it might present no direct menace to them, and whose abilities promptly secured them employment elsewhere. Above all, there is no accounting for the deterrent effect of Trygve Lie's policies on those who might have wished to serve a differently administered United Nations Secretariat.

The difficulty of arriving even at a close estimate of the number of dismissals made directly as a result of United States pressure at this time is further complicated by the fact that, at the height of the furor, Trygve Lie instituted an administrative survey of the Secretariat — which, undertaken by a "Selection Committee," resulted in nearly sixty terminations, declaredly for reasons unconnected with the political purges. Several of these dismissals were challenged, without success, before the United Nations Administrative Tribunal, on the grounds that they had been "improperly motivated." (In one such case, where adverse comments were found to have been falsely included in a claimant's personnel report — as a result, the UN administration stated, of a "pure typographical error" — it was declared by way of excuse that "mistakes were not infrequently found in the fact-sheets" submitted to the Selection Committee, with the "reassurance" from the Committee members that such inaccuracies "could in no way have affected" the judgments made.) Whatever the motives in inaugurating this survey, its timing served, as pointed out by staff representatives, to confuse its victims "in the minds of the public, and of prospective employers, with those terminated for political reasons." This committee's records were immediately destroyed.

Of the many strong impressions that remain from a reading of the principal papers relating to the United Nations purges of the McCarthy era,* two that carry both public and private im-

---

* Among the mass of which, the volume of the McCarran Subcommittee Hearings for the autumn of 1952, the Brief on Behalf of Nineteen Applicants submitted to the UN Administrative Tribunal in 1953, the

plications may be particularly noted: the indifference, already mentioned, of authority to the human consequences of its activities (and, in the case of the inquisitors themselves, a sadistic relishing of the suffering inflicted); and the inescapable conclusion that worth and ability are specific targets of the investigators and that certain of the victims have been selected precisely because of exceptional qualities that both made them conspicuous and moved them to speak out against the injustices of the times.

In the first instance, there is nothing to indicate, in the revelations of the McCarran Subcommittee hearings, that State Department officials relaying adverse ratings to Byron Price and his cohorts felt responsibility for wrecking careers and lives. Mr. Carlisle Humelsine, explaining "what the score sheet was on getting rid of individuals," describes the examination of dossiers on United Nations personnel by security agents at the State Department as follows: "I think they would go so far as, in certain cases, to say 'I think this particular individual is a very bad fellow, indeed.' " And an existence was promptly blown to smithereens. The objects of this process appear either as disposal problems for the State Department and the United Nations administration, or, to the investigators, as victims to be baited for meretricious political purposes and out of perversion, ignorance and insecurity.

It is left for the United Nations Administrative Tribunal to reveal, in its records, that a mutilated human existence and a destroyed human potential stood behind each of the references to "individuals," "adverse comments," and "derogatory evaluations": the public humiliation and private destitution of separate persons is spelt out clearly enough in their applications for

---

relevant volume of Judgements of the United Nations Administrative Tribunal (Numbers 1 to 70, 1950–1957, UN document AT/DEC/1–70), Trygve Lie's memoirs, *In the Cause of Peace*, the Secretary-General's Report on Personnel Policy (A/2364) of 30 January 1953, and the UN Staff Committee bulletins (SCC series) for the years 1950–1953 must be considered indispensable to any full consideration of the events.

redress and in their evidence that they have been "blocked from earning" even a subsistence wage by the combined antics of the State Department, the investigating committees, the United Nations administration, and the press. It should be emphasized that, although the Tribunal made compensatory awards — of ten, twenty, thirty, and forty thousand dollars — to holders of permanent contracts who were fired from the United Nations in the McCarthyist purges, the majority of the dismissed held "Temporary-Indefinite" contracts and were ineligible for compensation after Trygve Lie's 1951 revision of the staff regulations.

As to the impression that a number of the victims were picked out because of conspicuous abilities, one may first consider the following comments, to be found in the McCarran Subcommittee records, from Mr. John D. Hickerson, United States Assistant Secretary of State for United Nations Affairs:

It was agreed between the Department and the Secretary-General that actual operations under the arrangement would have to be handled in a most highly confidential manner. . . . In discharging such employees for cause, the Secretary-General had to contend with the fact that many of them had satisfactory efficiency ratings. Further, he had to contend with an appeals procedure which could bring into play a joint management-staff appeals board, with recommendatory powers, and an administrative tribunal, with power to demand a reversal of the Secretary-General's action or damages in lieu thereof. The obstacle presented by the administrative tribunal is apparent in its decision that the Secretary-General is required to make a statement of cause in discharging an employee.

The provisions for due process originally invested in United Nations bodies of appeal are here regarded as an inconvenient "obstacle" to the illicit activities of Lie, his associates, and the United States authorities; courts might, in the same way, presumably be regarded as an annoying impediment to crime. Correspondingly, the fact that the afflicted employees "had satisfactory efficiency ratings" appears as nothing more than

37

another exasperating obstruction. It would not be easy to discover, in the United Nations Secretariat today, a body of persons whose experience and capacities meet the official descriptions given in the appeals and judgments of the early 1950's (where detailed records of professional competence were submitted as evidence of extraneous motives for termination). One example of this extirpation of quality has already been given. Numerous others may be examined in the Administrative Tribunal's judgments — where one reads of "resourcefulness far above average" or "exemplary performance," or discovers that the post held by one appellant was abolished "for the reason that the work done by the Applicant has since been divided among several persons, a tribute to her abilities and the importance of the position she held." Such are the professional histories of the staff members dismissed by Trygve Lie "in the interests of the Organization."

The Brief on Behalf of Nineteen Applicants concludes its study of this aspect of the matter with the following statement:

The unquestioned capability of each of the terminees completely satisfied the interests of the United Nations as the Secretary-General has defined those interests; however, the political interests of the United States were not satisfied and therefore the capability standard was discarded.

A feature that recurs, in the records of the dismissed, is one that has been all but obliterated from recruitment requirements in the upper levels of the present United Nations Secretariat — that of specific, and in some cases unique, professional excellence in a particular field. An instance of this may be given by quoting from a judgment made by the Administrative Tribunal in 1953, in awarding damages to one dismissed senior official:

The Tribunal awards $40,000 in lieu of reinstatement and notes that in the computation of the amount regard has been paid to the following factors:
(a) Applicant's "outstanding professional competence" as consistently referred to in his annual reports;

(b) The very limited and specialized nature of his profession as anthropologist and African specialist whereby the opportunities of further employment are rare;

(c) The fact that he joined the United Nations at the special request of Mr. Ralph Bunche, Director of the Trusteeship Division, thereby terminating his previous career.

Within a few years Africa would explode into United Nations deliberations; the United Nations mission to the Congo would be staffed and directed, for the most part, by persons having little or no previous training in African affairs; and Dag Hammarskjöld was to declare that the Congo operation had demonstrated that the United Nations Secretariat "does not dispose of a sufficient number of highly qualified senior officials."

In an election-eve appearance with McCarthy's committee in 1952, Whittaker Chambers gave his opinion that a certain leading United Nations official might be a "subversive" who had previously used another name, though conceding he had never met either the official or his alleged alias. This case, an American against whom, as the Secretary-General himself admitted, there was not a shred of evidence of any kind, and whose distinguished rank and reputation presented dismissal difficulties even for Mr. Lie, denied Chambers' accusations under oath. He was ultimately hounded into resigning by the inquisitors' expedient of persecuting employees in whose recruitment he had concurred — a device not unworthy of a Solzhenitsyn novel; and, it was said, at the private insistence of Lie. Trygve Lie, in a public statement, accepted the man's resignation with regret and praised his outstanding contribution.

Another departing senior officer was publicly assured by the Secretary-General that he could "take real pride in his contribution to the United Nations," but that Mr. Lie had no option but to accept his resignation.

Various employees who were offered resignation instead of dismissal by the United Nations administration testified to the Tribunal that they had been assured that the Secretary-General, in seeking their resignation, had no complaint against them but sought to avoid possible embarrassment to himself arising from future publicity.

One might here recall the terms of the United Nations Charter: "The Secretary-General . . . shall not seek or receive instructions from any government or from any other authority external to the Organization." Lie tells us that negative evaluations from the State Department were transmitted orally in the single word "Reject," and adds that, although such comments were helpful, he "could not and would not" act on them. Yet that is exactly what he did. The archives of the McCarran Internal Security Subcommittee contain the following statement by Mr. John D. Hickerson, Assistant Secretary of State for United Nations Affairs at the United States State Department:

It is true that United Nations officials expressed the wish from time to time that they could have detailed information or evidence. However, to my knowledge there was never at any time a statement from the Secretary-General that the secret procedure was unsatisfactory in the sense that he would not act on the basis of the comments being supplied and that these comments were useful only as a basis for further investigation. If there had been, we would have taken steps to try to work out a new procedure.

One United Nations official interrogated by Senator McCarran's group replied as follows: "I am proud to be attacked by Senator McCarran, whom I consider a political mad dog and a subversive influence in the United States. I am not and have never been a Communist. I believe I am a vastly better patriot than Senator McCarran." The man was duly terminated, but Trygve Lie himself probably did not doubt the truth of that statement.

"Quietly, and in accordance with the Staff Regulations. . . ." The degree of quiet that attended these events continues to reverberate in the ears of those who lived through them. At the United Nations, the staff could naturally talk of nothing else. New York had seven large-circulation newspapers then, four of them active on behalf of Senator Joseph McCarthy and only one of the others (the *Post*) consistently and aggressively critical.* Pronouncements by Trygve Lie contribute no small part to the innumerable headlines, editorials, front-page articles and savage cartoons chronicling the UN experience of 1951–1953. Messrs. Walter Winchell and George Sokolsky got seemingly endless mileage out of the UN cases both in the press and on the air. A courageous exception was provided by Leon Edel,† the future biographer of Henry James, then reporting on UN affairs for the *Daily Compass*, who wrote:

The UN has arrived at the method of summary judgment and presumption of guilt before innocence is proved. The picture isn't a pretty one. . . . In acting as he has done Secretary-General Lie has made it clear that the UN is not prepared to offer any American called before a Grand Jury the presumption of innocence, and protection of rights as an international civil servant. . . .

A shocking aspect of this situation is that high UN officials, including Lie, have not had the courage to defend the staff they themselves hired. . . . What these officials avoid discussing is the fact that member states are obligated not to interfere in the internal affairs of the UN. In failing to make an issue of this matter and in failing to back up his personnel as well as his own authority to determine how and where his staff should function, Lie is understood to have been motivated by fear of decreased US appropriations for the UN under the McCarthy-McCarran type of pressure.

Here, for the first time, we have a reference to the crux of the matter; and a translation into simple English of the "host country" formula. The silence, or acquiescence, of other UN member governments throughout this time is a disheartening

* Of the magazines, the *Nation* and the *New Republic* put the case for the UN staff. An example of the other extreme is an article entitled "The Sinister Doings at the UN," published in the *Saturday Evening Post* in November 1951.

† Mr. Edel also tackled Lie on the issue during a 1952 television program, getting falsehoods and evasions in return.

tribute to what was then a worldwide "fear of decreased US appropriations."* (The Soviet bloc, led by Andrei Vishinsky, poured scorn on Lie — accurately enough — as "the tool of the United States arm-twisters," but their attitude — inevitable in the circumstances — had already been fixed by the Korean War, and in any case had nothing whatever to do with upholding civil liberties.) An intensified attack on the United Nations by anti-Stevenson forces in the United States during the 1952 presidential campaign (a headline, typical of many, declares: "NIXON BLAMES DEMOCRATS FOR REDS IN U.N.") at last precipitated criticism of Lie's policies in the General Assembly that autumn, in particular from the delegation of France, as the situation built itself up to an explosion.

On 10 November 1952, shortly before the French Foreign Minister Robert Schuman was to speak, Trygve Lie claimed the floor to offer his resignation. (At the time, there was very real doubt as to the sincerity of this offer; Lie's resignation in fact took effect five months afterwards.)

Three days later, on 13 November, the General Legal Counsel of the United Nations, Mr. Abraham Feller, committed suicide by jumping from the window of his New York apartment.

That Abraham Feller, the Secretary-General's partisan, friend, and faithful collaborator throughout the events leading

* "In the autumn of 1952 the other governments had little disposition for getting involved in the defense of the good name of the Secretariat though in the next spring, after it was all over, certain delegations were not slow to suggest how things might have been done in a different way." Trygve Lie, *In the Cause of Peace.*

Lord Gladwyn, who, as Gladwyn Jebb, represented the United Kingdom at the United Nations through these Trygve Lie years, makes no mention in his memoirs of the McCarthyist purges of the international Secretariat, although expressing his disgust for McCarthyism in the United States itself as follows: "You longed to be able to intervene in the controversy, which you obviously could not do, though in private conversation you could more or less say what you thought." Lord Gladwyn's unconsummated yearnings to intervene at this time were as nothing beside the desperate, though ever-diminishing, hopes of Secretariat members that at least one delegation would assume its responsibilities and intercede to protect the human rights and preserve the international character of the staff.

to Lie's resignation, was driven to his death by what Lie subsequently called "the purgatory of the personnel investigations" was affirmed both by Lie and by Feller's widow. Mrs. Feller attributed her husband's death to "accumulated tension from overwork, pressure at the UN, and Trygve Lie's resignation"; and Lie described it at the time as resulting from "the strain of defending American employees of the UN against indiscriminate smears and exaggerated charges."

In his memoirs Lie says that "Abe Feller was a victim of the witch-hunt, of the awful pressure of the hysterical assault upon the United Nations that reactionaries were promoting and using for their own ends. . . . He knew no American in the Secretariat had ever been indicted for espionage or any other subversive activity against his country. Although he felt as strongly as I that the United Nations officials who had pleaded the Fifth Amendment had betrayed their obligation and should be removed, he had a genuine sympathy for the victims of the headline-hunting investigations. . . . Day after day, he followed the Senate hearings and saw the tragedy unfold." The logic of this appears to be: "He knew they were guiltless, but felt they should be punished." The inference may be made from Lie's statement that the full meaning and consequences of the Secretariat position, foreseen by others at the outset, gradually revealed itself to Feller and engulfed him. There has been additional, uninformed speculation regarding this event. Senator McCarran announced at the time that Feller had not himself been under suspicion for subversion.

Under the impact of the drama, Trygve Lie lashed out briefly at the inquisitors; and promptly received a telegram requesting him to appear before the United States Grand Jury currently investigating "subversives" in the United Nations. This he declined to do (members of his staff were not so privileged); but he explained that he had intended no offense. The supreme irony of Lie, or any other UN official implicated in the conspiracy with the State Department, alleging that staff members "had betrayed their obligation" is consistent with what Lie himself described as "the atmosphere of Greek tragedy."

Dr. Ralph Bunche, then Principal Director for Trusteeship at the United Nations, also criticized "American pressures on the United Nations" in a speech made to the American Philosophical Society within hours of Feller's death; and asserted that there could be no question about the loyalty of "all but a few" of the nearly two thousand Americans employed by the United Nations.

These, such as they are, appear to be the only official statements issued to the public by the United Nations administration in defense of their staff. Shortly before the suicide of Abraham Feller, the Secretary-General's legal representative at the McCarran hearings addressed himself as follows to the presiding chairman of the subcommittee, Senator Herbert O'Conor of Maryland:

I should like to thank the chairman, Senator O'Conor, and counsel for the committee for their courtesies extended to me as the representative of the Secretary-General and for his conduct of the meeting in the spirit of complete fairness. I should like the record to show that in no case did the Secretary-General interpose any objection to a question presented to the witness, to any witness in the United Nations.

The record does show, and continued to show, as desired. Senator O'Conor responded:

Mr. Schachter, we are very happy to express concurrence in that observation and also to thank you for the many acts of cooperation which have occurred in the past days. You have been thoroughly cooperative in every way. I should also like very much, before concluding, to express commendation of the United States Attorney Myles Lane and the very able special Assistant to the Attorney General Roy Cohn, whose very outstanding work has been made known to the committee and of which more will be made known in the future.

In America, neither the press nor the public was more than passingly aroused in the Secretariat's favor by Feller's death.

In reporting the event, the New York *Times* discovered that "members of the Secretariat expressed their belief that the [McCarran] subcommittee had not confined itself to a search for employees guilty of espionage or of subversive activities, or for members of the Communist party, but actually is on the trail of all with a left-wing or New Deal background."

The press abroad, less submissive than foreign governments themselves, began to agitate for action to protect the principles and personnel of the United Nations. Leading newspapers in England and France, in Switzerland and Belgium, called for intervention by member states. Shortly after the Feller tragedy, *Le Monde** called for the removal of the United Nations from the United States, saying:

Many Americans will be shocked by such a proposal. Some from material considerations, not wishing to see abandoned the immense and preposterous building constructed at great cost for the Organization; others from a sentimental reaction or from mistrust. Could one not ask them to reflect with detachment upon the following: if the United Nations were to have its site at Leningrad, if the USSR provided 40% of its running expenses, if journalists and foreign observers (not diplomats) were experiencing difficulties in obtaining their visas, if a "Beria Committee" inquired into international officials accused of sympathy with America, if the chief of the legal services were to renew — like Feller — the last gesture of Jan Masaryk at Prague, what would be the reaction of the United States? Would they not think that the independence of the Organization demanded the transfer of its site to a territory less "committed"? And would they not be right in so thinking?

With the New Year of 1953, on a crescendo of terminations and suspensions, an official "security review" of all Americans in the United Nations was initiated by Executive Order of the United States government. That this review should be speedily implemented was the last expressed official wish of the retiring

---

* In an article of 22 November 1952 by Maurice Duverger: one of the most penetrating brief essays ever written on the internationalism of the United Nations Secretariat.

head of the United States delegation, President Truman's appointee Warren R. Austin; and it was hailed with satisfaction by the new, Eisenhower-appointed United States delegate to the UN, Henry Cabot Lodge — who made its inauguration his first official action — and by Trygve Lie.

The New York *Times* reported that "Mr. Lodge said the investigation would be 'more a question of security risks than disloyalty — you can be loyal and still be a bad security risk.' " The object of the review was the "clearance," or eviction, of every American in the United Nations Secretariat; Mr. Lodge appealed for, and received, the cooperation of J. Edgar Hoover to this end. Trygve Lie informed the press that his standard for dismissal in this new review would be "reasonable ground for believing that a staff member is engaging or likely to engage [sic] in subversive activities." In view of his later insistence that he did not for a moment believe subversives to exist within the United Nations, the terminations subsequently made on this basis must be agreed to defeat even Lie's powers of self-exoneration.

With the object of assisting the United States loyalty review, facilities for fingerprinting were set up in United Nations basement rooms. And, with Trygve Lie's approval, a branch office of the United States Federal Bureau of Investigation was installed on the third floor of the United Nations building for purposes of interrogating the staff.

The Secretary-General's decision to offer the FBI quarters on United Nations premises (that is, on international territory) is, for reasons additional to the obvious ones, a watershed in United Nations affairs. Trygve Lie's own account of the event expresses at the start his enthusiasm for the United States decision — made by the outgoing President Truman — to institute a full-scale security clearance of the United States component of the staff:

I welcomed it as giving help I had sought for years. A great many American members of the staff likewise welcomed it, believing it would enable them to clear themselves of indiscriminate suspicions, and were as anxious as I to get the investigation started quickly. Fingerprinting and the filling out of forms were the first steps, and the question arose as to whether I should allow these procedures to be carried out by United States authorities in the Headquarters building, which was international territory. There were vehement protests, mainly from European staff members and delegations, against my decision to permit them; but the Americans with whom I talked — they, not the Europeans, were the "victims" — took the decision as a sensible and convenient way of getting past the preliminaries quickly. Americans during the war, in government service or the armed services, had come to take fingerprinting as a matter of course, without the humiliating connotations of suspected criminality that it still has for so many people. I also permitted interviewing by the United States FBI and Civil Service agents of American staff members in their offices, if they chose. This also caused protests, again mainly from European staff members who were not involved. Most Americans preferred their offices to their homes for such interviews.

No other statement by a Secretary-General leads so directly to the question of high-level influences within the Secretariat. *"A great many American members of the staff likewise welcomed it"*: who comprised this multitude, and by what means was its favorable view made known? The reader may be assured that there was no canvassing whatever of Secretariat opinion, American or otherwise, on this matter; and that the FBI's installation (unmentioned by Lie, who speaks only of "admitting" the agents to the building) was already accomplished when the news broke with what can only be called horror on the body of the staff; even the staff representatives were given no advance information.

"The Americans with whom I talked": again, who are these? There would have been no point in seeking guidance from members of the United States delegation, since it was from that quarter that the FBI incursion had been proposed. Trygve Lie's official intimates in the Secretariat, as mentioned in his memoirs, were, like the subsequent cabinet of Dag Hammarskjöld,

predominantly Americans: Byron Price, the late Abraham Feller, Andrew Cordier, Ralph Bunche, Wilder Foote (of Public Information), David Vaughan (of General Services), Frank Begley (the Security chief, late of the FBI and the Connecticut State Police and of other investigatory posts, military and private, who had participated in Lie's discussions with Roy Cohn and with Robert Morris, special counsel of the McCarran Subcommittee) were among the senior American citizens having access to the Secretary-General during Lie's term of office — although of course Lie was in touch with other Secretariat Americans in varying degrees. The attempt to establish faces, rather than accept generalizations, in such matters has come to be considered impolite — particularly in such a case as the present one, where time and events have not favored Mr. Lie's sanguine view of his actions. Yet the answers to the questions raised by the Secretary-General's assertions are vital to any determination of the personal, national, and organizational forces at work in the UN Secretariat during Lie's term, and in subsequent years when many of the same persons held virtually the same positions and stood in similar relation to the Secretary-General.

It must first be said that Lie clearly intended to placate the United States authorities in these new demands, and that, as is obvious from his account, he sought support for "my decision" rather than advice upon it. He appears to have been constitutionally incapable of grasping issues of principle, an amalgam of stealth, expediency and platitude being substituted in him for that ability. The violation of United Nations territory, in its vast implications of subordination and precedent, is nowhere discussed. The "vehement protests" that came "mainly from European staff members and delegations" are likewise dismissed in a single phrase, in favor of the mysterious consensus of "Americans with whom I talked" — as if officials of other nationalities had no jurisdiction over the conduct of the United Nations Organization. That Americans "take fingerprinting as a matter of course" and that "most Americans" welcomed the FBI in their offices must remain Lie's own impression of attitudes in the United States.

It was Lie's belief that his deputies held him in high esteem. He tells us that when he privately announced his resignation to his assembled Assistant Secretaries-General "some sat numb and shocked, others looked almost desperate." Testimony from the survivors, as far as possible untinged by afterthought or wishful thinking, could be invaluable in identifying the sources of Secretariat responsibility in those critical years. Those who counseled and encouraged the Secretary-General in his course, and have continued to feel they were right, will wish to stand by their convictions; those who repudiated his view will, on the contrary, wish to dissociate themselves from his categorical assertions; and those who favored his position at the time and have regretted their stand can perhaps render a unique service to the history of government with the admission that they were wrong.

"If they chose." The "victims," as Lie repeatedly characterizes them, had no choice in the matter — short of heroism, which was in particularly meager supply at the time. It may be imagined what career, at the United Nations or elsewhere, awaited an American who declined to cooperate with the investigators. (A case in which damages were awarded by the UN Administrative Tribunal in 1953 concerns a dismissed woman employee who declined to fill out a United States "clearance" questionnaire, and the Tribunal's judgment includes the following account of the "choice" that was offered her: "She was informed by an official of the United Nations, Colonel Danielson, that she had the right to refrain from filling up the questionnaire. He nevertheless urged her to do so, and upon the Applicant's firm refusal he stated that he would be forced 'to turn her name over.'" Which he did. Like other "rights" of the time, this was one that could not be exercised with impunity.) As may also be imagined, FBI activities in the UN building were not confined to the interrogation of United States citizens. Opinions were continually solicited from UN personnel with regard to their colleagues' habits and characters. Although the practice, officially, was "strictly forbidden," staff of other nationalities were asked to appear in the "sensible and convenient" FBI offices: some agreed, feeling that refusal would go against them with the UN administration; others, the present writer among them, declined.

Suspensions and dismissals of course continued. In at least one case the vacancy so provided was filled by a Soviet appointee.

The condition of the staff's own defenses at this time may be gauged by the fact that a timid protest to the UN administration from the "reconstructed" Council of the Staff Association, expressing no direct objection to the FBI's presence in the building but merely regretting that staff representatives had not been consulted in advance, precipitated the withdrawal of a large minority of the Council's members — who wished to dissociate themselves from so disrespectful an approach to Mr. Lie.

Shortly before his departure, Trygve Lie presented a report on his personnel policies to the General Assembly. Making passing reference to the "confidential arrangement" with the State Department (which had by then been exposed before the McCarran Subcommittee), ignoring the resistance by, and reprisals against, the Staff Association, and dwelling emotionally on the administration's difficulties rather than reporting candidly on its role, this manifesto suppressed or misrepresented most of the events chronicled and documented in the present pages. A statement by Byron Price, appended to the report, excluded reference to employees dismissed on the administration's own initiative, and to enforced resignations and deportations prompted by political pressures; figures given for a small group of staff on whom "adverse" comment had been received from the United States authorities were beclouded by subsequent references to "several" others, to a further ten, and to yet another fifty of whom tidings were "awaited." Price's statement ends with an invocation of the high purposes to which the

United Nations is consecrated: "No organization dedicated to law and order can hope to survive if its own administrative actions are arbitrary and precipitate, based on mere suspicion and devoid of the due process to which all civilized peoples are dedicated." The report was acrimoniously debated by the General Assembly, which requested that a progress report be submitted to the next Assembly session by the incoming Secretary-General.

Such was the state of affairs at the United Nations when Trygve Lie's resignation took effect at the end of March 1953.

Three.

"Subversion"

The departure of Trygve Lie and the advent of Dag Hammarskjöld mark an apparent, though inaccurate, division between the subsidence of the McCarthyist purge of the United Nations Secretariat and the onset of the Organization's most effective years. That Lie's departure, even if a culmination of dissatisfactions, was directly occasioned by his handling of the "subversive" issue was clear at the time and is implicit in Lie's own account.* Those present in the General Assembly hall when Hammarskjöld took his oath of office were impressed by the earnest voice in which he undertook neither to seek nor to receive instruction from any outside authority. (Hammarskjöld recurred, in his public addresses, to this basic and complex issue; and his last speech in that same auditorium, a few days before his death, reverted to the same theme: "If the Secretariat is regarded as truly international, and its individual members as owing no allegiance to any national government, then

* Even a modest historian may feel despair on reading, in 1971, in an American newspaper the statement by a journalist long associated with United Nations matters that Trygve Lie was a casualty of Washington's resentment over "his defense of UN employees hunted during the McCarthy era."

the Secretariat may develop as an instrument for the preservation of peace and security of increasing significance and responsibilities. If a contrary view were to be taken, the Secretariat itself would not be available to member governments as an instrument, additional to the normal diplomatic methods, for active and growing service in the common interest.")

It would be pleasant to report that, as has been claimed, these vows were promptly honored by the new Secretary-General. They were not. The FBI agents remained on the United Nations premises throughout the first year of Hammarskjöld's incumbency — that is, until their purposes had been completely achieved. In a circular of 20 January 1954, ten months after Hammarskjöld's inauguration, the staff representatives deplored the continued presence of these "investigating agents of a national authority," and reported that "the Secretary-General has now informed the Staff Committee that interviewing by national agents in connection with the United States loyalty investigation of staff members of United States nationality is expected to come to an end shortly and that the submission of reports on present staff members by the United States Government is nearing completion."

Hammarskjöld is said to have expressed his disgust — privately — at the FBI's installation in the Secretariat building: its eventual removal, however, could not have been regarded, even by the FBI itself, as in any way premature.

Hammarskjöld also negotiated, privately, with the United States authorities for the restraint of American pressures on the Secretariat. *However, the United States security clearance for incumbents and new recruits was undisputed: and this amounted to a permanent, if less visible, FBI-oriented presence in UN affairs.* The clearance requirements in present use, agreed by Hammarskjöld with the United States authorities in 1953, will be found on page 285 of this book.

A reading of the judgments made by the United Nations Administrative Tribunal in late 1953 shows not only that UN responsiveness to the McCarthyist pressures continued after Hammarskjöld took office, but that a litigated case was upheld by the Tribunal and compensation awarded to the claimant. On 2 September 1953, five months after his appointment, Hammarskjöld informed the Tribunal in this connection, and with respect to the judgments of earlier successful appeals inherited from the terminal months of Lie's administration, that he had "decided that it would be inadvisable, from the points of view which it is my duty to take into consideration, to reinstate" the applicants. The pattern of Secretariat acquiescence was firmly set, and Hammarskjöld chose not to begin his United Nations career by audibly, or fundamentally, challenging it. Nor even, more curiously (and with few exceptions — of whom, however, Byron Price was one), by gradually retiring the group of senior administrative officers most implicated in the Charter violations of the secret agreement and the staff persecutions. Most of these, indeed, increased their authority at the United Nations in the subsequent years.

The holocaust of dismissals gradually ebbed away; but tremendous pressure to resign was put on the remaining "doubtful" cases — including such calculated humiliations as depriving a senior officer of his responsibilities and providing him with a worktable in a room occupied by junior staff, far from his previous site of authority. Those few who held out against this pressure were, as before, shunted into tideless backwaters. In the first months these things, though reduced in volume and far more discreetly conducted from the public point of view, were not radically different. The post-Lie victims of McCarthyism in the Secretariat were perhaps the bitterest, having hoped for better at the hands of Hammarskjöld.

The Staff Regulations were again "amended" — this time with some double-edged strictures about impartiality. The opinion of the International Civil Service Advisory Board, meeting in Geneva and New York, was sought in defining the conduct of the staff. The 1954 report of this body on the matter is currently made available to United Nations staff on their recruitment. (While concerning itself closely with the questions of integrity that had so recently exercised the Organization, and providing an exemplary set of standards for some ideal United Nations Secretariat that had not been exposed to the illegalities of Trygve Lie, the board did not address itself to the crucial fact that the problems of official misconduct and breaches of the Charter had not arisen within the staff itself *but from the actions of the Secretary-General and his deputies,* whose administrative authority is in fact reinforced by the board's recommendations.) The staff expressed certain reservations regarding this document at the time of its issuance.

Early in his Secretary-Generalship, Hammarskjöld showed signs of concern with the quality of his personnel; and a reorganization of the hapless staff got under way, initiated from within the Secretariat. The form and results of that renovation will be described later in this book.

What was lacking, of course, was some pronouncement on the fundamental issues, and any condemnation of the injustice done. There was nothing of this kind. Hammarskjöld's later references to his early brush with "the McCarthy issue" in the Secretariat suggest, also, that he took little cognizance of its infinite and ineradicable consequences for the United Nations Organization; to him it was "a short nightmare," and a "previous controversial chapter" that was closed in favor of "a new start." There is little evidence that he felt pain or indignation on behalf of the individuals annihilated in the witch-hunt, and no evidence whatever of a desire to make amends to them. But when his own turn came and Hammarskjöld was himself the object, during the 1960 attack by Khrushchev, of accusations against his integrity, he was to say:

Once an allegation has been repeated a few times, it is no longer an allegation, it is an established fact, even if no evidence has been brought out in order to support it. However, facts are facts, and the true facts are there for whosoever cares for truth.

In the coming months the hopes of Joseph McCarthy were to founder on the rock of the Pentagon during the Army—

McCarthy hearings. The domestic climate of the United States was to alter — though not necessarily the areas of pressure that had created it. With the death of Stalin, world attitudes were to undergo gradual, as well as precipitate change. Most of the McCarthyite desires had, in fact, been accomplished in the United Nations Secretariat by the time Hammarskjöld took office. His course of action, had this not been the case, remains an important question. Hammarskjöld too was to grapple with the menace of "decreased US appropriations," and with the expressions of that threat in complex questions of American influence exerted on world affairs both through and outside the United Nations; his relations with United States authorities were to become intricate and controversial. But it is extremely unlikely that he would have conducted himself before the world as Lie had done, once he had assumed his full authority. He was to assert, however, years later, that in response to the challenge of the McCarthy pressures "the Secretary-General and the Organization as a whole reaffirmed the necessity of independent action by the United Nations in regard to the selection and recruitment of the staff." That statement is quite untrue.

Hammarskjöld's most detailed public statement on this issue is brief enough, and forms part of a lecture, on "The International Civil Servant," delivered at Oxford University in May 1961. Excluding all reference to the destructive and formative experiences of the secret agreement and the complicity of high Secretariat officials in the witch-hunt of the 1940's and 1950's, it is a virtual rationalization of a *fait accompli* opposed to the original internationalist concepts of the United Nations Charter; and an instance — rare in Hammarskjöld's addresses — of an evasion of basic principle.

The dramatically demonstrated dangers of the Secretary-General's accepting "assistance from governments," as Hammarskjöld describes it, in the screening of personnel for shades of political and private opinion are passed over, in this speech, in administrative abstractions and in an inclusive reference to a

Secretariat policy of receiving "information that might be relevant to political considerations such as activity which would be
regarded as inconsistent with the obligation of international
civil servants." It is evident that such a definition could be extended or distorted to apply to almost anything. That "information" of this kind will vary greatly in nature and intention
according to the political climates existing in a diversity of
member states is nowhere discussed. (And it may be mentioned
that even the question of a record of criminal conviction, which
falls more properly within the province of advice acceptable
from member governments, might in certain instances be seen
as a political rather than a social reflection: United Nations
personnel, in the first, postwar years, included a number of
former Resistance members who had been confined in French
or German prisons, and contemporary analogies will readily
be drawn from other countries and circumstances in the
1970's.)

Hammarskjöld goes on to assert that, in negotiating procedures with the United States authorities for clearance of
candidates or dismissal of incumbents, "the Secretary-General
consistently reserved the right to make the final determination
on the basis of all the facts and his own independent appreciation of these facts." Yet that right, as we have seen, had in
fact been consistently forfeited by Trygve Lie; and the victims
of Lie's abrogations had been refused reinstatement by Hammarskjöld, and not even compensated in cases where there was
solely moral obligation.

The extent to which an "independent appreciation" can be
arrived at, in such a situation, is necessarily subordinated to the
information and presentation made by the national agency in
each case. From the entire Secretariat experience, past, present,
and cumulative, in this regard — and bearing in mind that the
administrative personalities involved were in many cases those
who had implemented the policies of Lie — it is obvious that
the instances where the United Nations Secretariat has recruited an American as a career official in defiance of a contrary

recommendation from United States official security clearance agencies will be minimal or nonexistent. (During my years in the Secretariat I never heard the United States clearance referred to as other than mandatory for American applicants, or knew of a case where a United States citizen was appointed over Washington's objections.) United States nationals, in General Service and Professional categories combined, now constitute over one-third of the Headquarters Secretariat work force — a situation which is in itself contrary to the concepts of the Charter.

The most significant aspect of the clearance requirement, however, does not lie in the exceptional circumstance of a candidate whose suitability may be contested between the Secretariat and the national agency, but in the pervasive and repressive atmosphere created by such a condition, and in the debilitating conformity it implies and imposes among the majority of the approved. (The simple instance may be given of Hammarskjöld himself — who, had he been a candidate subject to some such clearance system, would most certainly have aroused doubts in the investigators' minds by his singular and solitary nature, particularly if the tormented state of mind depicted in his now-published journal had come to light.) This essential factor is disregarded in Hammarskjöld's address, although by 1961 it had already shown itself to be a primary limitation on Secretariat capacity.

The desirability of an international civil servant's being regarded as a respectable citizen by his own national government is obvious (although to some extent dependent on the character, and fluctuations, of the government concerned). This reasonable criterion is utterly distinct from a formal process of passing such applicants through the Orwellian sieves of national surveillance agencies whose aims are notoriously directed not simply at the detection of serious transgressions but at the elimination of individuality and idiosyncrasy. Man is never nearer the grotesque than when enforcing on his fellows some arbitrary and topical concept of "normality" —

against which every significant action or utterance must thenceforward be consciously or unconsciously weighed, and which will inevitably operate at the expense of civilizing influences such as candor, magnanimity, and a sense of the ridiculous, and to the exclusion of abilities beyond the commonplace.

In acknowledgment of the situation, a few token organizational shifts were gradually made after Hammarskjöld's installation. The administrative chief, Byron Price, stepped down in 1954 — received, perhaps, back into censorship or film circles; his personnel remained. Certain staff members too patently active on behalf of the inquisitors disappeared from the corridors — dispatched, in their turn, to the ever-receptive UN missions abroad; others stayed on and flourished.

The dismissed staff members with contractual protection pursued, and won, their cases at the United Nations Administrative Tribunal. The judgment in their favor was followed by some deplorable discussion, in the General Assembly, as to whether the United Nations was obliged to give effect to the verdicts of its own tribunal; and the matter was referred to the International Court of Justice for "an advisory opinion." The World Court held the decisions of the Tribunal to be binding on the United Nations[*] — this result being followed, in its turn, by United States congressional anxiety that the damages should not be paid from America's contribution to the United Nations.

The other, larger group of dismissed employees — those in Temporary-Indefinite status — went to the wall. There was not, needless to say, any form of insistence, even from those who expressed themselves as appalled by the injustice, that the first category must be reinstated, or the second compensated: these possibilities of redress never seem to have been entertained by anybody — except perhaps by the victims themselves.

---

[*] In an earlier Opinion, of 1949, the Court had recognized the "international person" of the United Nations in law.

"An error which has to be corrected," Dag Hammarskjöld was later to say, in another context, "is a heavier burden than truth."

While the particulars were debated or ignored, an immensely significant change in the basic character of the United Nations Secretariat was accomplished without opposition — or, apparently, even comment — from persons in authority; but with the acute awareness of many members of the subordinate staff. Its implications were now to define the structure and spirit, and in consequence the effectuality, of the Secretariat as long as it may last in its present form. What had carried, in the early days, the aspect of a well-meaning confusion that would sort and stabilize itself, was now what one might call a chaotic fossil. "Clearance" had been effected, in the literal sense: the Secretariat was drained of impetus and vitality, and its most able and courageous officials had been either evicted or subdued. Those who had spoken up against Trygve Lie's misconduct, and been ousted, were precisely those who best understood and most valued the provisions of the United Nations Charter. The importance of human quality in the composition of the United Nations Secretariat had officially become — and indeed had always been — secondary, at best; which is to say, was actively opposed, since consideration for human quality is either first or it is nowhere.

In 1946 the UN Headquarters Commission had warned the infant organization: "The United Nations faces the choice: *Academism or Life. And this will determine its destiny.*" Academism is a euphemism for the choice now made by the United Nations. In accepting *permanently*, from its most influential democratic member state, the condition of official "security" clearance for its nationals before they might become candidates for even the humblest post in the United Nations Secretariat, the Secretary-General and his administration undertook to recruit only those Americans who met — or at least did not transgress — the standards laid down by J. Edgar

Hoover and his brethren, without regard to the nature, bias, or intent of those standards or to far more important qualifications that individuals might possess. It goes without saying that when such standards are arbitrarily imposed it automatically becomes unlikely that they will be notably exceeded.

That the nationals made available to the Secretariat by totalitarian states had been the subject of political screening in their own countries was of course a foregone if deplorable conclusion — originally unmentioned in the hope that time might wreak changes even in such matters as these.* That the United States, serving as the democratic model to United Nations membership and wielding an incomparable influence for good or evil over all the Organization's practices, should impose the same secret-police scrutinies on American applicants for United Nations positions, and with the heartfelt blessing of the United Nations administration itself, naturally closed the door forever on the possibility of an honorable, open, and freely competitive system of recruitment to the Secretariat.

Such a system of "clearance" would of course have been intolerable to the international Secretariat as originally conceived. It violated the United Nations Charter itself, and the administrative principles professed by UN leaders in the Organization's early years — as illustrated in the explanation given, by the State Department representative at the McCarran Subcommittee, as to why the "secret arrangement" contracted in the 1940's had not provided for a "full field investigation" (of the type to which American applicants for United Nations careers are now subjected by the United States Civil Service Commission): "The reason, as I understand it, that there was

* In his memoirs, Dean Acheson states in this regard: "Both [Trygve Lie] and we knew that citizens of Communist member states, some of whom would have to be included in the Secretariat, would be selected and directed by their respective governments, but neither of us wished United States citizens chosen by him to be in that category." A few pages later, Acheson makes a single, cryptic reference to the institution of the permanent security check on United States applicants for Secretariat posts, as follows: "The President tightened up the procedures."

no provision made for a full field investigation was that such an investigation would become known to the members of the Secretariat. . . . But because of the fact that the secrecy angle was made so positive and so important, they figured that it was better to do this limited job rather than no job at all." By the time the process was publicly accepted and instituted (and "welcomed" by Trygve Lie) in 1953, so many outrages had been heaped on the principles and statutes of the United Nations, and so little moral courage remained in the members of the Secretariat, that it appeared as just one more nail in the coffin of internationalism — and, in fact, as the logical conclusion to the events preceding it.

It is easy to imagine now, for example, the paradox — which has almost certainly arisen — in which a young person who had been prominent in a peace or civil rights movement would receive an adverse rating from the United States Civil Service Commission and the FBI, and be very probably refused employment by the United Nations; or that a lawyer who had participated in an academic seminar — such as that held at Princeton in 1971 — to study the practices of United States surveillance and investigating agencies would be debarred from a United Nations appointment; or that an economist whose thesis was opposed to established American concepts of industrialization or marketing might get a thumbs-down verdict. The bitter irony of these, and of a host of other such probabilities, is that United Nations operations, since the early 1950's, have suffered from chronic malnutrition in the matter of stimulating and contrasting views; and that much of the Organization's interior stagnation and conformity can be traced directly to the nullifying and intimidating effect of the clearance procedures officially instituted in 1953, and to the repressive atmosphere out of which these arose and which they in turn perpetuated.

A simple but acid test of the serious intentions of any United States official well-wisher of the United Nations is his record on this Charter violation — built in, now, to United Nations procedures for two decades — of American "security clearance" at the Secretariat. Few, if any, of such officials, whatever their favorable declarations regarding internationalism, will be found to have even alluded to it, let alone pressed for its abolition — although agitation to rescind it would disclose a depth and authenticity of internationalism infinitely outweighing all the tonnage of after-dinner speeches heaped on the United Nations in the past twenty years. It need only be realized that, under this scandalous arrangement, nearly half of the present United Nations Headquarters staff have been subjected to United States "security" approval, to perceive the impossibility of establishing, in such circumstances, any truly international civil service.*

For the adverse effects, both direct and incalculable, of such subservience on the recruitment of other nationals and on the international character of the Organization itself, there were ominous indications from the past. The decline of the League of Nations, dating from the rise of the Fascist states of Italy and Germany and their overthrow of principles that had been internationally agreed, was signaled by the League's acceptance of staff candidates imposed and approved by their governments rather than by the organization. Commenting on this deterioration — which, he wrote, "ate like a cancer into the living flesh of the entire international body" — Mr. Egon Ranshofen-Wertheimer, an official of the League of Nations and subsequently of the United Nations, has related:

The very qualities that had made a candidate from [previously liberally inclined] countries an ideal recruit, now invariably disqualified him in the eyes of his own government. . . . The Secretary-

---

* The present "clearance," under United States Executive Order 10459 of 2 June 1953, imposes an investigation of the most exhaustive and exclusively nationalistic kind by the U.S. Civil Service Commission, the FBI, and a battery of related agencies. The very nature of this investigation makes an absurdity of its claim to present only an "advisory opinion." That an applicant to an international civil service should be subjected to a preliminary — and obligatory — test of such extreme national orthodoxy is itself a violation of the Charter.

General was obliged to appoint persons he would certainly not have chosen had he retained a free hand. . . . To enforce the rules and regulations would have been desirable from the point of view of his own authority and of the morale of the staff, and would have been clearly within his authority. But . . . the Secretary-General of the League would have been pitted against a big power, and the outcome would have been a defeat for the Secretary-General.

The outcome, instead, was a defeat for the League; and its ultimate extinction.

Mr. F. P. Walters, in his *History of the League of Nations*, recounts the destructive effects of the application of national pressures to the Secretariat of the League, as follows: "The Governments of the Member States began to take a more active interest in the question of appointments; and in some cases to press the Secretary-General to nominate persons whom they regarded as reliable. . . . The smaller powers in the Assembly had always looked on the Secretariat as being with themselves the defenders of the international spirit. . . . They doubted whether this [international] role could be maintained by [those] who thought primarily of the interests of their own Governments."

When, with this history in mind, the question of a staff member's possible conflict with the policies and special interests of his own government was raised at the United Nations' formulation at San Francisco in June 1945, the following opinion of the founding fathers was recorded:

In answer to this question, it was pointed out that the experience of the League of Nations demonstrated that there was no practical difficulty in this matter except in the case of Fascist states.

Of a punitive bill introduced by Senator McCarran, shortly before the inauguration of the official security clearance in the United Nations, to prevent Americans from accepting United Nations employment without United States government approval, Trygve Lie remarks in his memoirs: "To my dismay the only precedent I could discover for such a law was the edict promulgated by Fascist Italy in 1927 to prevent Italians opposed to Mussolini from being members of the League of Nations Secretariat." And he ingenuously goes on to point out that Mussolini's penalties were far more lenient than those proposed by McCarran. Yet Lie accepted, with no expression of dismay — and declaring, in fact, that "I welcomed it as giving help I had sought for years" — the basic premise of this intervention in United Nations procedures, publicly stating that he himself would dismiss any United States employee he judged *likely to engage* in activities unacceptable to the American investigators.

It is only of recent years, when federal intrusion into American private life and thought has assumed dimensions openly incompatible with any democratic standard of liberty and order, and an estimated twenty million persons are said to have come under official surveillance in the United States, that the ultimate intentions of security agencies such as the FBI in noncriminal cases have been widely questioned, and investigations, both official and private, have been undertaken of the FBI itself. But there is no doubt that both Trygve Lie and Dag Hammarskjöld were well informed on the trends of thinking in United States investigating agencies when they permanently accepted, in 1953, the official screening process for United States personnel at the United Nations; and were aware that *there could scarcely have been a set of bodies more inimical to the concept of internationalism.*

At this juncture an opportunity was, for the second time, cast away for the United Nations to establish high standards of its own for recruitment. The recruitment machinery of the League of Nations, while less attuned to security interrogations, had incorporated a competitive entrance examination of serious standards — which naturally fell victim to the subsequent national pressures. The precedent had been ignored in the creation of the United Nations secretariats, where the initial stampede to produce "a staff" enrolled three thousand employees in the first nine months. A second chance now presented itself for the United Nations to repudiate the imposition of dubiously motivated hiring directives from national agencies, in favor of scrupulous selection practices of its own which would be aimed at forming an international cadre of the highest attainable quality. Incredible as it may seem, the possibility was never seriously raised by anyone in authority; and was forcefully advanced in United Nations governing bodies *only in 1971* — when it was vehemently advocated by the UN Joint Inspection Unit, in its Report on Personnel Problems in the United Nations, as a means of reversing the long, calamitous decline in staff quality and spirit.

Competitive examinations had been strongly recommended to the United Nations Secretariat in 1944, by an advisory group on the structure of the future body, and *in 1950* by the International Civil Service Advisory Board. This advice was ignored by Trygve Lie and Byron Price, and subsequently by Dag Hammarskjöld and U Thant; but the relevant passages of the 1950 report in which it appears are referred to, by the 1971 Joint Inspection Unit, as follows:

The further considerations on the evaluation of candidates which are set forth in . . . this report are worth thinking over, if only in order to realize how far we have moved away from the principles stated there.

And the report of the 1971 committee goes on to say, among much else in favor of competitive entrance examinations:

The fact is that *competition has never been openly practised in recruitment to the Secretariat;* we have already seen that, *in the only case in which it is practised* — the competitive examinations for translators and interpreters — *there is no recruitment crisis.*

It is self-evident that a system of examinations for entrance to an international civil service raises complex questions of establishing common standards. These difficulties are examined at length by the 1971 Joint Inspection Unit, which makes basic proposals towards resolving them. It is equally certain that such a system — if devised with wisdom and humanity, and with the objective of achieving a truly international Secretariat — would be, however imperfect, an immeasurable improvement over the present chaos of national pressures and bureaucratic confusions in which standards of competence are, at best, only intermittently applied. The worth and efficacy of any examining process lies, of course, in the quality and character of the examiners; and in this regard it must be said that the useful application of competitive examinations for recruitment to the United Nations must now await the installation of a new and radically different administrative establishment.

Beyond even these matters, the abysmal failure of United Nations authority in this first, crucial test of principle within its gates spread an implacable, demoralizing infection of fear, cowardice, indifference, and bureaucratic restriction throughout the Secretariat; and this was to work in chain reaction on human talents and conviction there over the next twenty years. It was the era of Adjust, as it was later to be the era of Protest; but Adjustment — a willingness to adjust to almost any adverse development and rationalize it as immutable rather than make oneself conspicuous by resisting it — took root in the United Nations and remained there.

An expert on United Nations affairs, Professor Thomas M. Franck, expressed the view, in 1968, that "the international service is only now beginning to recover from the blows dealt to its self-image during the McCarthy period by misguided American efforts to control the political beliefs of United States members of the Secretariat and force them to testify on matters pertaining to their employment, as well as the Secretary-General's failure to defend the independence of his employees against such role-destroying incursions." In truth, the international service has never recovered from these blows, which malformed its character from the earliest years.

The administrative deficiencies revealed in the McCarthy

crisis at the United Nations, far from being corrected, were consolidated and given prestige. "Power" at the Secretariat — power to penalize, with right of "emphatic refusal" to give reasons, powers of surveillance and intimidation — now resided with the administration; and it was an administration now composed of those who would welcome such a role or find it tolerable. Seniority, above a certain arbitrary Plimsoll line, implied a set of conditions greatly at variance with those obtaining in the rest of the Organization. Little enough effort, except in the form of official banalities, was thereafter made to convince the large body of junior staff that they had been specifically recruited to bring initiative to the service of the United Nations Charter — now spectacularly violated in the United Nations itself. And "local" recruits were hired into the Secretariat ranks as into the wildest parody of bureaucracy — to fill "posts," at the ultimate sacrifice of their capacities, their ideals and their self-respect, without career prospects and — in the case of United States citizens — with the satisfaction, merely, of having raised no doubts in the mind of agencies such as the FBI.

The Office of Personnel (as the Bureau was now rechristened), moved by the FBI example, reorganized — and extended into a vast system — a process whereby a secret dossier was, and is, maintained on every United Nations employee. Nothing can describe the repugnance felt by the staff for the "Confidential Files," never seen by the staff member himself but available to a variety of senior and administrative officials, in which any defamatory statement a colleague chooses to make may be commemorated indefinitely, uncontested by the object of it — who, indeed, has no means of ever learning of its existence.* Following the FBI pattern, anyone thenceforth dis-

---

* On the other hand, an empty show of "confidence" is made with an open periodic report on each employee, filled out by his seniors and witnessed by the staff member himself, regarding which the 1971 official Report on Personnel Problems has this to say: "The reporting system is satisfactory to no one and very difficult to use. . . . The compilation of personnel records . . . does nothing to enable the members of the [Promotion] Board or Committee to form an accurate idea of the real merits of the candidates under consideration."

senting, even mildly, against the system was a marked man and a "troublemaker." Critics who stuck to their guns were mechanically stigmatized as "embittered" or "disgruntled" — the administration never even troubling itself to inquire why numbers of its charges should become bitter or disgruntled, and merely chalking it up against them that they had let it be seen.

A show of gratuitous mistrust will inevitably be countered with the same. And if a conclusive act in the alienation of administration from staff was lacking, this network of secret dossiers and undisclosed black marks provided it.

Americans, or others, who find themselves wondering how the present quality of national leadership in democratic countries came to impose itself, or why the United Nations should so rapidly have retreated from its early promise, might reflect on the systematic expulsion of persons of character, intellect, and integrity from positions of influence and authority during the postwar years. Parallel to the destruction of enlightened and courageous elements in the executive of the United States ran the eradication of human potential from the Secretariat of the United Nations.

Subversion had, after all, occurred at the United Nations; though of a very different kind from that depicted by Senator Joseph McCarthy.

Four.

Effects, Ill Effects, and Aftereffects

"The fear of decreased United States appropriations"

Before turning to the events of the Hammarskjöld era, it is useful to trace the motives, and lasting effects, of the principal administrative actions of Trygve Lie's term of office. The United Nations is old enough, at twenty-eight, not only to be evincing incontrovertible traits and trends, but to have experienced whole cycles of internal development that have run their course from cause to effect to aftereffect. Of all that has passed, and been bypassed, at the United Nations since its founding, the events recorded in the preceding chapters are the most significant of member states' intentions toward the Organization; and of the character, imposed from without and nurtured from within, of the Secretariat itself.

"The issue in this case," states the Brief on Behalf of Nineteen Applicants submitted in 1953 to the United Nations Administrative Tribunal, "is whether the open declarations of the Charter or secret arrangements between the United States Government and the Secretary-General are to prevail in the United Nations. The issue is whether the Secretariat remains an international body within the United Nations or becomes an appendage of the Federal Bureau of Investigation and the State Department of the United States Government."

70

Almost twenty years later, the Chairman of the Foreign Relations Committee of the United States Senate was writing, in connection with the expulsion of Nationalist China from the United Nations, "Having controlled the United Nations for many years as tightly and as easily as a big-city boss controls his party machine, we had got used to the idea that the United Nations was a place where we could work our will."

It will perhaps have been seen that the fundamental issue of the struggle, in the Organization's formative years, for the United Nations' immortal soul was that of United States influence over the character and operations of the United Nations — this being pressed by American authorities in the plainest material terms of power and money; and that the outcome was the Secretariat's submission, with a consequent irrevocable casting of its personality.

The reader will not need to be told that, had a secret compact been uncovered between the United Nations Secretary-General and the Soviet government for establishing Soviet control over the administrative policy of the United Nations Secretariat — or indeed for any other purpose — and had the Soviet secret police been installed, by order of the Secretary-General, in the United Nations building, the international outcry would have been such as, in all probability, to bring down the United Nations itself; and the reaction in the United States would quite possibly have placed severe difficulties in the way of American participation in a future United Nations body.

No one can for a moment imagine that Trygve Lie would have abased the Organization and himself before the comparable demands of any other member state, host country or not — or that Hammarskjöld would have retained in the Secretariat the agents of any other nation. It would obviously be quite impossible to maintain, even for one year, an international secretariat in which staff tenure was subject to the domestic political fluctuations of every member state. The exception was made because the United Nations, as it then existed and as we have since known it, would have been unthinkable in the face of substantially "decreased United States appropriations" or American withdrawal; and because neither the other member nations — many of them dependent on American economic assistance themselves — nor the leading officials of the Secretariat could conceive of confronting such a possibility; or could conceive, far less, of a different kind of United Nations.

In November 1952 Maurice Duverger wrote in *Le Monde:* "The United States weakened the League of Nations by their estrangement from it. Will they enfeeble the United Nations by their proximity?"

The United States is the host of the United Nations not only in the basic fact of having invited the Organization to settle within its borders, but also in providing by far the greatest contribution to its finances — forty per cent in the early years, and over thirty per cent thereafter, until 1972 when the State Department recommended that the United States' contribution be reduced to twenty-five per cent. There were, as there continue to be, blunt references in the United States to "picking up the tab" at the UN; and, in some quarters, an almost equally blunt assumption that there has been purchased, along with this tab, an overriding say in the direction of United Nations affairs. In 1950 Senator Joseph McCarthy told the Tydings Subcommittee:

The financial contribution which the United States makes towards the running of the United Nations amounts to 45.57 percent. Actually, of course, we are paying practically all of that cost, in view of the fact that most of the Nations are contributing money we have previously given them. . . . I think one of the things this committee should spend some time on is the question of how . . . these . . . individuals with unusual backgrounds shift so easily from the State Department to the United Nations.

In December 1952, just before the United Nations' official acceptance of the United States security clearance program and the installation of the FBI in the United Nations building, the

New York *Times* reported a timely nudge to Trygve Lie from another Wisconsin senator:

Senator Alexander Wiley, a leading Republican foreign affairs spokesman, warned today that the new Congress would block United States funds for the United Nations unless there were security guarantees against "espionage and subversion" in the world organization.

And the New York *Post*, commenting on the same event, mentioned dissatisfaction in the General Assembly with the findings of Lie's panel of jurists:

However, any move by the Assembly to modify Lie's acceptance of the recommendations of this panel is likely to provoke open warfare with a sizable group of Senators. Senator Wiley (R–Wis.), who is slated to be chairman of the Senate Foreign Relations Committee, served notice on the UN he would oppose appropriating U.S. funds for the UN and its specialized agencies "unless adequate security procedures" have been worked out to guarantee that the UN and its organs do not remain a base for espionage and subversion. . . . No other delegation has asked for such an arrangement, and while it is conceded the Soviet bloc maintains an ironclad control over their nationals on the UN staff, no one believes Soviet practices should necessarily become the models of international conduct.

It was this same unself-conscious sense of ownership that surged into the headlines in October 1971 when, against the professed wishes of the United States government, Nationalist China was expelled from the United Nations in favor of mainland China (*whose entry the United States was supporting*), bringing a wave of resentment from a large segment of the American public, and a congressional gesture of cutting off American funds for United Nations programs. (It also brought the pathetic assertion from various UN delegates that the United Nations had thus demonstrated its "independence" of big-power pressures: in response to which it can only be pointed out that UN acknowledgment of mainland China was deferred for a generation at American insistence — almost twenty-five years passed during which Peking was in truth the Forbidden City; that it finally occurred within weeks of President Nixon's signal that he would seek better relations with Peking; and that the President's emissary was actually in the Chinese capital when the UN vote took place — a state of affairs as to which, as Senator Edward Kennedy politely put it, we may "never know the full considerations," but on which there must be certain speculation.)

Other member states have of course received far more direct rebuffs from the United Nations membership at various times:* the Soviet bloc, even aside from the Korean and Congo episodes, has been repeatedly at variance with UN decisions; Britain and France were trounced over their role in the 1956 Suez crisis; Israel, the Arab states, South Africa, and Portugal have been the object of UN censure. While there has been every indication that such decisions were unwelcome or unacceptable to the countries concerned, there has been nothing like the sense of almost personal injury that greeted the American defeat over Taiwan's expulsion — although there was no question whatever of censure in that case and the United States position, judged by actions rather than pronouncements, was at least equivocal.

Those who describe themselves as "realists" have insisted — starting from a posture of defeat — that United States ascendancy over United Nations affairs is a political inevitability: that is to say that, while America does not dictate the outcome of every issue raised at the United Nations, an immense American influence is both pervasively and directly asserted and that, even allowing for recent shifts of influence, it is as yet unlikely that the United States will be seriously crossed on

* As did also the United States, shortly after the China vote, when it was rebuked by the General Assembly for congressional actions violating agreed Security Council sanctions against the white minority government of Rhodesia.

major issues. (Certainly it is difficult to picture a United Nations in which the Secretary-General would be surrounded by predominantly Soviet or Asian or African advisers to the disproportionate extent that obtained with the American "cabinets" of Lie and Hammarskjöld, and, to a lesser degree, U Thant.) It is thanks, in part, to the supine acceptance of these "realists" that the situation has so far been able to impose itself largely unchallenged: no elected government will pursue a policy that leads it increasingly into public disapprobation and ridicule; but most governments will get away with what they can. (The eagerness, in United Nations circles, to embrace adverse developments as irresistible is a phenomenon that will be discussed.) It has been easier to submit to this passive and negative view than to face the great complexities attending its modification.

There is, in the first place, the undisputed fact that the United States, together with other member states, signed and ratified the United Nations Charter; and that the Charter enjoins governments in specific terms to promote international measures for resolving disputes and extending human well-being: the medium of these measures being a "United Nations" body whose internationality is to be scrupulously respected. The course proposed to governments by the Charter is of course beset by all manner of national and human obstacles, and could not, even in the best of circumstances, have run smooth. Yet it is, also, ultimately rational and feasible — infinitely more rational, it may be said, than the series of mass persecutions and annihilating wars that, culminating in the invention and use of atomic weapons, impelled the peoples of the world to call for a United Nations.

Those — and they are many — who contend that it is naïve and absurd to expect a nation such as the United States, in the prime of its great material and political power, to restrain its policies in accordance with internationally agreed treaties, or submit its disputes (such as American hostility to Cuba, or

American involvement in Vietnam) to a form of world arbitration, may be "realists" as they claim — if realism is equated with a basic resignation to chaos. Of such a form of realism, Bertrand Russell once had this to say:

I find many men in our dangerous age who seem to be in love with misery and death, and who grow angry when hopes are suggested to them. They think that hope is irrational and that, in sitting down to lazy despair, they are merely facing facts. I cannot agree with these men. To preserve hope in our world makes calls upon our intelligence and our energy. In those who despair it is very frequently the energy that is lacking.

Given the magnitude of United States influence in the world, any "realism" that excludes meaningful United States adaptation to the requirements of the international community must then be extended to the consequences of this approach in the contingent delinquencies of other nations; and to the resultant unlikelihood of the United Nations Organization's ever being taken seriously. Above all, it must reckon with the gradual alienation of citizens from governments which, piously embracing one set of attitudes before the world, pursue goals that are often patently opposed. Public confusion in the face of this "realistic" hypocrisy, and the rejection of valid principles because they have been emptily and cynically proclaimed, have contributed as much as any other single factor to the contemporary disaffection of the young and to failing confidence in constitutional authority throughout the world.

"WHITE HOUSE DENIES CREDIBILITY GAP" asserts a 1972 headline in the New York *Times*. However, our credence cannot be commanded or denied: it is something over which, in any long run, no government or person may exert control.

Thus when Mr. Kurt Waldheim tells us, on taking up his post as Secretary-General, that the peoples of the world expected too much of the United Nations at the outset, it might, in accordance with the dictates of "realism," be understood that we were somehow at fault for taking the pledges of our leaders seriously; and that our expectations should have been geared, less naïvely, to the low standard of intention and achievement that has in fact prevailed, instead of to what was proclaimed would be the case. The fact is — on the contrary — that high and sustained expectations, vigorously and intelligently pressed on national authorities, are the capital instrument by which the public raises the performance of government; and that without such expectations, which are standards in themselves, what small progress internationalism may claim would probably not have been accomplished, nor the United Nations brought into existence.

"As far as the United States is concerned," observes Senator J. W. Fulbright, "it is worth recalling that the United Nations Charter is a valid and binding obligation upon us, ratified as a treaty with the advice and consent of the Senate." The exercise of drafting a document, obtaining its approval in principle, and making it available for specific ratification has given an illusion of achievement to United Nations member governments, who have then felt free to disregard the provisions of the Charter in favor of their pressing national interests.

An anomaly of United Nations agreements and proclamations — such as the Charter itself and the Universal Declaration of Human Rights, and the many UN conventions relating to specific aspects of civil rights — is that, although their purpose, both immediate and indirect, is to secure individual and collective liberty and well-being, their influence is exerted mainly through national political bodies. That is to say, once again, that the "powers of compulsion" reside in those most likely to need compelling.

Many of the governments that endorse and invoke United Nations principles in UN meetings have, at one time or another, or continuously, violated these same agreements and usually with impunity. From the beginning the United Nations attitude to its conventions has been — as recently described by the Commission to Study the Organization of Peace — "more in the realm of what is desirable rather than mandatory," and importance has been attached to the formality of government endorsements of declarations in favor of humanity and justice, rather than to insistence on the active use to which these should be put — token approval being regarded as a strengthening of the judicial process in progressive nations, and a promising first step elsewhere.

The favorable consequences, within the domestic jurisdiction of member states, have naturally tended to show themselves in countries already amenable to enlightened legislation — where the Universal Declaration of Human Rights has, for example, been invoked and recognized in cases at law; and in the adoption of the Declaration into the constitutions of dozens of "new" countries. (An impeccable constitution of course carries no assurance it will be put into practice: even the Soviet constitution, for instance, sets forth the civil rights and moral duties of citizens in what might be thought an exemplary manner.) However, the United Nations procedures, being directed almost exclusively at a long-term official response, have also worked in a variety of other ways.

Threats to survival, both nuclear and environmental, and accelerating world emergencies of population and social disorder do not favor a slow accretion of legislative alleviations evolving without a parallel accompaniment of large-scale, vigorous action on behalf of individuals. "There is, I believe," says Professor Stuart Hampshire, "a growing sense that the usual calculations of recent past politics are scarcely worth making, and that short-term beastliness should not be tolerated for the sake of a supposed long-term future." When the government of Greece undertakes, in 1972, to submit a report to the United Nations on the condition of civil rights within its borders, United Nations officials welcome this arrangement as a gesture towards the eventual acknowledgment, perhaps in some future age, of international jurisdiction in such matters; others, of whom the present author is one, will find it farcical and will wonder whether the repetition of such empty exercises does not diminish, rather than contribute to, the stature and long-term potential of international controls.

The United Nations is unable to intervene in the domestic practices of its members; and, although the public retains the illusion that international bodies exist, like courts, for the redress of individual grievances, these bodies are in most cases powerless to protect petitioners or compel reforms; or even, in many instances, to discuss the questions raised. Open petition to the United Nations Commission on Human Rights by an individual human for his rights has, on a number of occasions, directly resulted in imprisonment of the petitioner by his government; and active humanitarian organizations, such as Amnesty, with nongovernmental accreditation to the United Nations, report total frustration in attempts to secure UN intervention in individual issues of civil rights.

It is this great dichotomy, this monstrous gulf between declaration and practice, that moved Aleksandr Solzhenitsyn, in his Nobel acceptance address released in August 1972, to pronounce the United Nations "an immoral institution."

This is an area where courageous Secretariat leadership would have made an immeasurable difference. There are persons in the present United Nations Secretariat eager to develop new and more direct approaches in such matters. But here again, authority has been timorous, and fearful of giving offense to governments or departing from established methods.

The paradox of course applies to many, many resolutions adopted on other issues by the United Nations that, irreproach-able in themselves, lead nowhere. In this respect, Academism — or Legalism — versus Life has reached a point where Daniel Moynihan, as a United States delegate to the 1971 UN General Assembly, could invoke the analogy of the League of Nations, declaring that "people caught up in the League of Nations system attached enormous importance to agreement on texts stating certain general principles and shared aspirations and under-standings — not on specific undertakings but rather on the way the world ought to be. It turned out not to be a very productive enterprise — and it continues here. . . . What I think we could usefully have less of at the UN is this quest for large pronouncements about things which are . . . impossible for governments to agree upon."

Nevertheless, the United States from the outset has had proprietary feelings toward the United Nations not only as the Organization's chief sponsor but also because the founding principles, the "large pronouncements," of the United Nations are parallel and complementary to stated moral precepts of government in the United States. (The Stalinist officials who signed the United Nations Charter on behalf of the Soviet Union presumably felt no such affinity, the various concepts of political sovereignty and human rights affirmed in the UN Charter being not so much a matter for debate within their domain at the time — despite the guarantees of a written constitution — as utterly disregarded.) Dag Hammarskjöld at various times referred to this kinship of the United Nations and the United States, and once described it thus —

When the United Nations was created, the founders had the experience of the League of Nations and also the experience of such a highly evolved constitutional pattern as that established on the American continent. A strong influence from both these experiences can be seen in the Charter of the United Nations.

For this reason, which is allied to their sponsorship of the United Nations, it was felt by many Americans, in government and out of it, that the United Nations was "good" in so far as it ran in harness with the United States' desires; and "bad" when it showed any sign of running counter. The overall result has tended to be, on what must be called a childish and demeaning level, the heaping up of presents to reward obedience; and the equally ignominious threat, at the merest suggestion of UN recalcitrance, to send the Organization to bed without its dinner. *Both* these manifestations have done harm to the United Nations.

The current "disillusionment" of the United States with the United Nations' role, and the recent decline in American involvement in United Nations affairs, can similarly be traced to an unreflective impatience with the natural consequences of debilitating national pressures such as those imposed on the Organization by the United States itself.

The UN body was of course led into temptation by the very generosity of the United States, which appeared, in the beginning, to make all possible; and by the determination of its members not to look a gift horse in the mouth. During World War II, experts looking to the creation of the future United Nations warned that "the main and probably inescapable disadvantage of location within the boundaries of a major power would be a tendency for the organization to be overshadowed by the international policies and relations of its host. It might even be affected by national political issues." The United Nations Preparatory Commission, meeting in 1945, also advised that "the United Nations should be so situated as to be free from any attempt at improper political control or the exercise of undesirable local influence." As late as 1946, the *Yearbook of the United Nations* recorded that the Organization "should not be located in the territory of one of the major powers, in particular one of the five permanent members of the Security Council."

These recommendations were overcome or ignored in determining the site of the United Nations Headquarters. The apprehensions expressed in them, however, were not only massively justified by events, but are literally and formally requited in the "host country" formula devised by Trygve Lie's triumvirate of jurists.

Doubts as to the suitability of the United States as the site for the United Nations have never been allayed in member nations; rather, the Organization's experience has confirmed and intensified them. In 1971, following a series of violent attacks on United Nations delegations in New York by dissident groups, the General Assembly set up a formal committee to replace informal meetings previously conducted on "relations with the host country." The possibility of relocating the Organization has been raised in this committee by Arab states, and by the Soviet Union and Cuba; but it has been a long-recurring theme among members less directly affected by the political climate of the United States.

The proposal that the United Nations be sited in the United States, though initially contested among the founding delegations, was quickly agreed.* The parsimony of other nations, or their postwar inability to make substantial contributions to the new organization, was not accompanied by forceful expressions of misgiving that a single powerful nation such as America should, at the start, place the United Nations under so large and continuing an obligation as her financial contribution of forty per cent implied: following the injunction of Mr. Doolittle, when temptation came they gave right in. That alternatives existed, or that, in a different sense, they have continued to exist, seems to have been difficult to credit at the time, and unimaginable later.

There was then, as there has never ceased to be, the possibility that a rational ceiling, say, of ten per cent, might be set on any single nation's share in maintaining the United Nations

* Trygve Lie had been in favor of the United States as a UN site all along: "In London, at the height of the war I had discussed America's future stand with my closest personal advisers, and put forward what I thought a daring and somewhat adventurous solution: Why not locate the headquarters of the future international organization within the United States' own borders, so that the concept of international cooperation could match forces on the spot with those of its arch-enemy, isolationism — utilizing at all times the American people's own democratic media?" It cannot be said that when the archenemy isolationism reared its head there was much matching of forces with it on the part of Mr. Lie.

Dean Acheson, on the other hand, in deploring the political exploitation by the McCarran Subcommittee and the 1952 federal grand jury of investigations of UN Secretariat staff, remarked — still without reference to the State Department's own long-standing secret activities in the same field — "If I needed confirmation of my opposition to having the UN headquarters in New York — which I did not — we had plenty of it during the autumn of 1952."

and its programs, the total — if necessary, a reduced one — to be made up by correspondingly increased payments shared among a large number of other member states. There is no question that the United States assessment of twenty-five per cent is unhealthy and inappropriate, and ought to have been reduced long ago: it needs no isolationist to point that out to us. On the contrary, a balanced United Nations to which all member states were proportionately committed in material terms would have been to the ultimate advantage of the United States.

There was also the possibility that the United Nations might have been launched, without its trappings of size and affluence, as a nucleus of quality and authority — rather than as a sprawling, extravagant bureaucracy, vulnerable in its formlessness and mediocrity, ever extending itself into a quicksand of discussions and procedures and new affiliates that its preordained size seemed to call for. Size, and financial increase, has throughout been equated with stature; only recently has there been a turning away from this misconception and — from a minority — a call for retrenchment. Delegates have proposed the "elimination of deadwood," the consolidation of useful functions and the abolition of others. Mr. Maurice F. Strong, the Canadian Secretary-General of the 1972 United Nations Conference on the Human Environment, has recommended "some drastic staff reduction — up to 50 per cent in some areas — and a major redeployment of UN resources in those tasks in which it can be most useful to its members and the world community. . . . Reduction of permanent staff need not reduce the amount of talent available to the UN to deal with important international concerns."

There were, in addition, possibilities of maintaining the Organization's integrity even under the pressures exerted by outside material and political forces. The very word integrity after all implies resistance to external influence. The courage and conviction, personal, official, and collective, required for such a course emerged at the UN, not in the member states or in the

Secretariat hierarchy where it would have been of incalculable value, but in the ranks of the Secretariat, where it was promptly crushed and expurgated by the United Nations administration itself — despite its endorsement by the UN's highest tribunal of appeal. "The United Nations is what the member governments want it to be — neither better nor worse," says Trygve Lie in his memoirs, echoing the favorite catch-cry of all who would comfortably absolve themselves of a responsibility in United Nations affairs: yet no one has been offered, and thrown away, a plainer opportunity to hold member governments to their own solemn pledges of what they wished the United Nations to become, and to elevate the standing and intentions of the Organization in its formative years.

Similarly, the economic and social aid programs of the United Nations have been bedeviled from the first by regular threats to withhold American funds unless, or because, such-and-such did, or did not, take place — culminating, in 1971, in the United States appropriation for UN aid being voted down by Congress a few days after the United Nations vote on the China issue. This particular congressional appropriation has been a periodic cliffhanger for twenty years, but is on each occasion greeted at the United Nations as a fresh consideration, to be taken up on immediate grounds rather than examined as an issue of principle. In 1971 the isolationist exertions of Representative John Rooney* of Brooklyn were blamed, along with those of the Buckley brothers, in UN circles for the menace to the UN aid appropriation — as if the situation had sprung newborn out of Mr. Rooney's dubious imagination and might be traced to a single culprit rather than understood as a whole series of related factors.

The only effective response to blackmail is to grasp its nettle: the United Nations, whatever its professed ideals, will never

---

* The hostility of Representative Rooney has also combined forces in recent years with American union leaders to hold a financial and political knife to the throat of the International Labour Organisation, a United Nations agency that dates from the era of the League of Nations.

attain to authentic internationalism until this spell of the "decreased appropriations" is exorcised. The following argument might therefore be made: that there will never be freedom from national pressures is self-evident in the nature of all United Nations business. There will always be, too, nationalistic groups inimical to any United Nations concept — in short, there will always be a Congressman Rooney. Faced with this prospect, the United Nations, both as a political body and a bureaucracy, must either acknowledge its subservience to these forces and, as in the past, make every effort to placate and rationalize them; or take measures to challenge and neutralize them with the object of becoming an independent and effective instrument for peace. It is as yet very unlikely that the United States will withdraw from the United Nations Organization; it is not even likely that the United States will wish to relinquish the influence wielded by its material commitment there, or allow other nations to assume this by default. There is in America a substantial, thinking public that does not support a stranglehold policy by its government towards the UN and its agencies, and would vehemently protest the discontinuance of United States membership in the Organization — to say nothing of the spectacle America would make of herself in the world's eyes by leaving the UN or driving it out of the country. But if United Nations action is to be forever circumscribed by such a condition then it might reasonably be held that the Organization should be judged a failure on that fundamental ground, and might do well to reestablish itself, should it come to that, on some quite other and more independent basis.

The obstacle to this nettle-grasping philosophy lies in the vicious circle of United Nations quality. Any challenge of the kind can only be made from conviction — that is, from moral strength. Had the United Nations shown itself of increasing value to the world, had it steadily commanded the respect and attention of a wide public by its actions and character, neither Congressman Rooney nor anyone else would be in a position to make political capital out of its deliberations — and in fact would damage themselves by attempting to. But the world's public, having watched the United Nations evade one crucial issue after another over the past decade, has not been encouraged to place its confidence in the United Nations or to feel that the Organization's usefulness speaks for itself. Still less is the inner climate of the UN Secretariat one of assurance and self-esteem; or even of unity of purpose. Few of its senior officials deeply believe in their ability to animate a newly constituted United Nations reduced in scale but directed at a higher quality of performance; or that the components of the present organization have an indispensable contribution to make in whatever straitened situation fate chooses to place them.

Nothing could make this plainer than the paltry and irrelevant arguments produced by leading UN officials in favor of continued American appropriations for the United Nations. An article in the New York *Times,* in November 1971, by the Acting Director of the UN Political Affairs Division, an American citizen, was almost exclusively concerned with demonstrating that local expenditures by UN personnel counterbalance, and justify, United States financial participation in the Organization: "The present assault on the UN is not only a political tragedy but it is also extremely bad business. The fact is that at least $120 million annually flows into the economy of New York City alone as a result of the UN's presence. . . . Expenses include staff salaries, office rentals, residences for top personnel" and so on. A plea for United Nations indispensability is also made by a New York *Times* UN correspondent: "Although there has been pressure in Congress for a cutback in American funds for the United Nations and other international bodies, the fact is that the United Nations has become big business for the city." The article goes on to fling purchases of "furniture and appliances, air conditioners and freezers, refrigerators and radios" into the void apparently created by the absence of more cogent reasons for the United Nations' continuance, and reports that "no matter how much the United States pays into the United Nations programs the cost is offset by the financial profits of having the world organization here."

If this is truly the level at which the United Nations now seeks to justify American financial participation in its programs, the increase or decrease of the appropriations might be thought to be of little consequence.

"The internal destruction of people and projects"

> Was he free? Was he happy? The question is absurd:
> Had anything been wrong, we should certainly have heard.
> — W. H. AUDEN
> "The Unknown Citizen"

The fatal pattern of national ascendancies over Secretariat affairs had been given. Confronted with massive and successful United States intervention to manipulate the United Nations international staff, other countries were moved to varying degrees of emulation, cumulatively exerting pressure for recruitment of their own chosen nationals — often simply to fill geographically numbered posts in the Secretariat as a matter of prestige and "influence." This was precisely what the founders of the United Nations had sought to avoid.

The United Nations Charter lays down ability and integrity as the first considerations for Secretariat recruitment, as follows:

The paramount consideration in the employment of the staff and in the determination of the conditions of service shall be the necessity of securing the highest standards of efficiency, competence, and integrity. Due regard shall be paid to the importance of recruiting the staff on as wide a geographical basis as possible.

The administrative course, since the Organization's founding, has been progressively to appease the innumerable national pressures, which have reached the pitch of lunacy with the influx of dozens of small "new" nations into UN membership, each clamoring for its complement of staff members in the

Secretariat; and, in corresponding ratio, to allow the standards of competence and integrity to lapse.

The second clause of Article 100 of the United Nations Charter reads as follows:

Each Member of the United Nations undertakes to respect the exclusively international character of the responsibilities of the Secretary-General and the staff and not to seek to influence them in the discharge of their responsibilities.

Not one Secretary-General has so far availed himself of the clear mandates of the Charter to do unrelenting battle against the ludicrous and self-defeating results of the "geographical" appeasement, whereby Professional posts of even the most minor significance are filled by national distribution with little — and sometimes no — deference to qualifications. The effect on the (often modestly placed) staff member who finds himself doing his own job and that of his "geographical" chief, with no prospect whatever of filling the senior post himself, may be readily imagined; less obvious is the dispiriting effect of such a policy on the "geographical" national himself, who, whatever his abilities, can never feel that he shapes his own career.

Several offices I worked in at the United Nations in the 1950's had their statutory Soviet staff member, who whiled away a two- or three-year assignment at the United Nations Secretariat by reading *Pravda* and taking marathon coffee breaks before disappearing back to what one trusts was the more demanding routine of some Muscovite ministry; and a much-quoted UN witticism of the early years was the question-and-answer, "What do you do at the United Nations?" — "I'm a Saudi Arabian" (or other rare national bird). Nowadays these appointees would tend to be the Grand Old Men of a situation that, catastrophically out of control, remains basically uncontested by the United Nations administration — even though it has now actually become a subject of criticism from certain delegations.

"The Secretariat," said Dag Hammarskjöld, "is international in the way in which it fulfills its functions, not because of its geographic composition. . . . If that had not been the view, the Charter would certainly have made wide geographic representation a primary consideration, instead of subordinating it to a demand for integrity." Despite his grasp of the matter, Hammarskjöld gave a decreasing impression of repulsing the burgeoning national cries for "More," or of challenging their interference with the competence and integrity stipulated as first requirements in the United Nations Charter.

By 1971 U Thant was giving official assurance to a United Nations committee that the geographical basis for recruitment, in conjunction with competence, "is now well established"; and blandly adding that of course the equal treatment of all staff is an imperative — as though the precise opposite were not the inevitable prevailing state of affairs and a ruling grievance of the staff. At the time of U Thant's retirement, the New York *Times* reported the view that "as far as is known he never challenged a member government when it nominated an ill-equipped man to a position on the staff." An official United Nations handbook, *Everyman's United Nations*, candidly informs us that, with regard to the composition of the Secretariat, "the main concern has been to ensure a more equitable geographical distribution."

It will be recalled that, in 1953, it was demonstrated that competence and integrity would carry no weight with the United Nations administration if powerful national pressures were ranged against them: "The political interests . . . were not satisfied and therefore the capability standard was discarded."

An excellent comprehensive statement on causes of the demoralized condition of the United Nations staff was issued in July 1971 by the Federation of International Civil Servants Associations (FICSA), a body of leading UN staff representatives having its headquarters in Geneva. This important, outspoken, and long-overdue summary of the extraordinary administrative situation that has come to exist inside the United Nations system had the following — among other things — to say on the subject of the geographical distribution of staff:

Increased interventions by delegations with the Executive Heads and Chiefs of Personnel, in order to propose the recruitment of their nationals at higher levels, or to influence the grade and step which might be offered [raises] the question in the minds of staff members as to the extent to which the Member States are committed to an efficient Secretariat. This factor . . . has a profound and adverse impact on the staff of the UN secretariats.

In 1943 Mr. C. W. Jenks — later to be Director-General of the International Labour Organisation — surveyed the administrative problems likely to face a future United Nations. Writing in the *Public Administration Review*, Jenks stressed *quality of leadership* as the element that would, through the top echelons, affect all UN staff and operations, and listed as desirable "integrity, conviction, courage, imagination, drive, and technical grasp — in that order." Commenting on this article in 1970, the UN Under-Secretary-General for Administration and Management, Mr. Andrew A. Stark, wrote:

But, alas, it is patent that, just as the achievements of the League of Nations in its lifetime and of the United Nations in a quarter of a century are pitifully small against the background of man's highest aspirations for the achievement of one world, the Secretariat falls short of the high standards of efficiency, adaptability and initiative which the world Organization should be able to command.

Stark went on to deplore "too great a degree of conservatism, too great a resistance to change, too great a weight of inertia in the Secretariat's administrative methods," and to point out that "far less than 10% of the Secretariat Professionals are under thirty years of age." (This latter figure at present stands at four per cent.)

A situation of this kind does not come about without a history and a continuity of causes. We have seen some of the shaky, not to say hollow, foundations on which the present administrative edifice was raised; and can now trace its principal aspects through two intervening decades, to the present point of deterioration.

In eradicating the various elements unpalatable to Joseph McCarthy, Pat McCarran, Roy Cohn and J. Edgar Hoover, it may be imagined that the United Nations had also eliminated from its ranks the persons who might have brought a larger dimension of thought, cultivation, and imagination to the Organization, and a measure of life-giving singularity. The "efficiency surveys" of the staff set up both by Lie and by Hammarskjöld (and supposedly independent of the McCarthyist purges) were doubtless influenced by the basic need of meeting "security" requirements and helped seal the Secretariat's fate by jettisoning, along with some deadwood, a number of oddities and extravagances, a heterogeneity that had given character. To stay on what was imagined to be the "safe" side, they inescapably favored the unresisting, the bureaucratic, and the philistine. The aims and composition of review groups then and thenceforth have been implacably directed at retaining only the completely fathomable.

The structure of the present United Nations Secretariat (and, to a large extent, all secretariats of the United Nations system), as conceived since 1951 and as illustrated by the geographical distribution of posts, is something that, if it makes sense at all, makes sense only on paper: a Dead Souls arrangement without reference to the living persons employed or the work required of them. Budgets and manning tables are drawn up with the overriding aim of satisfying the administrative and budgetary committees of the General Assembly from which funds and criticism, and a torrent of written and spoken verbiage, annually flow. (The 1971 FICSA report observes that administration is directed at "what governments will or will not buy, rather than the need of running the Secretariats efficiently.")

No reckoning has ever been taken of the consequences — reflected in almost every detail of United Nations operations *and present by implication in many United Nations failures* — to the individual and overall spirit of the Organization under such a policy, the abundant manifestations of which have been doggedly ignored or ruthlessly suppressed until, during 1971, they at last erupted into an outpouring of resentment and the threat of strike — and were made the subject both of the courageous FICSA summary, and of a devastating two-volume official report commissioned by the General Assembly.

It is significant that rebellion against the twenty-year attrition of staff quality has been initiated in United Nations agencies abroad, and has taken years to find outspoken staff advocates at UN Headquarters in New York — which provides the model for subsidiary and affiliated bodies, and where in fact the central problem lies. The internal events of the 1950's, and the reprisals then taken by the UN administration against its critics on the staff, made their enduring impression on Headquarters personnel; bureaucratic attrition did the rest.* It has not been possible to maintain an identical passivity elsewhere in the UN system. In 1967, a group of outside experts reported on conditions at the United Nations Food and Agriculture Organization at Rome, where staff dissatisfaction had risen to a crescendo. The secret report emphatically condemned an overconcentration of abused power at FAO Headquarters, intense interdepartmental rivalries, and extreme slowness of operations compounded by an absence of either long-range or short-range planning; it cited divisions so overloaded with administrative pressures that they were virtually stagnant and were not giving adequate attention to basic functions. At the time, the *Guardian* described the FAO administration as "the final proof

* When I was an elected member of the UN Staff Council in 1955–1956, it was virtually impossible to persuade staff members in either the General Service or Professional category to attend our meetings or take any but the most perfunctory interest in our deliberations — which were in fact almost exclusively concerned with salary adjustments and material conditions of work.

of Parkinson's Law." Years before, during a crisis precipitated by a staff suicide, the FAO staff had collectively appealed for action to remedy "persistent low morale," and got nowhere. By 1970, the FAO staff was again in crisis, and on strike; and in 1972 a new report on yet another administrative crisis was marinating in an FAO think-tank.

In 1970 a confidential report was prepared through the initiative of the staff association of UNESCO in Paris, excoriating the entire administrative setup there. This report, and staff petitions in support of it citing "frustration at all levels," brought reprisals against staff members by UNESCO administrators. Commenting on the situation exposed in the staff's report, the *Bulletin of the Atomic Scientists* had this to say:

We have known this for years, but governments who have been told have advised their representatives not to take any action. It is only through the courage of individual members of the staff and sections of the French press that the real internal destruction of people and projects has been brought into the open.

The United Nations Office at Geneva — which, with a staff of two thousand persons, is housed in the Palais des Nations, former headquarters of the League of Nations — has also been the scene of staff protests and strikes in recent years. And it is at Geneva that the Federation of International Civil Servants Associations has its headquarters, and that the Joint Inspection Unit presenting the current Report on Personnel Problems is based.

At New York, conditions of what can only be called despair have been tolerated for nearly a generation by a staff without administrative leadership or, until recently, energetic representation of its own — periodically placated by an official "review" which, purporting to concern itself with the malady, dealt with nothing but symptoms, if with those. "There is a sense of malaise, of dissatisfaction within the staff," the Under-

Secretary for Administration told the General Assembly in 1968, as the result of yet another official raking-over of productivity and morale. Superficial alleviations — always inadequate in the case of salary, except at the very highest grades where they are excessive* (and where they have not, due in part to the "geographical" factor that is paramount at this level, resulted in attracting a commensurate show of talent to the Secretariat hierarchy in general) — have tended to rest on the demeaning assumption that man can live by bread alone, and that a system of vacations, sick leave, and pensions can reconcile almost any employee to the atrophy of his faculties. If the UN pension fund is a dominant topic of conversation among United Nations personnel, and if the liberal annual leave of six weeks is excessively dwelt upon, that is because hope of other fulfillment has long since been extinguished. One cannot give rational meaning to a job through the amount of time one may spend away from it; nor to a career through its retirement benefits. One staff member has remarked that the Secretariat obsession with retirement and pension shows "a touching faith in life after death." The staff as a whole has been forced back on the material considerations that many of them, in enlisting, were willing to make secondary.

Of this prolonged folly, the rigidly enforced distinction between General Service and Professional categories has been, along with the geographical absurdity, the most destructive, and self-destructive, element within the Secretariat, and until now the most unrecognized. Unlike the Professional personnel,

---

* Although General Service salary scales are regularly published and Professional salaries may be calculated from complicated listings of pay and allowances, there appears to be no document providing totals of salary-plus-allowances in the most senior grades. Press reports have estimated the Secretary-General's *total* remuneration at approximately $100,000 per annum, and that of Under-Secretaries-General at something over half that amount. Senior Secretariat officials have consistently maintained that their pay is scarcely adequate to an appropriate standard of comfort and safety in New York City: a moment's reflection will therefore suggest to them the correspondingly magnified plight of the staff body. A bilingual General Service clerk starts at about $6,000 per annum.

the General Service are not recruited from political and geo-graphical considerations; there are few "international" re-cruits among them (that is, employees with rights of home leave and expatriation allowances), although it is a multilingual cadre in which many nationalities are represented — the larg-est component by far, however, being American. (All United Nations staff must be able to work in English; but, although bilingual qualifications — i.e., the ability of English-speaking persons to work in at least one other of the UN's official lan-guages* — have long been made a condition of General Service advance, they have not been required from Professional em-ployees, and at the highest levels the suggestion did not seri-ously arise until 1971.)

The General Service provides the major portion of the United Nations staff at New York and abroad: of about 35,000 UN employees, approximately 18,000 are General Service; of the New York Headquarters total, General Service constitutes almost two-thirds. These are people who have joined the Or-ganization independently, out of altruism and what might be called a spirit of adventure, ungratified by high salaries, pre-rogatives, or illusions of power; they have often paid their own way, to New York or some other UN center, for the purpose, and enter the United Nations with the idea of "serving." Al-though the lack of formal education is mechanically (and fatu-ously, since education is neither guaranteed by a diploma nor absent because uncertified) put forward by the administration as an impediment to their advancement, any number of them are college graduates, not infrequently more highly educated than their chiefs.† They represent the United Nations' great

* Bilinguality, in my day, commanded a welcome — and even crucial — extra ten dollars per month for a General Service employee. This has now been increased to $294 per annum. By some curious process of ad-ministrative reasoning, competence in a third language rates only half that amount, $147 per year.

† The myth that the Professional category comprises the formally edu-cated contingent of UN staff should be dispelled once and for all by the following revelation from the Report on Personnel Problems in the United Nations submitted to the 1971 General Assembly: "It is a re-markable fact that a very large number of Professional staff have never

untapped resource of enthusiasm, idealism, and variety. They would be the natural mainspring of any institution.

By a personnel policy which, had its declared purpose been the eradication of talent and vitality *in this major category of the staff*, could not have been more systematically destructive, the United Nations has deprived itself of a crucial stream of energy that was there for the taking; and saddled itself instead with a body of malcontents whose sense of grievance is the measure of its thwarted goodwill. More goodwill has perhaps been brought to the United Nations Secretariat than to any other modern organization, and more wasted there.

It is hard to avoid the impression that a desire to be of service to the United Nations is just what UN leaders least wish to discover in their personnel. The fruitless struggle of the General Service to make itself useful to the Organization has evoked, for the past twenty years, the wretched response of a Personnel bureau literally pitting itself against the human wish for growth and activity, seeking ever more ingenious methods of short-circuiting the currents of energy brought to the United Nations, in order to reserve senior appointments and advancement for the geographical candidates served up by governments — and, indeed, out of an apparent compulsion to perpetuate an ill-founded, inequitable, and archaic system. A junior functionary seeking to use his faculties will be rebuffed with as much insolence as if he were seeking special favors. Many of the least active areas of the United Nations emanate exhaustion: it is the fatigue that comes from resisting limitations imposed on capacity, rather than from using oneself.

It has often been observed that the members of the General Service category are regarded and treated by the United Nations administration as third-class citizens. It would perhaps be truer to compare their lot to that of the provincial auxiliaries of the Roman legions who, serving under Roman officers, might

---

attended a university. . . . Only 65 per cent of the [Professional] staff appear to have reached or passed first-degree level (i.e., to have completed three or more years of university studies), and *more than 25 per cent seem never to have attended an establishment of higher education*."

qualify for Roman citizenship after twenty-five years of un-blemished service — if, indeed, they survived a quarter-century of fighting the Empire's battles.* A General Service employee can be promoted into the Professional category only after a generation of service, by the acquisition of a rare and topical nationality, by gross favoritism or by some totally exceptional administrative circumstance. This is not made clear in the be-ginning, but allowed to dawn on the new recruit in his first months of employment. The vast majority, needless to say, never reach this heady reward; but if they do they usually find themselves merely continuing the same task they may have performed for the past twenty years.

(The last several years of my own decade in the United Nations General Service Category were spent filling a Profes-sional post and functions — a situation common enough in the General Service. It is perhaps worth recording that, in response to requests from supervisors that I be exalted to the commensu-rate rank, one personnel official declared I should be content with having these higher duties to perform; while another as-sured me that it would be simpler to make the Professional promotion if I resigned from the United Nations altogether and reapplied, rather than convulse the bureaucratic firmament by advancing me from the General Service after a mere ten years.)

It may be said conclusively that there is no system whatso-ever of reward for merit within the service of the United Na-tions.† Let a staff member demonstrate what abilities he will, these will receive no official recognition, and may even hinder

---

* Even so, Gibbon reports that Roman leaders familiarized themselves with the condition of their soldiers: "It was the policy of the ablest gen-erals, and even of the emperors themselves, to encourage [the troops] by their presence and example; and we are informed that Hadrian, as well as Trajan, frequently condescended to instruct the unexperienced soldiers, to reward the diligent, and sometimes to dispute with them the prize of superior strength or dexterity."

† "Many professional staff members are compelled to conclude that, in the long run, the quality of their work is less important to their career than cultivating a network of personal contacts within the Secretariat and even among delegations, and securing assignments in which they can make a name for themselves" (Report on Personnel Problems in the United Nations, 1971).

his prospects by making him appear suspiciously singular. Under this treatment, demonstrations of capacity almost invariably give way at last to apathetic conformity, or to resentful babbling about a withheld promotion. In ten years at the United Nations I never saw a single case of an intelligent employee's being encouraged to fulfill himself, let alone being rewarded for doing so — though considerable talents were displayed and exploited before arriving at their ultimate discouragement. This situation is not confined to the General Service, but persists up into senior ranks of the Professional category, being influenced throughout of course by the necessity of reserving appointments and promotions for the geographical candidates. Those who do slowly advance under their own steam are not infrequently those who have demonstrated least initiative, or have been least sensitive to the spiritual depredations of such conditions.

Rarely does a United Nations department head or divisional director seem to feel himself charged with the professional nurturing of his staff. Often he may know nothing of those beyond his own suite of offices, except for the senior members with whom he continually deals; and, for many of the hierarchy, prestige appears to demand that they not circulate freely in their own bailiwick but make others come to them. Few instances are as extreme as the celebrated case of a director on the 38th floor who in ten years is not remembered to have once visited the site of his responsibilities, more than twenty floors below; or of an Under-Secretary whose staff, attending a farewell party on his retirement, were moved to murmur, "So that's who he is"; or of another Under-Secretary who, having overreached retirement age, had *his* farewell party on a Friday and turned up again on Monday with a new Under-Secretary-Generalship (in which he remained for a dozen years), this time in charge of activities with which he had had no previous connection whatever. But innumerable lesser examples permeate the Secretariat (a section in which I worked for two years was visited only once or twice by its section chief, who had his office on another floor), and are but signals of a general condition.

Most senior officials apparently consider they have done all that could humanly be required of them by endorsing the "geography" or "longevity" advancements that come to their attention, without having to seek out, or inform themselves upon, any other abilities that might lie fallow in their domain; or without having to intercede on their subordinates' behalf against oppressive and debilitating procedures. A remarkable feature of United Nations life is the indifference of almost every senior official to the growth of demoralization around him and to the fate of the staff as a whole: it is quite impossible to retain their attention on this subject for as much as two minutes together, and no one with direct experience of the staff's predicament need ever expect a question on the matter from these quarters. (Delegates, of course, almost never come into contact with junior Secretariat staff; many General Service employees go through their entire UN careers without encountering members of delegations.)

As for the situation of the General Service, leading Secretariat officials and heads of delegations will receive with astonishment any suggestion that they should personally interest themselves in its human realities even for a moment — although proposals for its administrative fate are plentiful from such circles. In keeping with the secession of officialdom from life in our times, they would greatly prefer to authorize a series of ultimately ineffectual surveys at a cost of millions, and disseminate a plethora of documents, than inform themselves at first hand — with a commitment of time and attention, and a displacement of information in favor of knowledge — on the confusion that surrounds them.*

* This urge to govern human affairs while avoiding contact with them was given sublime expression by President Nixon when, in an American magazine, he wrote of his daughter's friends, during the same week that he set up a commission to report to him on causes of unrest among the young, that "when we sit around the table in the White House, they don't — understandably — talk much about politics to the President."

In this connection, the texts of the respective governmental views submitted in 1972 to a Special Committee for the Review of the United Nations Salary System largely ignore the questions of principle, and of morale and efficiency, raised by the division of categories; and in many cases exacerbate these fundamental problems by basing their recommendations on the perpetuation of the schism, some governments ignoring the human implications of the class system completely, others hoping to overcome them by correcting the grosser discrepancies of salary (as in the proposal by the government of Japan for improved alignment of General Service and Professional salary scales, made in the belief "that this arrangement would go a long way towards the harmonious relationships between the Professional category and the General Service, which increasingly have been endangered in not a few headquarters").

Here again, as in so many United Nations studies, the difficulty lies in bringing the simplest truths to light or getting the obvious into UN print. The grievances of a "lower" category whose upper ranks are fulfilling tasks in many cases identical to those of the "higher" grades directly above them, or whose members are — in a very considerable number of individual cases — required to cover and compensate for useless "geographical" superiors, or who may be by education and experience more highly qualified to perform functions to which they are told they may never aspire, can only be appeased by the application of justice and logic to its situation, and by an injection into its professional existence of at least the possibility that a show of ability will be recognized and advanced. The obstruction to bringing realities of the kind before any United Nations body is that the United Nations has taught itself to address responsibility as an abstraction; and that — as in world events themselves — consideration of the United Nations role veers away at the point where it would become seriously and specifically — and constructively — unflattering to those in Secretariat authority, and where it would require direct concern with human quality rather than with bureaucratic and political designs.

Among the numerous writings on United Nations operations published commercially by high UN officials there is scarcely a book or an article that comments on the existence of the General Service body, let alone takes cognizance of its numerical preponderance and adverse situation. Whole studies have been made of United Nations administrative affairs without a mention of it. The desire to present "administration" as abstract power, and to depict oneself as being where the action is (or, as all too often in the United Nations' case, where the inaction is), appears to result in a virtual obliteration of the administered, or their fusion into the gray shadowing on a graph. *Bearing in mind that the General Service category comprises the major portion of United Nations staff throughout the world*, such imperviousness can recall Lord Lucan and Lord Cardigan in the Crimea: it is tantamount to a general's having no interest in the condition of his troops.

In this connection I have read with wonder, in the Report of the Joint Inspection Unit on Personnel Problems submitted to the 1971 General Assembly, that

There is a keen desire [among the Directors of the various units of the Secretariat] that drastic changes should be made as quickly as possible in order to make available the competent staff they need; only in a few cases is that desire tempered by scepticism as to the very possibility of such a solution.

Here is the paper conscience that makes tragic nonsense of much governmental reporting — depicting, for the sake of "order" and *amour propre*, a state of affairs the precise opposite of the prevailing one. It is through the negligence of this very cadre "in charge of the various units," and its collaboration in the long-standing long-discredited personnel policies of the United Nations, its lack of either human or professional concern for the staff body and its reluctance to protest the system, that the present shambles has come about. How could a situation deplored in endless detail throughout a two-volume study conceivably have come into existence without the connivance — and, in some cases, instigation — of the Organization's senior officials? What *is* UN administration, if not the directors of the Secretariat, most of them long-term incumbents and some of them original fixtures from the inaugural days of Trygve Lie? One of the complaints listed by these directors in their enumeration of Secretariat deficiencies is "lack of leadership": *where was leadership to come from, if not from them?*

Reading this extraordinary appeal for reform, one might almost feel that the consistency of the "few cases" where "desire is tempered by scepticism" is preferable to the hypocrisy and self-delusion of the remainder.

The attempt to detach themselves from the sinking administrative ship cannot in any case be made by these officers without reflection on their own respective areas of responsibility. The interaction of quality and operation in the United Nations Secretariat is such as to create an almost indivisible whole; and the Report on Personnel Problems points out: "It is hardly necessary to add, however, that programming in the personnel sector would serve no purpose without a considerable improvement in the definition of the Organization's work programme."

In the same way it appears impossible to winkle out any senior official who will assume responsibility for the administrative policy that has dominated the United Nations' internal affairs for the last twenty years, with incalculable adverse effect on the Organization's world role. *It is as difficult, now, to discover an administrator who stands by those procedures as it was, in the past, to find one who would depart from them.* (U Thant's last statements in the face of the administrative nightmare seem to contain — apart from acknowledgments that "we have all long been aware of the need to put our house in order" — no expression of personal responsibility or of regret for the organizational chaos which, after a decade of leadership, he bequeathed to his successor.)

Inflexible in its enforcement, impervious or retaliatory to the most urgent staff appeal,* administrative and personnel officials yet show every reluctance to stand by the system they have so long perpetuated — and, now that it is under irresistible official attack, claim to have been seeking its reform all along. The 1971 Report on Personnel Problems informs us that "the officials responsible for recruitment to the Professional category are the first to desire drastic changes in the methods they are at present obliged to use" — as if this very area did not contain some of the long-term warhorses of the Secretariat who have had twenty years in which to agitate for "drastic change"; and as if they had been bound to the present methods by anything other than their own compliance.

Pressures from governments are of course blamed for the geographical candidates — who in fact have for decades been arbitrarily imposed on their reluctant colleagues by the UN administration with no expression of opposition or regret. (Indeed, in these and other matters, some UN administrators have so thoroughly presented themselves as the helpless pawns of delegations that one wonders why they are there at all.) However, at the 1971 General Assembly one delegate observed "that the relative importance of the two separate criteria of individual competence and geographical distribution required further clarification from the Secretariat." Even a sense that the administration took the staff's part in such matters would have been an alleviation, and a weapon towards reform, throughout the years when, quite on the contrary, continual

---

* For many years the notorious oral response of the United Nations Office of Personnel to staff appeals against the system was "You can always leave"; while written pleas for administrative improvements went unacknowledged. An account, by the Vice-Chairman of the Staff Committee, of salary discussions with UN administration representatives in 1971, produces a chilling echo of the events of twenty years before: "When one engaged in salary talks with the Administration, one learned that they were neither 'negotiations' nor 'consultations' in the normally accepted meaning of the words. They were more like courtroom proceedings, each side putting forward its evidence and trying to rebut the other's arguments. The difference was that at the end of the proceedings the verdict was rendered by the prosecuting attorney, i.e., the Administration representatives."

public assurances were forthcoming to delegations that their nominees would be accommodated as speedily as possible.

A curious feature of United Nations staff policies is a history of outright discrimination against women in the Secretariat. The United Nations maintains, among its governmental organs, a Commission on the Status of Women, and a section on Status of Women is incorporated into the UN Secretariat Division of Human Rights. The General Assembly has adopted numerous conventions on the equality and protection of women throughout the world, and other UN bodies have made studies and recommendations concerning women's rights in professional fields. Nevertheless, we learn from the 1971 Report of the Joint Inspection Unit on Personnel Problems that within the UN Headquarters Secretariat itself

Of the total of roughly 3,000 staff members in the [Professional] category, about one-fifth are women.

The proportion of women is extremely small in the higher grades [zero, until 1972, at the Under-Secretary-General level, 4 per cent at the Director level, and 8 per cent in the immediately subsidiary grade; thereafter the percentage increases in direct ratio to decreasing responsibility].

The total proportion of [Professional] female staff is 19 per cent.

As women have had an influential role in the application of United Nations personnel policies, and even in their formulation, this situation also raises an interesting and by no means unique question of discrimination by women against their own sex under a male system. The most striking example — and the one most alluded to, though certainly not the most important one — of Secretariat discrimination against women was until recently the absence of any female appointment at the Under-Secretary-General and Assistant Secretary-General level, where dozens of males of greatly varying competence have come and gone throughout twenty-seven years and where there were, until 1972, at Headquarters alone, approximately a score of exclusively male incumbents. A token appointment or two in this area — now achieved as the deficiency became more and more exposed in the light of contemporary agitation for women's rights — will do nothing to solve the much larger issue in the Secretariat as a whole, or to correct discriminatory provisions, adversely affecting women, in the United Nations staff regulations.

Recent General Assemblies and meetings of the Status of Women Commission have shown themselves slightly self-conscious on this point — as has Mr. Kurt Waldheim, who early in his appointment fulfilled his intention of installing a female in an Under-Secretary-Generalship. As the United Nations' own related bodies have been able to accomplish nothing, over twenty years, towards the reform of the general situation, however, it seems likely that significant change will come about only through outside pressure.

The administration of the United Nations Organization is accordingly seen to be based, not on "the highest standards of efficiency, competence, and integrity" with due regard to geography, but on an incapacitating system of geographical — that is, of national and political — discrimination; and to pursue a policy within which other, related forms of discrimination are at work against capacity: discrimination against youth (a crucial factor, to be examined later in this work), against women, against talent, candor, and singularity; and, above all, against those without official geographical advantages who have joined the Organization from a spontaneous wish to serve the world community.

In the past decade it has naturally grown more and more difficult to recruit and retain qualified staff on these terms. (The 1971 statement by the Federation of International Civil Servants Associations notes: "Lack of job satisfaction and anonymity, when added to the inevitable problems of expatriation, lead to frustration and discontent and it is surprising that it does not accelerate the high withdrawal rate.") This has been particularly true of the General Service, which is not forcibly fed from delegational pressures. For a time the United Nations administration attempted to meet the General Service lack by operating a system through which virtually indentured workers were hired as secretaries, mainly from Australia and the Philippines, by a series of irregularities and deceptions — eventually finding themselves stranded in the United States under threat of deportation if they left UN employment, and obliged to work their passage home as best they might. This unsavory arrangement was adversely publicized in newspapers abroad, and has supposedly been modified. The uppermost General Service salary scales, when laboriously attained, overlap with the lowest of the Professional category; it is into these lowest Professional grades that a General Service employee will be promoted, if ever, and with practically no expectation of rising further. His satisfaction is therefore to derive from a tiny increase in salary, a few perquisites, and the uncertain glory of his Professional designation. His duties and prospects remain about the same. It is a class distinction, and one long-term Secretariat member sums it up as follows:

We have a privileged class here and an under-privileged class, both represented by the same staff union. Why, for example, should the children's allowance be bigger for Professional than for General Service, when everyone knows that Professional children don't require bigger dinners? — one could go on and on. And just what is the profession that Professionals are skilled at? For the most part it is simply the same sort of insignificant paper work that is demoralizing us all.

Deploring the inequities between the grades and pointing out that "the present serious anomalies have no place in the United Nations, to which the world looks for human equality," the statements presented on behalf of the staff by FICSA in 1971 go on to say that "the system of two categories gives rise to serious psychological problems, an air of class distinction in dividing the two categories on the basis of the kind of work they do, and ways must be found to overcome the difficulties."*

In this connection, the treatment of the General Service issue in the two-volume Report by the Joint Inspection Unit on Personnel Problems cannot be sufficiently condemned, as it concerns itself with recruiting (by "junior competitive examination") a large body of lower staff who would, in accepting their inferior status, renounce any possibility of rising in the service. Although going on to assert that *"the efficiency of a modern civil service depends upon the degree of competence of its staff and the climate of incentives in which they work,"* the report favors discontinuance of promotion of even such few venerable General Service employees as have hitherto been elevated to the Professional category, on the grounds that this plays havoc with "the principle of geographical distribution," and "is a major factor in the aging of the Secretariat" because of the advanced years of the ultimately favored few. The recommendation concludes, with evident satisfaction, that "the application of the new rules . . . should in the normal course of events put an end to the practice of recruiting General Service staff, near the end of their career, to the Professional category."

It only remains to ask what caliber of person will enroll under such a system, which categorically excludes the possibility of his growth; and what sort of service will be obtained from an organization of which such persons comprise two-thirds. The United Nations, it would seem, believes in "development" everywhere but inside its own walls.

On the other hand, an artificial "solution" — the possibility of which is also raised by the Joint Inspection Unit — has been proposed by the Assistant Director-General of the United Na-

---

* "Obviously not everybody in a career service can expect to get to the top, but everybody should be able to hope to do so when he enters the service. What matters, at the time of recruitment, is the maximum attainable point. Career cadre in the UN organizations will not attract the most competent and dynamic staff member which the Charter requires unless the average competent official has an assured career span, can reach a reasonable grade at a reasonable age, and the exceptional man has a *chance* — even if it is only a small chance — of going much further."

tions Office at Geneva, a UN veteran who was Headquarters Director of Personnel in the days of Byron Price. Recognizing that the General Service contains "a number of highly qualified technicians," and that at present "the United Nations has no way of retaining the career prospects and perhaps the services of these staff members, except by promotion," this official proposes the creation of yet a third category, to be called "Special Service," which would provide an illusion of graduating from the General Service and into which General Service personnel could, as he puts it, be promoted "without diluting the quality and characteristics of the Professional category." The full offensiveness of this phrase, and of the proposition itself, can perhaps be measured by imagining the General Service to be comprised of an ethnic minority — in which case, of course, the expression would not have been used and the situation might long since have been rectified.

Even the FICSA statement, while pressing for dissolution of the division between the two categories — whose abolition should have been demanded decades ago, as a matter of basic principle and for the health of the Organization itself — reluctantly envisages the possibility of their retention by the UN administration. So long as this is the case, many of the grievances aired in the FICSA summary and in the Report on Personnel Problems will continue to erode UN potential — "A Personnel establishment which has become, by and large, more of a recipient than an initiatory body," "lack of modern personnel policies, and a certain administrative timidity," "a consequent loss of credibility in the system," "an almost absent coherent career policy," "no coherent system of training," "increased interventions by delegations," "relative slow pace of promotion for talented and gifted staff members and recognition of work well done"; and so on, and on. The FICSA representatives conclude:

Whatever the structure, it must allow for opportunities . . . through merit, whose basis would be proven ability to perform the job. It is a known fact that the splitting into two categories had unfavourable repercussions on staff morale. . . . FICSA is indeed greatly conscious of the practical difficulties involved in returning to *the system which existed prior to 1951* [author's italics]. . . . However . . . we can envisage both difficulties and immense advantages from a return to the old unity in the International Civil Service, with a possible impact on morale and efficiency.

So we are back at 1951 again, and apparently hoping for a second chance.

In 1971, an article was published in the *Saturday Review* by Mr. Hugh L. Keenleyside, former Director-General of the United Nations Technical Assistance Administration and UN Under-Secretary-General for Public Administration, describing the political and administrative crisis of the United Nations. The following extracts may be given here:

The dimensions of the tragic deterioration of the Secretariat are in part the result of the general financial situation, but lack of funds is not the whole, or even the main, root of the evil. When in 1970 the Fifth Committee [of the General Assembly] received demands for a major increase in the salaries of all professional staff members, it started a debate that lasted on and off for several weeks and that unveiled much more about general conditions in the Secretariat than some delegations and U.N. administrators wanted to have disclosed. Dissatisfaction with the work of the organization had been increasing among the more serious delegations over a number of years. It was obvious that productivity was low and getting lower. Many of the better people were leaving. Morale was deplorable; discontent was endemic. At one time during the salary debate there was even a possibility that the professional staff might strike. . . . The continuous rise in the cost of living in the New York area was an obvious factor. Even more important was the brutal deterioration of a city where congestion and pollution were matched by the increase in crime and in outbreaks of racial and politically motivated disorders.

But beyond these circumstances was the organizational chaos within the Secretariat. Here it was agreed that the two most important factors were (1) the way in which the principle of "geographical distribution" was being applied in appointments and promotions, and (2) the manner in which member governments were interfering with the efforts to establish and maintain an authentic and trustworthy international civil service. . . .

This means not only that persons of less than satisfactory quality are added to the U.N. staff but that, because they tend to move in at relatively high levels, they block the paths of able young officials seeking promotion through the ranks. Thus any serious efforts at career planning and in-service training are also stymied. Ambitions are thwarted and incentives dissolved.

This "competition among incompetents" also has resulted in an organization that is, in many areas, overstaffed. The work must be done, and if some staff members are incapable of doing it, others must be employed. Consequently, there are pockets of idleness that, in turn, become infected with sloth and a lack of discipline. Intrigues and bitterness, sometimes exacerbated by racial or other antipathies, soon follow. . . .

Members of the Secretariat cannot all be expected to understand and make allowances for the difficulties facing the Secretary-General. This contributes to a feeling that U Thant is not, in fact, much interested in people (which is certainly false) and even less in administration. Other critics charge that, unlike Hammarskjöld, he will not really fight for the principles on which the service was originally established. Faced with external pressure, he will give way; presented with internal problems, he will hesitate, delay, and when possible, evade the issue or pass it along for solution to an aide. . . . Some critics of the current administration tend to minimize the role of U Thant and to attribute the present distemper instead to "the 38th floor," by which they mean the "Establishment" in general. . . .

It is not surprising that many highly qualified professional members of the Secretariat, aware of past failures and present difficulties, frustrated by what they consider favoritism, by persistent interference from governments, by the absence of in-service training, by the blockage of planned careers, by conditions of life in New York, and (in some opinions) by inadequate salaries, have become disillusioned and embittered — especially when they see that violation of the rules often appears to bring the offenders appointments, promotions, and general success.

Looking toward the Joint Inspection Unit Report on Personnel Problems, then in preparation, Mr. Keenleyside added, "It would be unrealistic to expect that any really significant improvements will follow this report. Far too many governments have a vested interest in the present deplorable situation, and far too many others are looking forward to short-term profits from it." While conceding that the deficiencies of Trygve Lie and the high qualities of Hammarskjöld had their respective direct — and contrasting — repercussions on the Organization's standing, Mr. Keenleyside expressed the belief that heightened international tensions left the Secretary-General little time for administrative concerns, while "almost intolerable pressures" from member governments brought "inevitable compromises" from the United Nations administration on staff matters. The lack of Secretariat leadership, and of almost any degree of Secretariat autonomy, depicted in this article move one not to thoughts of reform for the existing apparatus, but of its demolition and reconstruction in some refreshed, independent, and uncorrupted form.

The following items form part of a list of United Nations present shortcomings incorporated in the Joint Inspection Unit's Report on Personnel Problems as giving "some slight idea" of the present predicament. I should emphasize that these are not conjectures by the present author, nor even assertions by UN staff spokesmen, but statements obtained through a consensus of United Nations senior officials and embodied in an exhaustive study commissioned by the United Nations itself:

Clogging of work programme with projects which cannot possibly succeed;
Paucity of modern working equipment;
Slowness of procedure in all personnel matters;
Acceptance of patronage in recruitment;
Lack of leadership; erosion of discipline and morale;
Difficulty of terminating incompetent staff members;
Lack of in-service training and of career prospects;

Lack of long-term policy;
Erosion of ideals.

Those who will trouble themselves to refer to United Nations records of exactly twenty years before will find, in a 1951 appeal to the administration from staff representatives, an almost identical listing of what are at that early juncture characterized as "the outstanding problems — or, indeed, opportunities" of the United Nations Secretariat.

That the "difficulty of terminating incompetent staff members" has been most severe in the Office of Personnel itself, and in other branches directly concerned with the United Nations' internal affairs, is self-evident in the present crisis. Commenting on the Organization's expansion, the Report of the Joint Inspection Unit on Personnel Problems observes that "the general conception of administrative methods, especially those concerned with personnel policy, has failed to evolve at the same rate." A partial solution might be found by applying in this area the suggestion made by a delegate to the 1971 General Assembly that "Professional staff lacking in motivation could be retired early." Even a complete change of personalities in the administrative sector, however, would be useless without a correspondingly revised context of attitudes and objectives throughout the Organization.

In that connection, Mr. Maurice Strong, Secretary-General of the United Nations Conference on the Human Environment, had this to say in 1971:

Yet the question remains: how in practice to revitalize a flagging organization which is somehow out of tune with the needs and the moods of the times? . . . I believe that a shock treatment is called for and the present moment provides a unique opportunity to apply that treatment. . . . I have come to the conclusion that the only practical way to revitalize the organization is through a major consolidation and regrouping. This must be no mere cosmetic surgery. It would require some drastic staff reduction — up to 50 per cent in some areas — and a major redeployment of UN resources in those tasks in which it can be most useful to its members and the world community.

In December 1971 the Council of the Federation of International Civil Servants Associations drew up its recommendations for the reform of staff conditions in the United Nations system and creation of a career service. Addressing itself to the necessity, stipulated in the United Nations Charter, "of securing the highest standards of efficiency, competence and integrity," the officials of FICSA went on to say:

Few would dispute the fact that conditions of service in the Secretariat are no longer adequate to secure a reasonable supply of staff of the quality described in the UN Charter. In addition there have been weaknesses in the recruitment process itself: inattention to candidates' levels of training, responsibility and experience, artificially restricted choice of candidates, failure to use properly the probation period . . . submission to pressure from delegations, personal bias, delay and uncertainty in offers to candidates, absence of a coherent career policy and of effective in-service training. All these factors are prejudicial to high quality recruitment. Internal selection committees have tended to fall into disrepute and have permitted practices to flourish which encourage the view of the staff that the International Civil Service is in a process of decline.

A study of the FICSA statements of July and December 1971 and of the current two-volume Report of the Joint Inspection Unit on Personnel Problems in the United Nations leaves the reader with the conviction that all these documents are calling for a new United Nations. There is no possibility whatever that reforms of the magnitude recommended in those papers can be accommodated by the present Organization, or even that the necessity for them will be properly understood by — indeed — the very administrators who created and nourished the present emergency. Capacity for reform is an instrument that must be kept tuned: there is little indication that it has ever been in functioning order at the United Nations.

"Of luxury or of simplicity"

While irrational distinctions of rank do their work among the lower grades, great contrasts of privilege isolate the hierarchy and the delegations from the entire body of the Secretariat staff. Only a very literal, or "unrealistic," person would have expected delegates and top UN officials to take all they have and give to the poor; and certain superfluities were no doubt envisaged by the signatories of the United Nations Charter. There might even have been, for generous spirits, a vicarious pleasure in the thought that the United Nations was the scene of an occasional celebration or good tuck-in. Adherents of the New York *Daily News* would possibly have made capital out of any normal standards of remuneration to, and diplomatic representation by, UN dignitaries, and the United Nations would have had to bear with equanimity this usual if regrettable quota of carping. But the excesses of self-indulgence to which UN senior social life has habituated itself, and its ever-extending network of allowances and other bonuses at the top, make a staggering contrast with the lot of the Secretariat as a whole, and indeed with any rational concept of comfort, or even luxury.

Although the "taxpayer" approach, in criticizing the United Nations, should be made on the highest level of public involvement rather than, as it has usually been, on the pettiest, there is no reason whatever why a preposterous show of extravagance and greed should be regarded as immune to intelligent public comment or as in some way unmentionable, by UN supporters, in the cause of peace.

While the United Nations Chief of Protocol describes, in an interview, the "strain" of a "digestion-challenging round of 300 to 400 parties, receptions and dinners" during the eleven weeks of the annual General Assembly ("the Turkish-born official says he loves it"), a circular informs the staff (the vast majority of whom are strictly excluded from these jamborees) that "anyone eating in the Cafeteria will do so without taking the dishes and utensils from his tray, and after eating will deposit the tray with its contents on a special rack in the premises." A former United Nations Under-Secretary comments: "The irresponsibility of many member governments is illustrated by the not unusual custom of a national delegation from an impoverished country holding a cocktail or buffet reception in a New York hotel at a cost of $15,000 to $30,000 at the same time that its government is far behind in the payment of its meager U.N. assessments." Interviewed in his eighteen-room official residence in the Waldorf Towers, the United States Ambassador to the United Nations, George Bush, a Texas millionaire, remarks, "We're in the process of adjusting to all this opulence." An array of delegates unself-consciously discuss their preferred restaurants with the New York press, lamenting the astronomical charges. The wife of a former United States representative to the United Nations recounts, "It was a rewarding experience. We had a huge car and a chauffeur to drive us about. When we left the UN we went back to taking taxis."

As the Permanent Observer of the Holy See to the United Nations succinctly puts it: *"Dopo le sedute . . . comincia il carosello."*

The unfailing assertion of the partygoers, that "much of the Organization's business is conducted" at the four hundred blowouts, is perfectly valid: the results can be seen for themselves each General Assembly. Anyone who believes that useful business can be done in such an atmosphere — and at a concentration of parties unapproached even in Hollywood's golden days — may follow his theory to its logical conclusion in the summary and verbatim records of successive Assembly deliberations during the past few years.* It is all there — the

---

* Even the assumption that more sober contacts between national representatives are invariably fruitful has been warned against by historians of the League of Nations — who are at pains to illustrate that, along with such advantages, came "the danger in basing diplomatic relations upon the accident of personal association."

same babble of voices, the same ingrown exchanges, the same circulation of drinks, self-importance, and hot air; the lack of reflection, silence, and self-doubt, and above all the lack of painful, invigorating contact with a larger dimension of intellect and reality. Pleasure is good for people: but it is hard to imagine any rational person deriving pleasure from this lunatic round of revels.*

It is not enough to say that if the United Nations were vigorous and productive these perquisites might be disregarded: an effective organization could not conceivably be disporting itself in such a manner. If evidence were needed that a new and grotesque variety of imperviousness has been hatched from the UN cocoon it would be supplied in this ability to pass without a qualm from day-long discussions of destitution and catastrophe to a nightly ritual of "three or four cocktail parties, crowned by a dinner" — the marathon sustained for months at a time, and resumed periodically throughout the year wherever the United Nations conference flag is unfurled.

There are, of course, exceptions — a few senior officials who privately deplore the "*carosello*" and its implications. But these are few enough, exceptional enough, and private enough; and in the United Nations tradition have never found it necessary to oppose the system publicly or attempt to change it. Here is an aspect of United Nations conduct where the "radical reforms" vaguely alluded to as necessary, from time to time, by UN leaders might long since have been specifically and easily applied. U Thant, who, like Hammarskjöld, did not relish the parties, apparently felt no urge to propose their reduction.

The merry-go-round of high salaries and allowances, abused immunities, incessant parties and earth-girdling trips is important in its implications, and its repercussions in the Organization's performance. One must also consider the extent to

* If UN business gets done at the parties, it predictably takes a beating the morning after. The Secretary-General reported in 1971 that the 1970 General Assembly lost more than 424 hours' working time because of the lateness of delegates and the early adjournment of meetings.

which it appears to matter to senior United Nations officials and UN delegates, its inappropriateness to the declared purposes of the Organization, and the monstrous discrepancy between the saturnalian free-for-all and the skinflint conditions imposed on the Secretariat as a whole. (In the latter respect it may be said that extras seem to be made available at the top by withholding necessities from the most junior grades — as in a recent suggestion to increase certain subsistence allowances, paid only to senior officials, and restrict overtime pay, paid only to junior ones.) Were a lone staff member to crash one of the innumerable galas, he would be ordered off by a UN guard; but it is an unfathomable mystery that the Secretariat staff *en masse* has never staged a sit-in at some such event.

In 1946, the Report of the United Nations Headquarters Commission posed the alternatives: "a spirit of luxury or of simplicity, these are as yet unsolved." That quandary was speedily resolved by apportioning luxury at the top and austerity at the bottom (although it might be said that *simplicity* — as distinct from the present United Nations extremes of indulgence or hardship — has never been a concept of the Organization, and it is interesting that the word was originally used). In the same report, Le Corbusier made the plea that the Headquarters of the United Nations "not become 'great' like Babylon." A United Nations delegate who lives in the Hotel Pierre or the Waldorf-Astoria, publicly commenting on the "opulence" of his situation, may — and apparently does — regard this as an entirely appropriate use of public funds; but he might also ask himself whether such a state of affairs enhances his credibility as a spokesman for humanitarian causes, or his right to present himself — as some UN personages unabashedly do — as a dedicated, and even sacrificial, servant of the world.

Although United Nations officials dismiss even passing reflections on the Organization's incipient Babylonianism as petty and sordid (and detrimental to world peace), it is difficult not to feel that the UN has entered into a species of involuntary alliance in this matter with the reactionary tabloids it abhors — providing them with a wealth of evidence of excesses and inanities which, even if usually denounced for meretricious reasons, might perfectly well be criticized from sincere and rational ones. There can be no question that the flaunting in the press of a scale of living unknown even to many affluent businessmen offers a weapon to the Philistine that a more reasonable distribution of UN comforts would have withheld; and that the already immeasurable distance between the majority of United Nations personnel and their leaders is only resentfully increased by this corrupt and unnecessary spectacle.

In 1971 the Secretary-General secured increases in pay and allowances of sixteen per cent for upper grades, and proposed a straight five per cent for the drastically underpaid lower ones — the latter ante being subsequently upped to eight per cent in the face of a staff call for strike. At the 1971 General Assembly, the Secretary-General's salary was increased by an annual $12,500; and the Secretary-General's pension was doubled, for U Thant's retirement, to $31,250 per year, tax free. In 1972, the Secretariat staff, through the Federation of International Civil Servants Associations, presented an impassioned appeal — this time to the committee reviewing the UN salary system — for redress of the severe inadequacies and inequities afflicting majority categories of United Nations personnel throughout the world. And were ignored.

The myth that the annual United Nations budget runs around $200 million was circulated for so long that even UN leaders appeared to believe it — or at least to perpetuate it in official statements. Declaring the United Nations' cost to be "less than that of the Fire Department of New York City," Kurt Waldheim echoed, in 1972, the UN's favorite, and unfounded, slogan. A recent schizophrenic UN press release entitled "INITIAL BUDGET ESTIMATES FOR 1972 TOTAL 207.7 MILLION" goes on to remark some pages later that "the Secretary-General notes in the foreword to the budget estimates that Member States are contributing about $870 million a year to the United Nations system of organizations."

While little enough of the actual total* (about $160 million out of an approximate total of $1 billion) is spent on costs for the staff in general, the public moneys annually expended by the United Nations and its agencies are of course not limited to administrative outlay, and include such major items as the UN Development System of economic and social aid to under-developed countries (which currently consumes a quite separate $360 million annually, with a 1975 target of $500 million, and, as its former director Paul G. Hoffman puts it, "will hopefully allow $1 billion worth of development activities to be carried out by the Programme and the low-income countries in 1976"); food and relief programs, and immensely costly and prolonged ventures such as the emergency operations set up as a result of the Suez crisis in 1956, and in the Congo and Cyprus. (These undertakings include some of the most commendable and controversial of UN enterprises, and the present purpose is not to assess their value in monetary terms — an impossibility in any case — but rather to attempt to arrive at a realistic concept of overall United Nations expenditures.) UN reiteration of the meaningless "Fire Department" figure — which should at last have been stifled as a result of the public airing of UN finances that took place after the 1971 China vote — is not only misleading but self-defeating, as presumably administrative costs would have greater justification as part of a vastly larger and more ambitious operation.

Any accurate assessment of the world taxpayer's contribution to the United Nations undertaking will of course include the costs of reciprocal activities entered into by member nations, and the considerable expenses of maintaining national

---

* United Nations budgetary figures also vary according to the methods of computation, and sometimes exclude important but indeterminate figures, such as direct reciprocal participation in United Nations projects on the part of individual member governments.

delegations permanently at New York and elsewhere for over one hundred thirty member nations and making governmental deputations available at thousands of UN meetings around the globe.

References to waste, in United Nations circles, are cheerful — "I'd be satisfied," one official declares, "if what we're doing is fifty per cent effective." (So, in point of fact, would the public.) Achievements are cited, and re-cited, with triumph and even with wonder — as if an organization that has, over nearly three decades, employed tens of thousands of persons at a cost of tens of billions of dollars could scarcely have been expected to have much to show. In some United Nations operations the effort to augment funds has consistently taken precedence over the need to develop quality. An attempt at public discussion of United Nations financing will bring the Pavlovian and often belligerent reply "Only a fraction of what nations spend on armaments" — as if *any* public expenditure were not fractional in comparison with the arms race; and as if public moneys *not* spent on armaments might be wasted with a clear conscience.

Long before the emotional and financial United States reaction to the expulsion of Nationalist China from the United Nations, the UN was technically bankrupt and plagued by unpaid national assessments — particularly for ventures, such as the Congo operation, not unanimously supported by its members. In his repeated impassioned appeals on behalf of the UN budget, U Thant did not always avail himself of the discrepancy between United Nations expenses — even accurately computed — and the hundreds of billions of dollars governments annually spend on weapons of war. In asking the 1970 General Assembly to meet a $5.5 million deficit in the $50 million budget for relief of Arab refugees, the Secretary-General might have called upon delegates to make some proportionate adjustment of their entertainment habits — setting the example with the sacrifice of certain superfluities by his own top personnel and even by himself; instead, he pointed out that it was "the sum recently paid for one painting [the Metropolitan Museum's Velásquez] or for a racehorse." The purchase of a great picture by a public gallery may be thought a poor example of extravagance; and, if one is to descend to that level of comparison, it is certainly a far more defensible expenditure than the millions annually spent on UN parties, or for UN overflow space in luxury apartment buildings, or for the creation and maintenance of a group of top-ranking Secretariat posts whose principal function is to placate geographical pressures or to postpone retirement for some ancient cornerstone of the Establishment.

It is obvious that self-indulgent expenditures — while indeed representing an abuse of funds that must be culled from individual citizens throughout the world — are neither the crux of the Organization's present financial plight nor, in themselves, an issue that need be dwelt on at length. As with many questions raised in this work, their importance lies in signifying aspects of an entire organizational condition; and in revealing attitudes and vanities in those who foregather at the United Nations with the responsibility of alleviating the world's emergency.

"The fears of others that kept them silent"

Of all the regrettable legacies from the moral collapse of the United Nations in the early 1950's, the most insidious has been timorousness. The United Nations' motto might, by the 1970's, be said to have become *"Sauter pour mieux reculer."* A group of leading officials who stood by with scarcely an audible word of protest while scores of their subordinates were, with formal United Nations sanction, made victims of a national reign of terror, and the founding principles of the Organization itself torn asunder, could hardly have been expected to grow braver with the years; nor have they. And their attitudes have permeated the entire UN body — gathering momentum, so to speak, as they merged with the not inconsiderable tributaries of native bureaucracy. Two expressions are constantly repeated at the United Nations these days, in response to any outside plea for more constructive approaches, past or present: *"It wouldn't have done any good"* and *"It's inevitable."*

An interesting question of our times is posed by the incapacity of public men to take public issue or make public renunciation. And it *is* an issue of our times, a reflection of a much wider, corporate condition in which a defector from current and accepted attitudes is regarded as having exposed himself and failed others; and as being, in some way, cut off from grace. Even our multitudinous nonconformists come, these days, not singly but in battalions, and minorities run in the millions: the very word "individual" has come to have a computerized ring to it. Courage is required not so much to be "different" within the recognized spectrum of disorder, as to be singular and to set oneself intelligently apart.

A Stevenson, despite repeated humiliations inflicted by the White House, will thus cling on — at the United Nations; a McNamara will transfer from the Pentagon to the World Bank without a public murmur; a Humphrey, as Vice President, will keep any doubts about American policy in Vietnam strictly to himself, then seek the Presidency on an antiwar platform; a Goldberg will move on from the Supreme Court to . . . the United Nations. Many are the resignations from ill health or pressure of private affairs; few, or nonexistent, are the resignations on principle. The Big Noise, these days, tends to be one of the Silent Majority.

"A shocking aspect of this situation," wrote Leon Edel of the purges of the United Nations Secretariat in 1951–1952, "is that high UN officials, including Lie, have not had the courage to defend the staff they themselves hired." And, in a letter to the New York *Times* immediately after the suicide of Abraham Feller, Mr. Telford Taylor observed: "If, indeed, Mr. Lie rightly diagnosed the disease, Abe Feller was the victim not of his own fears but of the fears of others that kept them silent. . . . What voice has been raised to say that the United Nations is the creature and vehicle of all the nations . . . to point out that the notion of political conformity within this staff can, and surely will, be applied to the grave disadvantage of the democratic cause? Instead, two Senators, one of whom ought to know better, have declared that these basic issues should be solved with the hack of a butcher's knife, or else the United Nations should be sent packing from these shores. Upon these gross and crude misconceptions there has been, so far as I know, no official comment to help set the matter straight. Perhaps for lack of expression from others whose duty is to see and describe what lies beyond our own noses Abe Feller has dropped out of the race."

The question as to who, and how many, of the United Nations' leading officers were aware of the illicit "secret arrangement," contracted in violation of the Charter between the Secretary-General and the United States government in the 1940's, before it was exposed in all its significance at the McCarran Subcommittee hearings in 1952, and the further questions raised by their silence or acquiescence over this conspiracy will perhaps be explored eventually. It is scarcely conceivable that top officials in the Bureau of Personnel could have gone in ignorance of the existence of such a pact, whose consequences vitally affected the management of staff affairs; or that the legal chiefs who prepared the briefs for Trygve Lie against the appeals of early victims of the secret arrangement were unaware of its existence. These are specific questions to be considered within the whole — as are also the cases of officials in the State Department itself or serving on the United States Mission to the United Nations who, though vocal enough since then in the cause of internationalism, are not known to have said a word on its behalf in that hour of trial. In the wider realm of those senior Secretariat officers whose knowledge — like that of the body of the staff — was derived from the events themselves as they unfolded, and who provided no leadership to the considerable segment of the Secretariat willing to make a stand for the principles of the Charter, and afforded no protection or support to the victimized, a very contemporary set of official inhibitions and passivities presents itself for study.

It is not without meaning that, twenty years later, the mildest intimation that a different course of action lay open to United Nations Under-Secretaries and other UN leaders during the McCarthy persecutions can cause angry outbursts of self-justification, and abuse of the propounder; or merely aloof and sorrowful silence over the unseemliness of such a matter being mentioned at all (and indeed, in an organization that specializes in an outpouring of verbiage, it is almost impossible to find a single retrospective allusion to these crucial events). I have yet to meet a United Nations official of any seniority who — the matter being drawn to his attention — does not express repugnance for the injustices of that era; and some of them expressed repugnance at the time. (The Under-Secretary, a Canadian national, of the department in which I worked at the United Nations during the McCarthy years called his staff together and forthrightly condemned the whole affair; this same official also authorized at least one member of his staff to cite his name as a character reference in testimony before the McCarran Subcommittee.) But the idea of action, concerted or individual, never seems to have arisen, nor is it now accepted as a decent subject for speculation. And should the eye of any leading Establishment participant happen to fall on the suggestion here it will most assuredly meet with indignation and surprise, and with volumes of authoritative explication as to its impracticability.

On no subject is the cry "It wouldn't have done any good" more vehemently uttered.

As to present expressions of repugnance, a public that has now witnessed the rehabilitation of the United States Far Eastern experts Owen Lattimore, John Service and John Paton Davies, and heard the Chairman of the Senate Foreign Relations Committee pronounce them "vindicated," might wonder whether some form of official redress might not, even yet, be forthcoming for those dismissed under similar circumstances from an international organization whose leaders now seem generally agreed on the injustice and impropriety of the terminations. No single gesture from United Nations leadership — unless it were the repudiation of the security clearance stranglehold — would more eloquently express a desire to turn at last to the establishment of a true international civil service.

The fact is that the United Nations, like the United States itself, has never wished to atone to its casualties of McCarthyism. While most Americans would agree that respectable citizens were victimized by McCarthy and his followers, very few would care to be reminded that the victims still stand in need of redress. There has been a guilty compulsion to stifle the whole unresolved phenomenon of McCarthyism in America, and to minimize as a regrettable episode this pathological manifestation, many of whose characteristics — and leading characters — are now embodied in the processes of government.

Bearers of high office at the United Nations exact an almost priestly — or what used to be priestly — immunity from critical comment on their official actions. Nevertheless, there is no telling what effect a show of opposition within his own top staff might have had on Trygve Lie or others, or what even a threat of high-level resignations over his policies might have done to galvanize fearful delegations into protective action. (Few who saw the stand made by Joseph Welch against Senator McCarthy are likely to forget that turning point, even though Welch had doubtless been assured by the fainthearted that "it wouldn't do any good.") Beyond this, there are the considerations of conscience and self-respect.

Had Trygve Lie, instead of offering public assurances of his cooperation to the inquisitors, made plain that he held them in contempt — as he revealed years later in his memoirs when he castigated the "vicious and distorted" attacks of "headline-seeking Congressional Committees"* and ascribed the American hysteria to "unreasoning fear and intolerance" — the Secretary-General would have inspired quite different sensations in his personnel and, ultimately, in the public in general; as it was, he confined himself to a single critical public statement, at the time of Feller's suicide, after which dismissals continued and the FBI was installed in the United Nations building. In the same way, if governments, instead of offering Lie an extended term of three years when his first appointment expired in 1950, had acted on the misgivings that heads of delegations are said to have expressed,† the United Nations Organization might have taken a different and positive turn in its early years. Or, more simply, had the staff known the low esteem in which a number of Mr. Lie's senior colleagues now claim to have held him at the time, and the opposition now said to have been offered to his dismissal policies behind closed doors, a very different spirit would have animated the Secretariat during the early 1950's when the staff felt themselves utterly abandoned by all who had the duty of rising to their defense. (One high-level officer, an Englishman, did refuse to concur in the firing of his staff, and quickly found himself translated to another continent.) We also learn from his intimates that Trygve Lie was given to ungovernable rages — the favorite tale in this connection being the "Walls of Jericho" story that

---

* Lie characteristically goes on to say: "I felt strongly that a United Nations official should cooperate fully with investigations conducted by an official agency of his own government" — the agency in this case being the very same "headline-seeking Congressional Committee" of the "vicious and distorted attacks." The expression "witch-hunt" is readily used by Lie and by other senior United Nations officials to characterize these persecutions they did nothing to impede.

† Lord Gladwyn expends, in his memoirs, few words on the character of Trygve Lie, and none at all on his McCarthyist misdeeds. He concedes that "Trygve Lie was by no means an intellectual. The people he liked associating with for the most part were American tycoons," but goes on to assure us, "Still he was a good Secretary-General, in the sense that he was genuinely impartial and something of a father-figure."

originated in a scene in temporary quarters at Lake Success, where Lie literally brought the house down when the scrim partitions of his office gave way under the reverberations of his screams.

If senior Secretariat officials had given support and stature to the Staff Association of the United Nations in 1950 and 1951 when, *with the endorsement of the Administrative Tribunal,* its leaders stood out against Lie's collaboration with McCarthyism, an honorable fight might at least have been made for the principles of the UN Charter within the Organization itself. Not only did they, for the most part, keep notably aloof from any opposition movement, but some of them, in the 1970's, are still expressing disapproval of the bad form shown by the staff's unruly protest meetings of the time. In such matters, much will depend upon one's ultimate definition of good behavior.

One need not return to the gestures of Cato or Seneca for higher examples. To recall that the McCarthyist persecutions were under way four years after the termination of World War II is to be reminded of the countless instances of self-sacrifice that were then fresh before the world. That Trygve Lie, for example, was a national of a country many of whose citizens had resisted their German overlords at fearful risk throughout the years of Occupation, is to make his falling in — whether as United Nations Secretary-General or in any other capacity — with the incipient Fascism of the Un-American Activities Committee almost incomprehensible. The Italian anti-Fascists who were exiled, imprisoned, tortured and executed through the 1930's and early 1940's might, no doubt, have more easily convinced themselves that their resistance "wouldn't do any good," as for many years appeared to be the case; nevertheless, those of them who survive are the Italians one would prefer to know above all others. Reason and justice are kept alive in mysterious as well as obvious ways, and the fact that one may see no immediate result of a sacrifice for principle may be one of the best reasons for making it.

In this matter of action or inaction towards protection of the Charter principles, it should be recalled how limited was the risk involved for the most senior officials of the United Nations. Not only was physical courage not required of them, or the all-encompassing heroism of a Solzhenitsyn (or, to draw a closer parallel, of Major Georges Picquart, who staked his career on telling the truth in the Dreyfus case, and went to prison — and was vindicated), but their positions to some extent protected them from the degree of retribution wreaked on other members of the staff. United Nations Under-Secretaries would not, in all likelihood, have been obliged to become handymen or janitors, as was the case with the more junior officials in whose dismissal they tacitly or otherwise concurred. As later in the case of a McNamara, some at least would very possibly have gone — had it been allowed to come to that — from one well-paid and prominent position to another. However, fear and material considerations most certainly played their part among those to whom the situation was unpalatable; and, although the story is more subtle than that, these principal elements must be included.

Any United States citizen who spoke against the inquisitions of the time instantly exposed himself to persecution. For that matter, any non-American at the United Nations who similarly raised his voice would have incurred some form of the investigators' wrath (it will be remembered that Trygve Lie himself was asked to appear before the federal grand jury for making the single criticism which he subsequently retracted), and indubitably that of the Secretary-General also. Not only were the inquisitors perfectly capable of inventing "subversive" pasts for those who obstructed their path, but Lie actually sent to Washington the names, for example, of persons on the United Nations Staff Committee regarding whom it would be convenient, from his point of view, to receive an "adverse" rating; and employees who had previously been cleared were subsequently revised to "adverse" designations as the political pace quickened. A number of leading Americans in the Secretariat were erstwhile New Dealers — indeed, that had originally been a motive for their recruitment — who asked nothing better than to lie doggo, or bend over backwards, until the storm had passed. No one can relish the public blackening of his reputation, or wish to find himself without the means of supporting his family; but, unless we are to abandon questions of principle entirely, they must be discussed in a context of sacrifice. As long as some few among us are capable of risking themselves for principle, the question will arise as to why others of us are not — most particularly if those others continue emphatically to profess the same standards.

The absence of bodily risk, and an unlikelihood of imprisonment, which should simplify the choice, complicate it: for, with this alleviation, the chips are no longer down and the sophistries set in. Endless assertions and circumlocutions will then be adduced to prove what, were the choice otherwise, would speak for itself. And the argument will never be settled: for its essence is an attempt to convince the unpersuaded self.

All such considerations of risk, which bear on the single self, are magnified in the bureaucratic collective. While material factors might have been uppermost with some unknowns who had tumbled, through accidents of timing and nationality, into the high ranks of the United Nations Secretariat — and who in certain cases would possibly have been little moved by these particular questions of principle — they would not necessarily have weighed conclusively with the few whose very standing might have made their protest influential. What is interesting here is the mesmerizing effect of "official life," even on men of integrity and achievement. Action, an action that would run counter to what the establishment of the moment insists upon, becomes a psychological — almost, one might say, a physiological — impossibility. The bureaucratic addiction, with its vitiation of character and proportion, is insidious, and its power is only felt to the full under the challenge of withdrawal.

There is, also, a contemporary lack of confidence in the vindications of posterity: a lack of confidence, that is, in posterity itself. When, in a great passage of his *Mémoires*, Chateaubriand recounts the publication of his excoriation of Napoleon over the murder of the Duke of Enghien, his fearless, prophetic statement asks no requital but the judgment of later centuries — "Nero prospers in vain, for Tacitus is born within the empire. . . . What are our sufferings, if our name, pronounced by posterity, will move a generous heart two thousand years after our death?" In the past, the certainty — or illusion — of future both consciously and unconsciously informed courageous action: there was a sense not only of an infinity of time but also, within the timeless community of an enlightened few, an assumed constancy of standards through which sacrifice might be commemorated and spiritualized. Today, the present itself is made precarious by the absence of an apprehensible future; and the public, inundated with "news," is quickly indifferent to individual gestures, whatever the importance to their originator. Wonder may not last out even its allotted nine days' span, and there is no assurance that our best actions will stir a generous heart two weeks, let alone two millennia, after the event.

Neil Sheehan, in his introduction to *The Pentagon Papers*, describes the formulators of the United States' official policy towards Vietnam throughout the 1960's as "confident men — confident of place, of education and of accomplishment. They are problem-solvers, who seem rarely to doubt their ability to prevail." This was emphatically not the case with the United Nations leadership of the Trygve Lie era; nor, with the single spectacular and total exception of Dag Hammarskjöld, has it ever been. Lie himself, as his memoirs show, was a mass of contradictory impulses and inferiority complexes; among his deputies, equivocation and pusillanimity even appear, in some cases, to have led to certain positions being taken — as illustrated by the administrative chaos. If one considers that the Secretary-General's legal representative was thanking the McCarran committee for its "spirit of complete fairness" with regard to investigations of UN staff just three weeks before the legal chief of the United Nations committed suicide on the issue — with Trygve Lie attributing that death to the committee's "indiscriminate smears and exaggerated charges" — it will be seen that excessive certainty of its position was by no means the difficulty in the UN's highest echelon at the time; and that insecurity was, in fact, at the root of much of the trouble.

As with the United Nations itself, in its inability to entertain a prospect of reduced circumstances where all would devolve upon belief and initiative, those of the UN hierarchy who inaudibly deplored "the witch-hunt" of the 1950's were apparently insufficiently self-reliant to detach themselves from the organizational position. Once banished from the confraternity of authority, a "leader" has no assurance that public office can be held again, or public influence directly wielded. It is only a conviction of ultimate capacity to fulfill oneself and be of use without official standing and even without public prominence that makes the severance possible: and that is why it is so rare.

It is a short step, in bureaucratic circles, from "It wouldn't have done any good" to "It would have been harmful." The rationalization that actual good was done, and the United Nations preserved, by allowing the Charter to be violated on United Nations premises over a period of years, may be considered in the light of the subsequent effectiveness and prestige of the Organization. Certainly opposition would have required great resolve, and would have had to be offered out of moral conviction and not from calculation. It seems highly unlikely, however, that outspoken resistance to Trygve Lie's policies from a group of top officials would have proved fatal to the United Nations; and one could at least as well argue that it would have been life-giving, or that the dissenters might have later returned in triumph to lead a revitalized organization. Or, for that matter, that the departures or dissenting proclamations might have been as quickly passed over by the press and public as was the suicide of Abraham Feller. From the officials' own point of view there would, presumably, have been the indubitable and lasting dividends of self-respect.

The assertion that the world organization would have been damaged in such a matter by its top officials' speaking out in any case raises the interesting hypothesis that the United Nations could be destroyed by a stand on its own principles.

As it is, no topic comes up less, in United Nations circles, than the 1950's schism and its long aftermath (and one will search in vain for a reference to this formative crisis in UN administrative studies — including the current two-volume report, where the years 1950 and 1951 appear, merely, as a politely indicated point of departure from certain standards). No topic, coming up, could be less welcome. It inspires the involuntary horror of the *fonctionnaire* at the inference that "policy" is ultimately attributable to individual responsibility. What might be openly discussed, were conscience easy, leads instead to anger or silence, and to minimizing falsifications ("Only a dozen were dismissed"). It is as if one single expression of remorse would — like Trygve Lie at Jericho — bring the whole flimsy house down.

In 1943, it will be remembered, Mr. C. W. Jenks* emphasized that quality of leadership would dominate the effectuality of a future United Nations Organization; and listed as the desirabl? attributes of an international civil servant "integrity, conviction, courage, imagination, drive, and technical grasp — in that order."

Much has since been said and written towards defining the obligations of a United Nations official, rather than his desirable attributes. The International Civil Service Advisory Board opinion of 1954 is still circulated to the staff. The oath administered to the new UN recruit requires him to exercise his functions "in all loyalty, discretion and conscience." Dag Hammar-

---

* Since 1970, Director-General of the International Labour Organisation.

skjöld wrote at length on the subject, and had — among much else — this to say:

The international civil servant must keep himself under the strictest observation. He is not requested to be a neuter in the sense that he has to have no sympathies or antipathies, that there are to be no interests which are close to him in his personal capacity or that he is to have no ideas or ideals that matter to him. However, he is requested to be fully aware of those human reactions and meticulously check himself so that they are not permitted to influence his actions. . . . If the international civil servant knows himself to be free from such personal influences in his actions and guided solely by the common aims and rules laid down for, and by the Organization he serves and by recognized legal principles, then he has done his duty.

In response to this, we have Conor Cruise O'Brien asking, in 1962:

What sort of creature can be guided *solely* by the Charter of the United Nations, the Staff Regulations, the Resolutions of the General Assembly and the Security Council, and textbooks on international law? . . . I should like to suggest, with due diffidence — granted the example of Hammarskjöld's life, and the authority of experience behind his [above-quoted] lecture — that the good international civil servant must necessarily be guided not solely by the factors mentioned . . . but also by what he thinks is right, and that his idea of what is right is historically and culturally formed.

The concept of the international civil servant, and of his ideal attributes and necessary loyalties, has not of course remained static and subject merely to more exact definition. Consciously and unconsciously it has been adapted to the nature, and likely requirements, of such an organization as the present United Nations. In 1958, in considering an extraordinary case of staff insubordination which will be summarized later in this book, a Joint Disciplinary Committee composed of four senior members of the United Nations Secretariat declared that "the staff member must accept the findings of the higher authority or leave the service." This disciplinary body, finding heavily against the "defendant," went on to state:

> While recognizing that the obligations of members of the Secretariat are basically the same, whatever the nature of the duties which may be entrusted to them, the Committee considers it particularly important that the staffs assigned to the secretariats of political bodies, operating either at Headquarters or in the field, should not only subordinate their personal views to the decisions of their responsible superiors in the Secretariat, but also understand and accept the overriding authority in all matters of substance of the bodies themselves.

This important statement goes far beyond the obvious requirements of impartiality and professional rectitude: it abrogates conscience. Although applied with special emphasis to "the secretariats of political bodies" at the UN, it concerns itself with the conduct of all United Nations personnel, and perfectly reflects the attitudes, as they have evolved since 1950, of administration to staff. It does away with at least the first five of Mr. Jenks' requirements, and substitutes in their place the philosophy of Adolf Eichmann.

The "personal view" of a reasonable being is not a mere hodgepodge of latent partiality over which some arbitrarily designated "responsible superior" may confidently assume supremacy, but necessarily includes the dictates of justice, of humanity, and of self-respect. No organization or person is entitled to command, from any human being, a spiritual subservience of the kind required by the 1958 United Nations Joint Disciplinary Committee; nor can a body prosper that succeeds in exacting it. Persons who have formally ceded their ultimate responsibility for their own actions may make good servants, but they cannot make good servants of peace. And, as we have seen, leaders who require such renunciation from their subordinates are in their turn enslaved.

The case considered by the 1958 Joint Disciplinary Committee is a particular illustration of the irrationality — not to say immorality — of such a position, since it in fact hinged upon the mental instability of the defendant. This defendant, in turn, had *his* subordinates — as he had held, for nine years, a senior position in the United Nations Secretariat: were they, according to the UN doctrine, to have accepted the "overriding authority" of a superior only to discover that an investigating committee subsequently found him "aberrant" and "not open to rational persuasion"? "Responsible superiors," in the UN Secretariat, are very often geographical appointees with a greatly varying regard for international scruples. Alcoholism has been a problem — particularly for those on the receiving end of inebriated judgments. There are any number of regula-tions defining the propriety of the international civil servant, w. .hout a totalitarian statement of the kind issued by the 1958 Joint Disciplinary Committee; there are ample restrictions on the career of a United Nations employee without depriving him of his immortal soul.

"As long as they keep talking"

AVENANT: *Allons. Du courage.*
              Naturellement, tu as peur.
LUDOVIC: *J'ai pas peur. Je réfléchis.*
AVENANT: *Ça se ressemble.*
              — JEAN COCTEAU, *La Belle et la Bête*

The present United Nations, viewed in the light of past events and non-events, sometimes gives the impression of a vast coop in which multitudinous chickens have come home to roost; or a deposit of ultimate pulverizations from the mills of the gods. Timidity has seeped down from the top, it is in everything.

Awareness that they could expect little protection from their leaders against any serious pressure, political or geographical, that outside forces chose to exert was absorbed by the staff both consciously and imperceptibly, in sudden shocks and by degrees. Senior indifference to other aspects of the staff condition was automatically and accurately foreseen. Little respect could be spontaneously felt for officials whose professional actions were so greatly at variance with their public protestations — although calls from on high for a one-sided show of devotion have never ceased to this day. The staff had seen the righteous forsaken, and forfeiture of one kind or another became second nature virtually to all.

The very name of action has grown inimical to United Nations personnel. The most inveterate complainer (and complaints, along with the Pension Fund, are a constant theme of Secretariat conversation) can be stopped in his tracks by the suggestion that he attempt to change the situation. *The energy expended in explaining not only why nothing can be done, but why doing nothing is the only constructive course, might, if differently directed, have moved mountains.*

An important United Nations survey, the 1969 *Study of the Capacity of the United Nations Development System*, comments as follows on this phenomenon:

Today, the UN system seems to be a disproportionately old and bureaucratic organization. Many governments, steeped in much longer traditions, are far more progressive and ready to respond to modern conditions. . . . The UN system has more than its fair share of "experts" in the art of describing how things cannot be done.

Another official survey, drafted in 1970 for the United Nations Institute for Training and Research, opens with the assertion that "training of staff of the U.N. agencies has not kept pace with that of national administrations," and goes on to observe: "It is remarkable that whilst several of the U.N. agencies had in their employment public administration specialists who advised governments of developing countries, their advice was not on the whole sought on the administrative and management problems of the agencies themselves, whose senior personnel and administrative officers seldom seem to have had any special training for these duties." This report comments on the "unhappiness on the part of some of the most thoughtful staff members at the middle level [who] felt that they were trying to operate an administrative machinery which was becoming more and more evidently less efficient than those of national governments with which they were dealing."

These searching, mature, and objective statements of the United Nations' condition are a far cry from the assertions more recently made by Secretariat leaders that the Organization is in its infancy and therefore cannot be held to adult standards. "We're still in the embryonic stage," a United Nations Under-Secretary declared in an interview in 1972. "Think how long it took the nations of the world to settle their internal, warlord differences before becoming nations. Centuries were spent trying to find a central order. . . . The international civil service, of which the Secretariat is a part, is also still in an extremely embryonic stage." By these Neanderthal analogies we should condone the failings of any legal or governmental system. The internationalist concept, though fifty years old in its present form, is, as Dag Hammarskjöld pointed out, the extension of a vast body of historical and legislative experience: falling back, in the most literal sense, on a plea of juvenility can only confirm the public's apprehensions of the United Nations' debility and further undermine the self-confidence of the Secretariat itself.

It is significant that the "excuse" of the United Nations' immaturity has been increasingly put forward of recent years — indicating, apparently, that the Organization is becoming more embryonic as it grows older. The present United Nations is quite obviously *not* in a bold and healthy state of growth; and there is a direct relation between the fear and conformity imposed on the Secretariat in its first decade — with consequent blocking of the arteries of healthful criticism — and the Organization's retrogressive attitudes and policies.

The influence of endemic timidity on the United Nations as an instrument for world peace will be discussed.

As early as 1950, an administrative "They" had irrevocably and intimidatingly withdrawn itself from the body of United

Nations staff. The lesson to be learned from the fate of staff representatives who had interceded for their victimized colleagues was taken to heart. If there was to be a dearth of any one thing over another at the United Nations Secretariat during the next twenty years, it would be the spectacle of anyone taking anyone else's part, however mildly, in the face of authority.

It would seem no simple task to have made a more or less uniform work force out of 35,000 persons of different nationalities and backgrounds, dispersed over the globe, whose very strength might have lain in a complementary range of attitudes. Yet it has been managed without — after the initial expurgations — much show of strenuous exertion and even without wholly conscious intention, the most significant restrictions being imposed by staff members on themselves in their acceptance of the situation.

Every institution is to some extent both Mother and Big Brother to its employees; but the diversity of United Nations personnel and the international aims of the Organization, together with its relative newness, make the example remarkable in the extreme. Again, the staff member appears to become hypnotized by the organization view of himself as a slot on the manning-table: even the unhappiest UN personnel cease to believe they might be better employed, or employable at all, elsewhere. Few maintain a body of outside friends and interests — even a person unfamiliar with UN affairs will sense the stale, repetitive quality of thought and talk in United Nations circles. (In this connection, one can scarcely credit the lack of imagination that, in 1970, endorsed a gigantic office and residential building project to house UN personnel together in their work area within a sort of bell jar — under a connecting dome whose eventual function all too vividly summons up Baudelaire's *"Couvercle noire de la grande marmite."* This undertaking — which was passed by the New York legislature without a proper hearing and had an initial estimate of $310 million — was described in the New York *Times* by Ada Louise Huxtable as "a monster, created by monstrous economics, that can both damage the city and set damaging precedents."* It was to some extent retarded by the withdrawal of the United States' financial support following the 1971 UN action on Nationalist China.)

The melancholy — or heartening, depending on how you look at it — fact is that many more imaginative approaches to the world's problems exist outside the United Nations' confines than within them. The severance from proportion, from a rational human ecology of diverse factors, has to a great extent been fostered by well-meaning public indulgence. The large public favorably disposed to the United Nations concept has been inhibited from asking nourishing, searching questions about the actual Organization not only out of respect for the high purposes for which the United Nations was founded but also for fear of giving comfort to jingoists and warmongers — who in fact, as we have seen, wreaked their will on the United Nations in the 1950's unobstructed by intervention from any such group. (And the weakness of the well-intentioned public attitude may be seen in this very failure to intercede on the UN's behalf when the Organization was subjected not to healthy criticism but to vicious attack.†) For its part, though cowed before its destroyers, the United Nations has exerted over its constructive critics a form of moral blackmail that is in itself something of an unconscious inheritance from McCarthyist techniques: any but the most reverential inquirer will find himself stigmatized as an enemy of world peace. If one raises facts, one is trivial; if quality, unrealistic; if principles, a perfectionist.

The impulse not simply to rebuff critics but to discredit them

* It may be mentioned that the United Nations Secretariat maintains a large bureau on housing, building and town planning, and administers advice in these fields throughout the world.

† Very few UN supporters rallied to the defense of the Charter against the McCarthyite purges of the United Nations in the 1950's. However, it should be said that more than one prominent New York lawyer undertook the defense of UN cases without charge. Members of the Secretariat staff subscribed towards the payment of other legal fees.

comes from the very heart of the UN matter. United Nations officials attribute sordid or self-seeking motives to their critics because they themselves can no longer conceive of higher reasons for concern over the Organization's fate. In their hearts they cannot bring themselves to believe that there are still citizens who care for the United Nations concept and potential enough to be sincerely indignant at its present standards. It is this profound lack of confidence that moves them, instead, to cultivate exclusively the less exigent — and indeed flattering — goodwill of a receptive, rather than inquiring, public.

The public's unexacting indulgence is perhaps the greatest single obstacle that the United Nations *idea* has had to contend with. Had the Organization and its deliberations been subjected from the first to a full measure of informed public criticism, had it — instead of posing as a convocation of higher beings — been required to justify its procedures in the face of enlightened public comment, or been obliged by its supporters to meet even moderate standards of coherence and common sense, its story would have been more of a struggle and less of a tragedy. Instead, a set of unassailable founding principles has been used as a talisman to ward off self-knowledge. The fact is that the public in general has never been encouraged to take the United Nations' existence seriously — that is, as an instrument whose ultimate usefulness depends on an implacable public willingness to hold it to serious standards of achievement. It is frequently stated that the United Nations is "our best hope for peace." Nevertheless, our best hope for peace continues to rest in the public's determination to have peace; and to create and maintain, by uncompromising public insistence, effective instruments for world order.

Public opinion is not "a factor" in the fate of the United Nations: it is *the* factor — as it is in all the interaction of contemporary world politics. The almost unexploited public capacity to influence favorably the authority and effectuality of internationalism is like the unrealized power of a beautiful woman

— inviting victimization from predators who can scarcely believe their good fortune. A refreshing draught of public indignation over their leaders' performances in United Nations assemblies, a sustained agitation for United Nations effectiveness from a huge body of world opinion, a concentration of unremitting demands for Secretariat initiatives — an emphatic show, in other words, of high expectations — would even now wreak vital transformations in all the deadly circumstances we have been discussing here. It may be guaranteed that even the first intimations of such treatment would do much to cure the national and international invalids of the United Nations of their hypochondriacal complaints.

As it is, the public has never understood, or been instructed in, its power in this respect; and few well-wishers of the United Nations are prepared to take the sacred cow by the horns. The many sincere and energetic proponents of a stronger United Nations have been unwittingly deflected into putting the Organization's views to the world, instead of forcing the world's emergency on the Organization. The United Nations exerts, in such circles, the strength of the weak — taking the position that exposure to any forms of criticism other than the "agreed" ones would cruelly endanger its frail hope of survival. Thus enfeebled by an ever more liquid diet of obligingness or indifference and demanding a bedside manner from the world, an Organization that might have been vitally charged with global life and death, with great issues of right and wrong, has been emasculated into a place of sweetness and light all too closely resembling a sickroom.

It is estimated that there are twenty-seven thousand persons in New York City alone associated with the United Nations; and a large number of these have undertaken the task of conveying the significance of UN operations to the general public. Why should infinitely more not be done by these groups and individuals to alert the public to adverse developments and deteriorating leadership within the Organization itself, and to press for correction? On the contrary, the United Nations condition — as delineated in the reports submitted to the 1971 General Assembly, for example — is ignored or concealed by the Organization's supporters and by the press as being "harmful to the United Nations mystique." "Mystique" is frequently invoked by United Nations officials themselves in special pleading for the Organization: like virtue or sensibility, however, it is a quality more blessed to possess than to claim on one's own behalf.

The numerous organizations throughout the world charged with supporting the United Nations are under no obligation whatever to limit that support to what is comfortable to UN bureaucrats or to national representatives, or to take UN pronouncements at face value, or to disseminate UN presentations without deep and continuing inquiry into the quality of operations; yet that is, in general, the way that much of this activity has so far worked. Few such groups have seriously interested themselves in the Organization's administrative crisis, or traced its repercussions in performance with a view to reform. The hankering to "talk to the man at the top," to be privy to the views of the influential, has in some cases also played its role — without much reflection as to whether the Establishment is likely to be an objective, or even knowledgeable, source on its own deficiencies. If delegates and United Nations officials were faced, in their deliberations and operations, with a less obliging scrutiny from informed internationalists, and a public airing of their effectuality, a different standard would unquestionably have to be attained.

The large and diverse group of nongovernmental organizations accredited to the United Nations is an important channel by which individual and communal rights and interests are presented to intergovernmental and international authorities. These bodies also, in urging United Nations action, are too frequently subjected, by UN officials, to encyclopedic enumerations of procedural impediments to intervention; or even themselves, in some cases, converted in the UN's proximity into apologists for the restrictive clauses of United Nations resolutions. Here too is an expression of a serious public concern that might be made more active in alliance with a vigorous Secretariat.

Books about United Nations affairs written, for public and academic consumption, by outside commentators in the economic and social field all too often tend to adopt an indoctrinated tone — in some cases so benignly instructive as to be scarcely adult; it is an unusual, and invaluable, work of this kind that imparts a measure of reality with regard to the Secretariat's basis of operations.

The press, on the other hand, has played an inconsistent, almost formless role at the United Nations, giving extensive coverage to political matters only and making little searching inquiry into the nature of the Organization itself. There are five hundred press representatives permanently accredited to the United Nations, with an additional twelve hundred getting temporary accreditation each year; many major news services have offices in the UN Secretariat building. Some of the long-term correspondents write about United Nations matters as if for a house organ, getting their information from the same eternal UN spokesmen and from press releases, and making — as it were — no trouble; and unconsciously adding to the general air of United Nations infirmity.

A cumulative sense of the Organization's interior mood and condition would in fact provide the press with crucial insight into all United Nations operations. There has been, so far as I know, no effort on the part of the American press to develop a serious, accurate, inside view of the United Nations, rather than that officially dictated to them. Press contact with the "staff" (that is, with the vast majority of United Nations personnel) has been nonexistent, beyond the occasional ladies' page article on how to drape a sari or make couscous; and the paralyzing staff conditions, including the desperate ructions and horrific official reports of 1971, have gone almost totally unreported in the newspapers. This has also been true of official United States studies of the United Nations in recent years which, although containing useful and realistic criticism, have been largely passed over in the press.

(Meanwhile, predictably, we find the New York *Daily News* piously lamenting, in the wake of the 1971 UN expulsion of Nationalist China, the fact that the United Nations "has dropped all pretense of living up to its ideals" and "has been but a frail reed from its founding," with no indication of the role that organs such as the *Daily News* itself have played in undermining United Nations principles and usefulness, not only in the Organization's formative years but on every journalistic occasion since.)

The press has, of course, a paramount role to play in the education of public attitudes towards the United Nations, and therefore in the Organization's effectiveness. Again, this influence has been left largely in abeyance — through indulgence on the one hand and cheap abusiveness on the other, and, above all, through indifference. A minor indication of the acute sensitivity of the Secretariat itself to the concerted influence of a powerful press is provided in the incident of the Taiwanese newsmen who were expelled from their United Nations accreditation over the New Year of 1972 by U Thant and Mr. Waldheim, at the instigation of the Chinese delegation: the taking up of the cause of these press representatives by their colleagues in the UN Correspondents Association and, most notably, by a deputation of the most powerful information executives in America who called on Mr. Waldheim in person, resulted in modification of the Secretary-General's categorically stated position. One might wish that a host of comparable — and, in some instances, far graver — improprieties, over many years, had been the object of similarly constructive attention from the press. It is not too late, however, for the development of more mature press approaches to United Nations affairs. Much has yet to be written about the United Nations; and there is little likelihood that the present tone will be maintained by a younger generation.

The Secretariat staff itself, with a handful of notable exceptions, is fearful towards public discussion of the inadequacies it continually laments — the general attitude being that the United Nations' interior condition should remain a secret shared among the initiated thousands. "Of course it's true, but he shouldn't have said it" has been the intramural response to every attempt to shed light on the situation — a recent example being the abuse directed from within the Organization at Mr. Maurice Strong, the UN Under-Secretary-General in charge of the 1972 Stockholm Conference on the Human Environment, who recommended that United Nations staff be cut "up to fifty per cent in some areas." *The Delegates World* typically quotes anonymous Secretariat officials "who, after reproaching Strong, said that there was still a lot of sense in what he said."

"Bureaucracy," said Karl Marx, taking issue with Hegel's more sanguine view, "is a circle no one can leave."

"As long as they keep talking" is the habitual public reproof to any expressed wish for a less ineffectual United Nations. The United Nations has kept talking through wars, civil strife, military aggression, religious persecution, tidal waves, starvation, and millions of violent deaths. It has not evolved a recognized machinery of mediation, or even coordinating services for the prompt and practiced alleviation of natural disasters in the world.* Its own repeated claim that it has prevented the ultimate cataclysm of worldwide atomic war, while letting "little" wars — such as those in Vietnam, Biafra, or East Pakistan — take place without United Nations intervention has been well described as analogous to the belief of primitive peoples that human sacrifices offered to angry gods produced beneficial effects on the harvest. The awful fact is that when the world came closest to nuclear war, during the 1962 Cuban missile crisis, the United Nations machinery was bypassed by the great disputants — as it had been, by the United States, in the previous Cuban crisis over the Bay of Pigs invasion, when the

* A service for coordinating disaster relief was approved in principle by the UN General Assembly only in December 1971.

United States Ambassador to the UN, Adlai Stevenson, was ignominiously uninformed of Washington's intentions and actions — and only put to use when the immediate danger was resolved. (In 1960, Cuba was prevented from bringing its apprehensions of the United States' attack before the Security Council by the then U.S. Ambassador, Henry Cabot Lodge; in an attempt to rationalize United States' preclusion of UN arbitration of the subsequent missile crisis, Stevenson painfully argued at the Security Council in October 1962 that the inter-American system was "far older than this one" — meaning the United Nations.) Nor is the United Nations a participant in the Strategic Arms Limitation Talks — described by the New York *Times* as "undoubtedly the most important diplomatic negotiations in the world today."

The greatest contrast of all to the "keep talking" slogan is provided by the assertion of Dag Hammarskjöld that the United Nations should be "an instrument for negotiation of settlements, as distinct from the mere debate of issues."

Five.

"The World of Action"

If the first months after Dag Hammarskjöld took office as United Nations Secretary-General, in April 1953, brought no striking outward contrast with the preceding ones, it was nonetheless felt throughout the United Nations that a contrasting personality had taken charge; and even Trygve Lie's former adherents were not heard to lament his departure. Hammarskjöld's candidacy for the Secretary-Generalship was formally proposed by the French representative at the United Nations, Henri Hoppenot, a critic of Lie ("They didn't like me because I didn't speak French," said Lie of the French delegation; but it is probable that, in proposing Hammarskjöld, the French were moved by more than his linguistic accomplishments), and seconded by the British. Like Lie, Hammarskjöld was apparently surprised that the choice devolved on him, his reported response to the first rumor of his nomination being "Amused but not interested."

Hammarskjöld came to the United Nations as a publicly unknown quantity — which, in a quite different sense, he remained; and his autobiographical writings show that he himself felt that fulfillment had been mysteriously withheld from him until, and for, this time. His figure was unfamiliar to the world at large, and to many persons in government: it is recorded by various biographical writers on Hammarskjöld that neither the United States Ambassador to the United Nations, Henry Cabot Lodge, nor the United States Secretary of State, John Foster Dulles, had ever heard of him before his candidacy was raised. To the United Nations staff in general he was no more than a delegational name, though he had had a distinguished career as an economist and diplomat and had held high posts in the service of his country, some of them related to United Nations affairs.

Hammarskjöld was forty-seven years old when he became Secretary-General, and had all his life been recognized by colleagues and acquaintances as having remarkable, as well as difficult, qualities. In his intellect and character, the powers of a logician, an intuitive thinker, and a man of action were combined in what must be called genius; his nature, as far as it can be inferred from his conduct and writings and from the observations of those who knew him, was cerebral, fastidious, solitary, and deeply masochistic. His posthumously published "journal," *Markings* — dismaying as it often is, with its righteous egotism, chilling puritanism, and deficient self-realization, its heartfelt allusions to Golgotha and Calvary — attests over and over to his sense of having been "chosen," and his dedicated acceptance of that selection. "Hammarskjöld did not say that God appointed him to be the Secretary-General of the United Nations," Professor Gustaf Aulén has written, "but he nevertheless received the charge entrusted to him, including all its responsibility, as a divine vocation."

It was a delayed vocation. "A distinguished career" such as Hammarskjöld had previously had leads a public man through a series of influential but supporting roles. And authority — even supreme authority — was traditional in his family. His father interrupted a long period as Governor of Uppsala to become Prime Minister of Sweden in 1914, a post he held during most of the First World War. Hammarskjöld's ancestors had been soldiers and servants of the state. He was brought up in a fortress, the Castle of Uppsala: a haiku of 1959, and an elegiac essay "Castle Hill" that was among his last writings, commemorate his childhood union there with the seasons and the earth.

Hammarskjöld's forbidding and despotic father, described by Sven Stolpe, a Swedish writer who knew Hammarskjöld from youth, as "a massive Småland block of granite," died in the year that his son was appointed to the United Nations. (In 1954 Hammarskjöld was elected, in an oedipal culmination, to his father's seat in the Swedish Academy, where custom requires that a member's inaugural address concern itself with his predecessor.) Hammarskjöld's close attachment to his demonstrative, spirited mother — whose last child he was, and fourth son, born when she was forty — makes a kinship in the face of what Stolpe describes as the father's "reserve and isolation." Yet, despite "a perpetual conflict with a dominating father-image (in many ways deeply unlike me) whose pressure I hated and whose weaknesses I consequently saw very clearly," the adult Hammarskjöld lived in his parents' home, and then with his widowed father, until he was himself over forty. And "reserve and isolation" mark the son's life early and seem to have reached a climax, judging from Hammarskjöld's own testimony and that of others, in the months and years immediately preceding his appointment to the United Nations.

Self-accusation and solitariness, and an inability to repudiate solitariness, are interspersed in his journal at that time with a yearning for "something to live for, great enough to die for":

How well I understand the mirror symbolism in Cocteau's *Orphée*. To break through the barrier which, when I encounter reality, prevents my encountering myself — to break through it, even at the price of having to enter the Kingdom of Death. Nevertheless — what do I long for more ardently that just this? When and how shall I find the occasion to do it? Or is it already too late?

— *Markings*, 1952

149

"The years before his appointment he appeared very frosty," is Sven Stolpe's artless comment on this period. Other accounts give what must be called a repellent picture of Hammarskjöld's twelve- or fourteen-hour working day, interrupted only for a dutiful return to his parents' house for meals; and one writer has sketched an intricate pattern of ability and ambition finding its way through a political and bureaucratic labyrinth with great tenacity. The "outside interests" that Hammarskjöld maintained under his grueling, self-imposed regime were, rather, *inside* interests — cerebral and contemplative pursuits of such astringency that it would seem bold to call them pleasures, and the physical diversions of solitary walking tours or expeditions in the mountains.

In view of Hammarskjöld's later show of pragmatism, it is interesting that a Swedish diplomat has said of his pre-UN career, "We knew him as the perfect bureaucrat." By every account, he became somewhat more approachable in manner when he found the release of sole authority.

A senior official of the United Nations Secretariat who was an associate of Hammarskjöld's throughout his Secretary-Generalship, Mr. Brian Urquhart, has written that "it is difficult to appreciate a man so strange and so important without either descending into cheap and impertinent analysis or getting lost in admiration." Not all analysis need be cheap or impertinent; still, it is true that, in *Markings*, the revelations seem too readily to hand: almost everything is indicative, and is countered, though not tempered, subsequently or at once by some other, "corrective" statement, so that one is always out of context to some degree. Yet the exposure is self-inflicted, and Hammarskjöld intended that it should be taken seriously.

To say that Hammarskjöld took himself seriously would be consummate understatement: and taking oneself seriously is a dangerous flaw, since it interferes with the perspective of all other seriousness. An early entry in *Markings* makes a plea for the higher strivings of earnestness ("That we all — every one of us — take ourselves seriously is not *merely* ridiculous");

but Hammarskjöld himself later comments on "the alienation of great pride from everything which constitutes human order." In the early years of his United Nations appointment, Hammarskjöld wrote to his friend Bo Beskow: "My salvation is to 'take the job damned seriously, but never the incumbent' — but it has its difficulties. The roads to a basic conviction that in the deepest sense is religious may be most unexpected." It may be that without "great pride" it would be impossible to accept high office in the spirit in which Hammarskjöld did — with the sense of predetermination that Winston Churchill described himself as experiencing when assuming the Prime Ministership of Great Britain in 1940. Churchill wrote: "I felt as if I were walking with Destiny, and that all my past life had been but a preparation for this hour and for this trial."

Hammarskjöld's reflections on his own assumption and exercise of office take equivocal forms:

You are dedicated to this task — because of the Divine intention behind what is, in fact, only a sacrificial rite in a still barbarian cult: a feeble creation of men's hands — but you have to give your all to this human dream for the sake of that which alone gives it reality.
— *Markings*, 1955

Success — for the glory of God or for your own, for the peace of mankind or for your own? Upon the answer to this question depends the result of your actions.
— *Markings*, 1957

It is as if, within himself, he approached power at once furtively and defiantly, both nobly and with shame. A premonitory entry, of 1951, is even coy —

A fable: once upon a time, there was a crown so heavy that it could only be worn by one who remained completely oblivious to its glitter.

Such a "fable" simply does not make sense. Apart from the fact that shine has nothing to do with weight, awareness of the necessary condition of obliviousness would disqualify the recounter of the fable from his obviously wished-for coronation. The analogy, and the manner of expressing it, leave a queasy sensation. Curiously, it is Churchill, frankly embracing glory, who seems less concerned with the gratifications of power.

Markings is an astonishing, and in some ways excruciating, testament. Not a few of its many readers* appear to value it as a set of inspiring maxims; and there is a tendency to regard Hammarskjöld himself as a species of Kahlil Gibran. Hammarskjöld described the journal as "a sort of *white book* concerning my negotiations with myself — and with God," and that is the light in which churchmen have made studies of it. Those who interest themselves in its inadvertent revelations mostly do so defensively and with every qualification, as if to ward off some interpretation that might detract from Hammarskjöld's "image." This, as I believe, occurs in the mistaken belief that to admit large, and even unappealing, complexities in a great figure is necessarily to denigrate him; or in the fear that greatness will be subjected to trivial considerations of form. Whereas, on the contrary, a brave and productive life is by far more moving when seen to be wrung out of, and to have transcended, private suffering and debilitating introversion. In fact there is something infinitely cheering about these acts of insubordination on the part of the psyche.

In the same way, writers have been at pains to deny that Hammarskjöld had homosexual tendencies — as though even a possibility of effeminacy, once allowed in him, might somehow lessen his stature. Whatever might or might not be learned in the future about Hammarskjöld's life in this respect, it is hard to see how it could, or why it should, diminish his achievement. (It cannot be said that the refutations of homosexuality so far published on his "behalf" are conclusive. His

* The United States edition of *Markings* (hard cover, Alfred A. Knopf, Inc., 1964) has sold, at this writing, approximately half a million copies.

much-quoted explanation of his bachelorhood, given to the Queen Mother of Sweden, that it would have been selfish to involve a wife in such a demanding existence as his, would not necessarily preclude some other reason, of inversion or celibacy, which it would have been less tactful to offer in conversation with a dowager queen. A letter from Judge Henrik Klackenberg of the Supreme Court of Sweden, an early friend and colleague of Hammarskjöld, states that there was no indication of "a sexual inversion" in Hammarskjöld and goes on to illustrate this by saying that they had had "lively and frank discussions" on the subject: "To me it is a completely absurd thought that I could have had these conversations with a person of homosexual leanings himself." Judge Klackenberg had obviously never been in a railway carriage with M. de Charlus; and, if he had read Proust's disquisition on this very theme, he had forgotten it. On the other hand, the accumulation of instances of Hammarskjöld's offensiveness to women and hostility to family life, while convincing enough, are countered by other testimony; and add little in themselves, since there are married misogynists and one even runs into the occasional disgruntled *paterfamilias* — Tolstoy might be thought an example of the latter, if Tolstoy can be considered an "example" of anything.)

The immature, and ultimately bigoted, view that serious discussion of Hammarskjöld's sexuality is disrespectful leads away from our understanding not only of this important man but, inevitably, of his career also. It seems, on present evidence, that Hammarskjöld's probable neuterness had a homosexual bias.

Markings might be said to be a document in which the unconscious cumulatively gains the upper hand — in the face of the contrary intention. In this connection it is important that Hammarskjöld foresaw the journal's publication, and left it to the charge of a friend with permission to that end, stating: "These entries provide the only true 'profile' that can be drawn." Mr. W. H. Auden, in his sympathetic foreword to *Markings*, regrets that assertion, pointing out that "no man can draw his own 'profile' correctly because, as Thoreau said: 'It is as hard to see oneself as to look backwards without turning round.' The truth is that our friends — and our enemies — always know us better than we know ourselves." Mr. Auden also believes, giving cogent reasons, that the journal was extensively revised by its author (a contention both supported and disputed by other writers on Hammarskjöld): "I should say . . . he went through it, cutting a lot, rewriting many entries, and, perhaps, adding some entirely new ones"; and goes on to say: "Some people, no doubt, will condemn such retrospective revisions (assuming they were made) as 'dishonest,' but such criticisms are unjust."

What might conceivably be criticized as "dishonest," of course, are not the retrospective revisions, which are Hammarskjöld's prerogative to make, but the failure to acknowledge them with regard to a work whose publication he himself foresaw: the absence of any notation to this effect, together with the retention (or imposition) of a sequence of dates, would amount to a misrepresentation that is perhaps significant only in reflecting Hammarskjöld as a man who wished to live, and to be understood to have lived, an arduous spiritual journey. It is *the wish to appear* that matters here.

Mr. Brian Urquhart contends that Hammarskjöld's desire that the journal be published posthumously "arose from his feeling of loneliness" — from the need of an intensely solitary man to communicate, after his death, the thoughts he could not share in life. This indubitable, and even conscious, impulse does not, however, account for the apparent revision of the book which suggests a counteracting wish to create a design rather than to offer, simply, spontaneous expressions of self; and which, revealing an ultimate incapacity to share, must make Hammarskjöld seem lonelier still.

A critic of *Markings*, the Danish diplomat Eyvind Bartels, has commented, "Strange that Hammarskjöld should care what profile other people drew." It will be said that everybody cares, to some extent, for the world's opinion; but Hammarskjöld's gesture is premeditated, and perhaps particularly relevant since the imperative need to conquer just such vanities is a major theme of *Markings*. If the diary was revised for continuity and "coherence," as seems probable, this raises at least a question of a distasteful and puzzling desire to leave an "image." ("You ask yourself if these notes are not, after all, false to the very Way they are intended to mark . . . and now you reckon with possible readers, even, perhaps, hope for them." — *Markings*, 1956)

In commenting on the "relentless earnestness and not infrequent repetitiousness" of the entries made during Hammarskjöld's first years as Secretary-General, Mr. Auden urges us to bear in mind that most of these "must have been written by a man at the extreme limits of mental and physical exhaustion." The wonder is that Hammarskjöld found time, and a state of mind, in which to make these entries at all; still more, that they should be dominated by a "narcissistic masochism" — to employ his own phrase — in itself consuming of time and energy even if the residue is subsequently turned back into fuel. The "spontaneous" condition of exhaustion will not necessarily have prevailed, if the journal was extensively emended, over intentions of revision; it might also be argued, "*In fatigatione veritas*." In these details Mr. Auden perhaps shows a forbearance that should probably be extended to all but is more usually reserved for those we like or admire.

Knowledge, insight, strokes of beauty, a lofty exactitude of thought and word appear in *Markings* side by side with an exasperating and sometimes histrionic solemnity, moments of triteness and of archness, and a monumentality as heavily delineated as heroic sculpture or patriotic art. To address or exhort oneself in the second or third person is an uneasy literary form at best; and for readers of a diary the indirection can create a third presence: there is relief when an outright "I" or "me" or "myself" irrupts into Hammarskjöld's catechizing of his "self." There is sarcasm, there is sometimes irony — but not wit; and we do not need Hammarskjöld's lines, "The fun/

You shall forget it," to remind us how completely, in his journal, he succeeds in carrying out that injunction. It is almost impossible to imagine an Anglo-Saxon of comparable education and background providing so unremittingly humorless, and self-humorless, a testament as his. Yet *Markings* cannot be said to be the journal of an ascetic. The observations of nature, the apprehensions of torture, are often sensual. Though the flesh is present mainly in its torments, it is there and unresolved.

Much has been made of Hammarskjöld's sense of his imminent death. Anyone who has a continual presentiment of death will, in the natural course of events, be justified. Hammarskjöld did not die in the natural course of events — he died a premature death as a result of what is presumed to have been an air accident, although the conditions in which his last flight was made were abnormally precarious. As Mr. Eyvind Bartels has written, the last entries in *Markings* are so prescient as to produce the hallucination that Hammarskjöld made them posthumously. The reader of *Markings*, however, will feel that Hammarskjöld's life was, in a sense, a long premonition of, and preparation for, death.

Hammarskjöld dwelling on his own obsessions gives the impression of seeking, almost childlike, to exorcise them by recognizing their existence. His death-wish, his appetite for power, his arrogance — these are reiterated without ever producing a feeling that there is a powerful wish to turn away from them: rather, in a context of self-mortification and acceptance, and — inescapably — of wallowing. The spiritual reality, of conflict and pain and aspiration, that infuses the writings is in no way inconsistent with this impression. What is necessary, rather, for the reader is to accept them as an intricate whole that will never yield a "profile," or the crude outline known as "image."

There could be no more unlikely comparison than that of the United Nations' first two Secretaries-General; and one wonders what might have become of the United Nations had Hammarskjöld been its first, instead of its second, executive head and had the forging of the Organization's character from the beginning. It is ironic that Hammarskjöld's initial acceptance by the great powers has been put down to his former bureaucratic self-effacement, which was apparently thought to indicate an obliging docility, as contrasted with the boisterous personality of Lie, which was mistaken for vigor. This is the eternal confounding of noise with strength, and bluster with ability.

Nor could there be a greater autobiographical contrast than these two men writing about themselves: the pettiness and self-praise of Lie, with his cheap asides about open zippers or the spilt gravy at a banquet, on the one hand; and, on the other, the somber, mystical musings of Hammarskjöld.

An enigma may be someone about whom too many have too often had their say. The views of Hammarskjöld's personality put forward by a number of his acquaintances and associates are, at times, an almost impenetrable mass of contradiction, some of this coming from the same persons. The propagation of a myth has set up a perhaps natural resistance, and even some proprietary feelings, among those who were in regular contact with the man. Gunnar Myrdal has written: "Those who knew Dag Hammarskjöld do not think of him as an unfeeling, coldly calculating person. On the contrary, his personality was explosively emotional, though the emotions were under control." Ralph Bunche declared: "There was nothing formidable about him; he not only tolerated but seemed to relish views at odds with his own; and if he had a messianic complex he concealed it well from his working associates." Many other impressions are recorded, some similar, some directly opposed, and some hostile, and others yet a confusion of all three. Brian Urquhart writes of Hammarskjöld's "august aloofness that discouraged intimacy," and goes on to say: "Hammarskjöld certainly knew that most people thought him aloof and unapproachable, and in later years his Olympian public position also set him apart. He did not discourage this picture of himself."

One might perhaps apply to Hammarskjöld words written

by André Malraux about de Gaulle: "Intimacy with him did not mean talking about himself."

Friends and colleagues of the eminent dead are not an impartial jury whose views will be of equal weight and detachment, or whose verdict is collectively arrived at. Much, if not all, depends on the character of the adjudicator, on his sensitivity, his powers of observation, his relation to the person concerned, and his reaction to the circumstances in which his judgment is sought. Some of the opinions expressed about Hammarskjöld by his acquaintances have the ring of perception and authenticity; others shed little light on the situation except to suggest limitations in the persons concerned.

At the extreme, there is the desire to bend over backwards to correct the impression of Hammarskjöld's aloofness and obscurity. Even without the evidence of *Markings*, one might feel wonder to read, in a statement by Mr. Andrew Cordier: "In my constant dialogue with him for eight and a half years, I never found him to be excessively complex and certainly not enigmatic." And something ominously called "a sense of fun" obtrudes itself: one biographer, Joseph P. Lash, reports of Hammarskjöld that "with a few friends and aides he engages in horseplay, exchanges highbrow jokes, makes up mischievous nicknames for the cast of characters that frequent the UN stage, and, says one of his friends, gives the impression 'he's really giggling inside all the time' "; another biographer, Emery Kelen, declares, "He could smile, but laughter was not in his repertory." Horseplay is the form of fun most dreaded by the witty. Witty comments, as distinct from sarcastic ones, by Hammarskjöld seem rarely to be quoted — although certain of his associates have mentioned his talent for lively and sometimes malicious description of persons and events. *Markings* — where one may read, in an entry of 1958, that "apart from any value it may have for others, my life is worse than death" — makes it clear that "inside" is just where Hammarskjöld was not giggling.

Hammarskjöld's capacity for anger, and his respect — or

lack of it — for others, are similarly the subject of conflicting comment. W. H. Auden, in his foreword to *Markings*, for example, relates that "Hammarskjöld's close colleagues in the Secretariat have all commented upon his exceptional patience in listening to what others had to say." Yet it may fairly be added that many of the same colleagues, including one thanked in Mr. Auden's foreword, have also commented, in conversation and in print, on Hammarskjöld's memorable and frequent shows of impatience, and his capacity for anger. Joseph P. Lash describes the Secretary-General both as "a gifted listener" and as "an indefatigable monologist," and Brian Urquhart tells us that Hammarskjöld "had the utmost difficulty in communicating on intimate matters with other people. A superb talker, he was basically a monologist." Hammarskjöld's own testimony appears in an entry of 1955 in *Markings:* "You listen badly, and you read even worse. Except when the talk or the book is about yourself. Then you pay careful attention. Are you so observant *of* yourself?"

Hammarskjöld's anger was legendary in the Secretariat. He could be gratuitously rude to outsiders; and offensive to the vulnerable, as the transcripts of his press conferences show. It is of course entirely possible that Hammarskjöld both listened patiently and let rip, though not simultaneously, and what remains to be established is the side on which the balance fell.

Brian Urquhart has written: "In life, Hammarskjöld's personality was elusive and impossible to label or pin down, and it seems likely that it will remain so." Mr. Urquhart's own study of Hammarskjöld's Secretary-Generalship, appearing after this book goes to press, will undoubtedly much enlarge our knowledge of Hammarskjöld's official actions and of United Nations political operations throughout his term of office. Nevertheless, renown awaits the biographer who can achieve a full-scale portrayal of the man, and illuminate the private and determining influences that bear on this extraordinary personality; who can give us, that is to say, insight into the human attributes that made possible the phenomenal career.

All published opinions, if they are to have depth, will have to grapple with the revelation and roadblock of *Markings*.

Public men must ultimately be judged by their public actions. What is certain is that this introverted and original man retained and practiced his concept of an active United Nations Organization to the end of his life.

> What distinguishes the "elite" from the masses is only their insistence upon "quality." This implies a responsibility, to all for all, to the past for the future, which is the reflection of a humble and spontaneous response to Life — with its endless possibilities, and its unique present which never happens twice.
>
> — *Markings*, 1959

The peoples of the world, at least in modern times, are inclined to show panic at the threat of being ruled, even through democratic institutions, by highly intelligent persons. (It cannot be said that at present they suffer from any menace of the kind.) Rather than choose leaders from what is pejoratively designated an "elite," they will give preference to those who openly express hostility to reflective, cultivated, or widely humanist attitudes: the brute who aligns himself with our worst limitations will be hailed, for a time, as a "man of the people," while the visionary is derided as an egghead. (On the other hand, those who propose a dictatorship of "elitism," or of anything else, are most often those whom any intelligent process of selectivity would exclude at the outset.)

Dag Hammarskjöld did not have to be publicly elected to his post, or pass through the processes of public exposure by which men nowadays attain high office. It was therefore as if by accident that the world acquired a significant political figure who was also a person of vision and intellect.

In our era, the road to holiness necessarily passes through the world of action.

— *Markings*, 1955

The political actions of Dag Hammarskjöld as United Nations Secretary-General represent, in detail, a density of fact and a ground for speculation which this writer has neither competence nor inclination to pursue. Much information on these matters is already available to the public; much has yet to be released; some things may never be known, or at least agreed upon. We must remind ourselves that there are, ultimately, no outsiders in world events; and that while "inside stories" may — or may not — alter our view of how certain developments came about, the events themselves and their consequences are irrefutable, if sometimes slowly delivered, testimony. The character and trend of large developments in the world, and the credibility or otherwise of public figures, are often more readily apparent to the public than to theoreticians or to those circling the inside track. What seemed at the time the most important and constant element in Hammarskjöld as a political figure appears even more significant now, in the light of its subsequent absence from the international scene: Hammarskjöld had a positive and dynamic concept of what the United Nations should and might be — as an instrument as independently as possible active for general good.

Hammarskjöld knew that governments, left to themselves, could not be trusted to make use of the United Nations' potential, and that their moral hand must be forced through guidance, intervention, and example from the United Nations entity itself. He knew also that this entity had yet to be created; and that it was a figment of faith, to be realized only by performance. In the process of that realization, his own inventiveness and creativity can be traced like those of an artist.

Brian Urquhart has written:

The Secretary-General, by virtue of his position and prestige, has

161

unrivalled possibilities for constructive and conciliatory action. . . .
Of all important public positions, his is perhaps the one in which
spiritual strength, integrity, and courage are most essential to effective performance, for without them the office, lacking the normal
trappings and supports of power, is an empty shell of high-sounding
principles and good but unfulfilled intentions.

As the effective is the enemy of the "inevitable," so Hammarskjöld is the enemy of all the ineffectual multitude who insist that "the Organization cannot be better than its members
allow it to be." His refusal to accept that simplistic slogan, par-
roted by delegates and press alike and by high United Nations
officials themselves, may be given in his own words:

It has rightly been said that the United Nations is what the Member
nations make it. But it may likewise be said that, within the limits
set by government action and government cooperation, much depends on what the Secretariat makes it. . . . Because the Secretariat
is a living thing. . . . It has creative capacity. It can introduce new
ideas. It can in proper forms take initiatives. It can put before the
Member governments new findings which will influence their actions. Thus, the Secretariat in its independence represents an organ
not only necessary for the life and proper functioning of the body,
but of importance also for its growth.

Not only, as Hammarskjöld saw, was the cardinal and original sin of governments in their attitudes towards the United
Nations neither fixed nor irredeemable among the great transformations of world events, but it was susceptible of positive
change *through Secretariat influence.* "The limits set by government action and cooperation" were, similarly, not immutable, and might be extended by the enterprise and stature of the
Secretariat. In addition, governments were subject to the national pressures of the peoples of the world — whose confidence, in turn, might gradually be gained by constructive
initiatives from the United Nations Organization itself. There
was no necessity whatever for the Secretariat to abet governments in their negative policies towards the United Nations or

to make national pressures an excuse for its own timidity or inertia: on the contrary, the Charter had specifically empowered the Secretary-General to work around and against destructive national pressures for the benefit of the international community.

Hammarskjöld understood that indifference or hostility to internationalism on the part of member states "favored" the passivity of the Secretariat — which had in fact been thoughtfully provided with a set of watertight procedural justifications for its own inaction. *He also saw that every invocation of such excuse diminished public interest and belief in the United Nations and fatally reduced the Organization's future possibilities.*

Hammarskjöld's determination that the Secretariat should, in his own words, "develop as an instrument for the preservation of peace and security of increasing significance and responsibilities . . . available to member governments as an instrument, additional to the normal diplomatic methods, for active and growing service in the common interest," and his insistence that "the United Nations is not an end in itself" but "an instrument for negotiation of settlements, as distinct from the mere debate of issues" may best be illustrated by passages from his several addresses on the theme:

I spoke before of what I called a continuous diplomatic conference without publicity, for which the Organization is a framework, side by side with the public debates. . . . It is possible, however, to go further and say that increasingly, although in a way difficult to define, something like an independent position for the Organization as such has found expression both in words and deeds. The roots of this development are, of course, the existence of an opinion independent of partisan interests and dominated by the objectives indicated in the United Nations Charter. This opinion may be more or less articulate and more or less clear-cut but the fact that it exists forms the basis for the evolution of a stand by the Organization itself, which is relatively independent of that of the parties.

I do not believe that the Secretary-General should be asked to act, by the Member States, if no guidance for his action is to be found either in the Charter or in the decisions of the main organs of the

United Nations; within the limits thus set, however, I believe it to be his duty to use his office and, indeed, the machinery of the Organization to its utmost capacity and to the full extent permitted at each stage by practical circumstances.

On the other hand, I believe that it is in keeping with the philosophy of the Charter that the Secretary-General should be expected to act also *without such guidance* [author's italics] should this appear to him necessary in order to help filling any vacuum that may appear in the systems which the Charter and traditional diplomacy provide for the safeguarding of peace and security.

Obviously [the office of Secretary-General] is a reflection, in some measure, of the American political system, which places authority in a chief executive officer who is not simply subordinated to the legislative organs but who is constitutionally responsible alone for the execution of legislation and in some respects for carrying out the authority derived from the constitutional instrument directly.

A biographer of Hammarskjöld, Joseph P. Lash, has said it was "Hammarskjold's view that his authority derived not only from the specific mandates given to him by the other UN organs but from the Charter as a whole." That is the crux of his contribution to the United Nations. A senior UN official has made of Hammarskjöld, in retrospect, the epitaphic complaint that he "exceeded his authorization": the truth is that he understood that authorization in its highest and most exigent sense, and gave it meaning.

Time and again, year in, year out, UN dignitaries will deliver what they evidently consider the conclusive riposte to outside pleas for United Nations intervention in vital issues: "No government put it on the agenda" — sinking back, one often feels, with a sigh of relief at not having had to come to grips with yet another onerous emergency, and with no recognition of the eventual consequences to the Organization, in world opinion, of a grotesque, legalistically justified incapacity to contend with one crucial matter after another. Hammarskjöld comments on the danger:

For the Secretary-General this course of action — or, more precisely, non-action — may be tempting; it enables him to avoid criticism by refusing to act until other political organs resolve the dilemma. An easy refuge may thus appear to be available. But would such refuge be compatible with the responsibility placed upon the Secretary-General by the Charter?

In all this there is the fundamental question of attitude. *Hammarskjöld did not want a "refuge"* of this kind. He did not start from a negative position, with phrases about inevitability trembling on his lips, but from a determination to act that, if forestalled in one outlet, would at once seek another. That Hammarskjöld stood ready to exercise the Secretary-General's prerogative, under the UN Charter, to raise critical questions in United Nations forums was in itself instrumental in having them raised there by governments, and acted upon. He sought to resolve and mediate, and to find imaginative methods of doing so beyond the often feeble or equivocal mandates of UN resolutions. This was the large view of his office that, despite compromises and failures, he retained and put into positive practice, taking risks in the process. His conviction of the United Nations' potential, and of the uses of his own post, is a far cry from the now widely accepted outlook expressed as follows in 1971 by the Washington *Post:* "The UN exists as a political forum and arena anyway, regardless of who is secretary-general, so there is good reason to think of him not so much as a political officer but as an administrative officer whose principal mission is to make the organization better fit for the political usages of its members."

One need only consider the Secretariat claims for a role in past UN achievements, or study the obituary of a UN Secretariat leader, to see that high United Nations officials are held to have initiated and shared in the positive actions of the Organization. How would this be possible unless positive opportunities were open to them, or without a negative converse? It is curious, too, that the word "idealist," constantly used in the past by Secretariat leaders to disparage the "impracticality" of those who call for a greater show of principle from the

United Nations (and leveled, like an accusation, at the present author on a variety of occasions) turns up in every eulogy of Hammarskjöld by his deputies; and that idealism is now in fact being urged on the public by United Nations officials — presumably as a "last resort."

United Nations intervention in the Suez crisis, UN failure to respond to the extremity of Hungary, the UN actions with regard to Lebanon in 1957, to Jordan in 1958, and to the Congo in 1960, the Secretary-General's initiatives in the 1959 upheavals in Laos, and his inability to terminate the prolonged exclusion of mainland China from the UN, are all, for better and worse, crucial indications of the extent to which Hammarskjöld could maintain his course among currents set up by the big powers. When his innovations had the stamp of authentic internationalism (as when, in creating, on Lester Pearson's proposal, the United Nations Emergency Force at the 1956 Suez crisis, he produced a body with irrefutably international characteristics, in which Scandinavian, Canadian, Yugoslav, Latin American, Indian and Indonesian troops served together, not to make war but to keep peace, with little parallel to the Korean enterprise), public confidence and imagination were aroused to an extent that influenced governments in their official attitudes to the United Nations. The mass convergence of world leaders on the 1960 General Assembly was a tribute to the stature and significance imposed on the Organization almost single-handedly by Hammarskjöld. When Khrushchev chose to lock himself in a feud with Hammarskjöld over the UN Congo operation, thereby ensuring that Hammarskjöld's career as an effective Secretary-General was at an end, we may suppose that — even beyond the displeasure raised in the Soviet mind by UN activities in the Congo — it was in recognition of Hammarskjöld as adversary and as an unlooked-for influence on world events: a belated awareness, in short, of UN potential as a brake on national policy — the very factor that had been the object of confused concern in the United States years before. Hammarskjöld's masochistic relishing of his "martyrdom" in their vendetta makes painful reading:

Dumb, my naked body
Endures the stoning, dumb
When slit up and the live
Heart is plucked out.

Yet vendetta it was, and it closed with his violent, even if accidental, death.

It has been said that the only honorable termination for a United Nations Secretary-General is to be fired — fired, that is, by irate member nations resisting his determination to give them peace. Since Hammarskjöld's disappearance there has been little likelihood of this form of honorable discharge for top United Nations officials; and one thinks back incredulously to the time when the public themselves coined the slogan, "Leave it to Dag."

We are told that no man is a hero to his valet. The paltry spirit of that cliché cannot be said to have circulated within the United Nations staff during Mr. Hammarskjöld's term of office: quite the contrary. The multitudinous valets of the UN Secretariat for the most part looked on Hammarskjöld with awe, albeit from very, very far afar; and, given the staff's somewhat plaintive conversational tendencies, his detractors were few. (In the final year, when he became *persona non grata* with the Soviet bloc, an inevitable anti-Hammarskjöld stance was adopted by personnel from the Communist countries, this being flaunted by their mouthpieces rather than themselves.) After Hammarskjöld attained world stardom, the staff member who might never set eyes on him from one year to the next — as was the case for the vast majority of us with the three first Secretaries-General — felt rather like some obscure country cousin repeatedly complimented on his connection with the famous relative who never sends him so much as a Christmas card.

When Hammarskjöld assumed authority at the United Nations he must certainly have been aware of the bewildered and demoralized state in which the staff had been left to him by his predecessor. As has been said, during his first year of office the new Secretary-General showed signs of administrative concern. Five years later, at the inauguration of his second term, he described to the staff what his first reflections on the matter had been:

I knew only too well that every real achievement, in whatever field it is, is always the work of many. I knew for that reason that, for me to meet in any way the demands put upon me in this job, it was necessary to build on the work of every single colleague in the staff, on the Organization and the staff as it had been built up over the years. For that reason, I also felt that the first duty of the Secretary-General must be to give to the staff and to staff problems their proper priority in the efforts. How can you possibly go into the field of political activity, try your efforts in the diplomatic sphere, if you have a feeling that the very basis on which these efforts have to be developed is a weak one — not in the professional sense, but in the sense of human satisfaction in the job, human feeling of belonging to the joint effort?

Hammarskjöld claimed, then, to recognize as paramount the importance of quality and a sense of purpose in his staff. We must now consider his efforts to achieve these. After his arrival at the United Nations, a "reorganization" of the Secretariat got under way — designated, with wild implausibility, as "streamlining" by the powers of Personnel. This was an early entry in the interminable list of efficiency scrutinies, management studies, and desk-to-desk surveys, all of them concerned with symptoms not disease; and more will be said of it hereunder.

There was an opening effort to improve — or, more accurately, to initiate — relations with the staff: Hammarskjöld lunched a few times in the staff cafeteria and traveled up to his office in a crowded elevator; in Trygve Lie's time elevators had been emptied for the Secretary-General. He also made a tour of the Secretariat building floor by floor.

The importance that United Nations officials, and writers on

Hammarskjöld, have attached to this tour of the UN building seems to require that some words be said about it here. It is true that it gives some indication of relations between the uppermost ranks of the Secretariat and the UN staff, and the little that is thought owing from the former to the latter. It was, so far as I know, the only occasion* in a dozen years or more when a Secretary-General or members of his immediate entourage visited the floor on which I worked, or most of the other floors in the UN building; and for the occasion of his lightning-swift passage we were enjoined to clear our desks so that they would bear as little resemblance as possible to their usual selves. The cordial, though surely not improbable, gesture of making such a tour was apparently regarded in the hierarchy as so extravagantly beyond the call of duty that its beneficence was impressed on us for years thereafter. Mr. Andrew Cordier referred to it eight years later, in the brief memorial tribute he circulated to the staff on the occasion of Hammarskjöld's death: "His concern for the staff marked by two visits to all of our offices, and in countless other ways, must now be matched by our increased concern for the future of the United Nations." The mere fact of mentioning the "two visits" puts the "countless other ways" in perspective.

The claims made by Hammarskjöld and his deputies for the efficacy of the Secretariat reorganization of 1953–1954 suffice to reveal the unreality of Establishment thinking as regards the staff, and the lack of communication between the two. Hammarskjöld's first reports and proposals on management policy, submitted to the General Assembly in late 1953 and 1954, opened the themes that were to dominate his administration: an almost total disregard of the necessity for proper standards and formal processes in Secretariat recruitment, for staff training, or for even minimal career prospects and incentives for the staff majority; indifference to, with consequent intensifica-

---

* It has been said that there were two such tours; if so, the second is not generally remembered.

tion of, discriminatory attitudes — such as those affecting women and youth — in Secretariat procedures; an obsessive desire to reduce the staff as a whole to anonymous, unreasoning servility in the name of an "internationalism" that was in fact to suffer incalculable harm from this debilitating legacy; an exaggerated confidence in contractual terms of service, conduct, termination and appeal as regulators of human situations; and, above all, the concentration of power in "a single supervisory level having the status of Under-Secretaries" who were to report directly to his own supreme authority "in order to bring more closely under my personal direction certain central control functions."

By this arrangement Hammarskjöld confined his acquaintance of his own headquarters staff to an increasingly clique-ish minority of senior officials; and the Establishment was sealed off more effectively than ever from a staff majority of whom the thirty-eighth-floor denizens saw, heard, and knew virtually nothing.

A set of generally grim recommendations for revision of the staff regulations and circumscription of employees' private activities — *with no compensating career encouragements to qualifications or merit* — were accepted by the General Assembly in December 1953, although Hammarskjöld's attempt to break the independence of the Administrative Tribunal was rejected. Objections from the Staff Association were, it need hardly be said, overridden — and a press release by the Secretary-General in November 1953 on this matter is remarkable for arrogance of tone. The present writer has been unable to find a single indication that the necessity of internationalizing the preponderance of Headquarters personnel (that is, of reincorporating the General Service into the career body) was ever considered, or the slightest reckoning taken of the consequences of an institutional situation in which the majority was denied advancement. The shifts of Secretariat structure, with the predictable cards coming again to the fore, concluded by Hammarskjöld in 1955 did not touch, except in platitudes and abstractions, upon the urgency for a transfusion of human quality and energy into the entire United Nations system; and the deficiency was to manifest itself at once.

From the beginning the staff representatives protested, to little effect, staff exclusion from any meaningful participation in the Secretariat reorganization and the absence of incentives from the Secretary-General's proposals. In the following years, as the demoralizing geographical factor continued to erode morale and competence and the inadequacies of Hammarskjöld's "restructuring" were increasingly exposed by the exigencies of his own political initiatives, governments themselves demanded investigation of the Secretariat condition. To the first of a series of such inquiries, which, in 1958, recommended that the Secretary-General delegate certain of his — by now severely neglected — administrative functions, Hammarskjöld replied:

My personal experience does not lead me to share the misgivings of the [governmental] Advisory Committee. Indeed, I should like to register the view that the present arrangements have proved entirely sound, and in practice have worked well. I do not myself see the slightest justification for proposing any changes.

This is Hammarskjöld at his imperious and inaccessible worst. Any member of his staff outside the hierarchical handful with whom he habitually dealt could have enlightened him as to the effects of his administrative arrangements; and he himself was to learn something of their adverse consequences before he died.

That politics soon engrossed the new Secretary-General at the expense of his administrative duties was said to be the staff's loss and the world's gain; that the Secretary-General refused to delegate effectively to anyone the administrative responsibilities he had progressively less and less time and inclination for, was everybody's disastrous loss. I say "refused," not only because Hammarskjöld was challenged on this question (though the Khrushchev revival of the "troika" proposal of a triumvirate Secretary-Generalship was scarcely motivated by pure concern for administrative effectuality), but because the lack of full and authoritative attention to the United Nations' internal structure and quality was a glaring and increasing deficiency throughout his term, and much commented upon. Consumed by the almost unimaginable demands of his political role, Hammarskjöld — while retaining his theoretical concept of an international civil servant — quickly lost interest in the tedious obscurities of his staff's actual condition. Once around the Secretariat domain was enough for him; few of the thirty-eight floors ever saw him again, and no more desks were hastily dusted in his honor; cafeteria lunches quite understandably palled (such self-conscious tokens of good-fellowship were in any case faintly embarrassing, and one of Hammarskjöld's many distinctions was his lack of folksiness); and riders of his elevator bank found themselves turfed out, on occasion, to speed the busy Secretary-General on his way to concerns quite other than theirs. The staff in general had, perhaps, been found wanting; but it had not been weighed.

If Hammarskjöld felt himself saddled with an assemblage of mediocrities that he would not himself have chosen, he did little, by his own appointments, to elevate its overall level. In any case it does not seem to have occurred to him that radical changes in the system might even so bring quality to light, or that such intervention was desperately required if the Organization was not eventually to founder on this very iceberg; nor that offices at Headquarters or missions abroad staffed by the demoralized, the fearful, or the incompetent would not yield useful performance or advice, or ultimately enhance the standing of the United Nations itself.

In the first years of office, Hammarskjöld seems to have felt that he could encompass all things. The extent to which he managed this, in fields other than the administrative, is testified to by his career as Secretary-General (and documented in transcripts of his press conferences, where a mastery of many

complicated issues is shown in his ready replies to a sometimes unpredictable variety of questions). Towards the end of
his life Hammarskjöld described himself as "on a sort of
steeplechase with problems involving peace or war racing
across his desk, with a mass of documents absorbing all his remaining time and none left for the long-term thinking that was
indispensable." It will be imagined what long-term, or even
short-term, thought was available, in these circumstances, for
the administrative vicissitudes of the Organization.

No officer of the United Nations has been as intelligently
concerned, in his thinking and pronouncements, as Hammarskjöld with the evolving identity and responsibilities of the
international civil servant. None appears to have been anything
like as aware of the immensely significant part to be played in
international affairs by a UN Secretariat in which individual
quality and initiative were at work for the guidance of nations.
*None has done less to create a career service with these objects
in view.* Any person who was a member of the body of the
United Nations staff — that is, representative of the majority
— during Hammarskjöld's term must read his thoughtful and
far-sighted writings on this theme with incredulity, recalling
the waste and demoralization that increasingly took hold in
the Secretariat in those years, and the crippling limitations imposed by an administrative neglect of which the 1971 Report
of the Joint Inspection Unit on Personnel Problems in the
United Nations is but the logical culmination. Except perhaps
in the circle of Hammarskjöld's intimates, and other established
sites of administration authority, few opportunities were created for Headquarters staff to use or extend themselves; even
in the Organization's expanded operations and on political missions, the chances for showing personal quality or initiative
were bureaucratically limited. The "geographical" encroach-
ments played havoc with any possibility of efficiency or unity
of purpose, and with "the sense of human satisfaction in the
job." No effective training programs were instituted for employees to develop their capacities, or for "geographical" ap-

pointees to equip themselves for useful UN service; while those who had come provided with skills were frequently permitted no use of them. Restrictive and conformist doctrines were promulgated by every organ of the internal administration. Every avenue was closed to progress through the ranks, or encouragement of the gifted. During Hammarskjöld's years of office some of the best remaining quality in the United Nations staff was starved out or died at its post for lack of any effective nourishment, and able persons whom he himself recruited into top positions quickly departed because they were allowed no scope for their talents.

From his writings and behavior, it is clear that Hammarskjöld knew nothing of the temper of the staff during his term. No institutional leader can have been more out of touch with the day-to-day conditions and spirit of the thousands working under him. The banality — and, it must be said, the condescension — of his occasional speeches and references to the staff are insufferable in the light of the conditions prevailing at the time and since:

Let me mention also the gratitude a Secretary-General owes to his collaborators in the Secretariat from the third basement to the 38th floor. He is fortunate to profit in his work from a team-spirit which renders him unfailing support. He can count on dedication, often to thankless jobs, necessary for the success of the joint effort. He can trust that a challenge will be met with a deep sense of responsibility, broad knowledge, and a truly international spirit.

There is only one answer to the human problem involved, and that is for all to maintain their professional pride, their sense of purpose, and their confidence in the higher destiny of the Organization itself, by keeping to the highest standards of personal integrity in their conduct as international civil servants and in the quality of the work. . . . Dejection and despair lead to defeatism — and defeat.

Did he really not know that the vast majority of his "collaborators" were given no possibilities for "professional pride" or "sense of purpose," or for turning out work of quality? Or that, with the best will in the world, they could not, in many cases, conceivably regard their "thankless jobs" as necessary but knew them to be the meaningless detritus of unbridled bureaucracy — posts, in fact, that would have to be organized out of the Secretariat if its operations were ever to become efficient? And that even meaningful work was often drained of significance by the impossibility of bringing any personal quality to it under the system? Did no one ever take courage to inform him that the "dedication" he counted upon, which had indeed been brought by many to the Organization, was being remorselessly turned into "dejection and despair" by the negligence and ineptitude of his own administrators? If he was as detached from the administrative reality as he appears to have been, it is an extreme and frightening example of the extent to which authority — even when vested in a highly intelligent person — can be cut off from vital information, by wishful thinking reinforced by the misrepresentations of the self-promoting or sycophantic, or of those who are themselves ignorant of the truth; by the systematic abstractions of documents; and in this case, also, by the consuming distraction of political activities which, ironically, depended for their ultimate continuance and success on a high-caliber United Nations Secretariat.

There is something demeaning in being told that one need look no further for fulfillment than someone else decrees is necessary, particularly when such passivity would clearly be quite unacceptable to the propounder of it himself. Sven Stolpe tells us that before Hammarskjöld's appointment to the United Nations "he had a tendency to appoint himself judge: to look *down* on people — however kindly"; and Brian Urquhart comments on Hammarskjöld's "consciousness of superiority." Hammarskjöld's autocratic injunctions to "serve gladly for the value of serving," his consignment of his "collaborators" to "thankless jobs" which must be borne with patient and even grateful submission are, of course, totally at variance with his rules of conduct for himself. "In our era, the road

to holiness necessarily passes through the world of action."
"Live your individuality to the full." "Forward! Whatever
distance I have covered, it does not give me the right to halt."
"Only he who at every moment is all he is capable of being
can hope for a furlough from the frontier before he dis-
appears into the darkness" — this is Hammarskjöld exhorting
Hammarskjöld. His own "submission" was an arduous translation of concept into practice. Even his reflections that "the
'great' commitment all too easily obscures the 'little' one," and
that greatness may "all too easily shut our hearts" to the "ordinary everyday" have a patronizing ring to them. The fact is
that, while lumping his staff benevolently if remotely together
in his mind as, presumably, "the little people," Hammarskjöld
rested his administrative confidence in a group of personages
who were in some cases unequal to the large responsibilities
they discharged on his behalf.

Hammarskjöld treated the staff body as a servant class; and
his rare addresses to staff gatherings had all the indulgent
authoritarianism of the master's annual remarks in the servants'
hall. The extent to which he was encouraged, by the deportment
of his immediate entourage, to regard this attitude as widely
acceptable, is suggested by the uncritical, almost worshipful
tone in which some of his intimates have spoken and written
of him since his death. His "tendency to look down on people,"
his "consciousness of superiority" — naturally more exposed in
general than in particular encounters — were inalienable forces
of his nature, and are imperative signals to those who will
eventually contemplate his personality profoundly. Within the
privacy of *Markings*, Hammarskjöld tormented himself, end-
lessly and fruitlessly, by taking the measure of this aspect of
his own character and of its isolating results, and even of its
destructive repercussions on others; but its effects on the Organization itself are reckoned with only obliquely, even there.

No one will imagine that Hammarskjöld himself would have
enlisted, and remained indefinitely, in a service that offered no
outlet for ability, and no prospect of attaining a holiness neces-

sarily approached along the road of action. This is not, of course, to say that all his neglected staff were incipient Hammarskjölds. But many had joined the United Nations with very much such sentiments as his; and would have accepted sacrifices had they been encouraged to fulfill themselves in the Organization's cause. Throughout the 1950's there yet remained in the UN Secretariat a nucleus of idealism — of persons who had truly come "for the value of serving" and who might have been galvanized into a productive and influential element in United Nations affairs. Far from inertly contenting themselves with "thankless jobs," they might have profitably been advanced to areas of authority, superseding the incompetents who have nurtured the Organization's present crisis. In 1973, there is still no provision for the exploitation of this resource — and little certainty that it still remains.

In all this, Hammarskjöld followed the management pattern set from the era of Trygve Lie: an administrative disorder perpetuated, for the most part, by the same persons and still in operation at this writing.

While the relentless injunctions to do our best continued, with few opportunities being provided for this optimum, Hammarskjöld never ceased to concern himself on paper, and no doubt in mind, with the role of the international civil servant. Were his reflections, often brilliantly expressed and pursued, on career internationalism intended to refer to some phenomenon of the future, or to those few sparrows on whom his own eye might alight? In any event, it was not long before his actual staff found themselves abandoned to the devices of a series of Personnel chiefs — now imported specifically from England on some vague assumption that Fair Play would perforce be among their native attributes; not all of these found favor with the Secretary-General when unpacked.

It may well be asked — but never was — why the staff put up with such a situation, in which hierarchical indifference, not to say contempt, towards them was undisguised. The Dead

Souls syndrome had taken over with a vengeance, and few appeared to feel that the Secretary-General or his counselors had fundamental obligations to interest themselves in the composition and management of the Secretariat. Leaderlessness in this respect was widely recognized, but there was even a humble suggestion of its being a shame to bother him when he had "real" things to do. If the staff did not find themselves interesting, why should the Secretary-General? And a staff union that had passed through the experiences of the Trygve Lie years was not likely to force its views on his successor two or three years later.

It is to be expected that Hammarskjöld's deputies in the Secretariat will not easily accept assertions that he could not effectively delegate authority, or that he had that other failing of the purposeful and self-sufficient leader — the accumulation and retention of weak subordinates. Those who were burdened with responsible tasks during the Hammarskjöld years, and those who felt they made a show of strength have naturally been resistant to a different perspective formed by Hammarskjöld's character and career and by the diminution of the United Nations' influence almost from the moment of his death; and even, perhaps, by a different understanding of responsibility and strength. Ralph Bunche has told us that, among his intimates, Hammarskjöld "not only tolerated but seemed to relish views at odds with his own"; and no intelligent person need believe that the Secretary-General conducted himself like a preposterous Napoleon among his entourage. These are, however, quite other matters from the incontrovertible emergence in the world of a leader who conferred authority but did not share it, and who did not attract to himself those who would bring the stimulus of independent views or would address themselves to his pace and level.

Hammarskjöld did not bring younger men to his circle — his top associates were his seniors in years, or contemporaries in whom the point of challenge had been passed. He wanted men around him who would follow his path and his directions:

performance must be the basis of our opinion that this was, in varying degrees, the case. In a memorial tribute issued at the time of Hammarskjöld's death, his Chef de Cabinet, the Under-Secretary-General C. V. Narasimhan, stated: "It was difficult for most of his colleagues even to keep up with him."

Hammarskjöld's biographer Joseph P. Lash recounts that, during Hammarskjöld's more youthful years with the Swedish Foreign Ministry, "he quickly brought together a small secretariat of outstanding young men." However, the account goes on, "It was 'not a brain trust,' one of its members observed, because 'he was his own brain trust.' " Conor Cruise O'Brien describes the meetings between Hammarskjöld and his chief officers as being like those "between a youngish headmaster and a bright sixth form." Again, it is not to be expected that the participants will necessarily recognize themselves in such a description; and, again, outcome must be the basis of our opinion. (There is evidence, too, that in his private friendships Hammarskjöld sometimes sought the company of those who would look up to him.) We may assume that senior officials who had not stood up to Trygve Lie on basic issues of United Nations integrity were unlikely to show themselves cantankerous with Dag Hammarskjöld over more obscure questions.

In Mr. Lash's biography of Hammarskjöld, a chapter entitled "One-Man Job," apparently founded on conversations with Hammarskjöld, gives the Secretary-General's reasons for exercising sole authority — among them, his responsibilities under the United Nations Charter. Lash goes on to say: "What was legally stipulated and politically necessary dovetailed with Hammarskjold's strong personal proclivities. Able to do three or four times the work of the average civil servant, a first-rate economist, diplomat and jurist, with standards 'too high, too quick, too critical' to permit delegation of authority, the top-level Secretariat soon after his arrival was reorganized around his extraordinary abilities and enormous capacity for work. . . . 'Delegate,' both friends and critics advised him. Yet this was not possible in the UN. . . . He wanted to reduce the one-man aspect, but he had not been able to come up with an alternative, although·he was very keen to do so."

Despite Hammarskjöld's presentiments of mortality, he made little preparation, other than his example, for a future in which the United Nations would be deprived of his leadership and in need of other strong and positive wills. This state of affairs was never more excruciatingly evident than in the days immediately following his death, when the assembled circle of his official intimates, most of them veterans from the days of Lie, gave an impression of being even physically divested of impetus.

If illustration were required of the extent to which Hammarskjöld was "his own brain trust," and how little, during his years of office, the Organization as a whole was reinforced and made confident, or an independent will for action infused into his deputies, it could not be more eloquently supplied than by the velocity with which, after his death, the United Nations abandoned his initiatives and his political designs. To anyone unaware of the Organization's internal condition, the instantaneous retreat must seem incomprehensible; to those who were part of the system, entirely predictable. The ardent disciples of his path in life did not rise to the momentous occasion of his death by embracing his message as a Testamentum Domini through which his vision and example might be vigorously pursued. Ground had been broken, trails had been blazed, models and precedents had been given; but there was little hewing, clearing, or emulation, from those who remained or came after, in the wilderness of calamities that has since engulfed the world.

In extenuation of the United Nations' diminished political influence since Hammarskjöld's death, it is pointed out by Secretariat officials and others that world hostilities have intensified (a claim that perhaps shows short memories for the brinksmanship of the Cold War) and international relations become more complex in recent years. That the world, in the past decade, has entered into a seemingly permanent state of emergency might, quite on the contrary, have been regarded as all the more urgently necessitating Secretariat courage and initiative, and as calling upon all conceivable United Nations efforts to meet the extremity. United Nations initiatives have in fact declined as world crises accelerated.

Mr. Eyvind Bartels has written that Hammarskjöld's death was "a full stop; a full stop to his political activity too, which lacked both supporting strength and roots." This was so; but it was totally and grievously unnecessary.

Bright things had once more come to confusion; or, rather, confusion, like a dark companion, had been accreting all along.

The reader may consider the following statements:

The first duty of the Secretary-General must be to give to the staff and to staff problems their proper priority in the efforts. How can you possibly go into the field of political activity, try your efforts in the diplomatic sphere, if you have a feeling that the very basis on which these efforts have to be developed is a weak one?
— Dag Hammarskjöld,
extemporaneous remarks
to the staff, 1958

The UN organizations, in my humble opinion, have never had anything that could fairly be called a personnel policy.
— Statement by the President
of the Federation of International
Civil Servants Associations, 1971

It must be said, however, that none of the lines of modernization which we have just mapped out will have any exact significance until such time as the concept of *career staff* has been clearly defined. . . . Under the present system, moreover, career organization for Professional staff members is left to chance. . . . No one has yet specified exactly what sort of distinction should be drawn between the different kinds of Professional staff that make up the Secretariat.
— Report of the Joint Inspection Unit
on Personnel Problems in
the United Nations, 1971

In listing the remedies now seen to be urgent if what it calls the "grave crisis" of morale and efficiency in the United Nations is to be surmounted, the 1971 Report on Personnel Problems has compiled a catalogue of the lost opportunities of three decades; and an administrative indictment of the United Nations' first three Secretaries-General.

If any senior official opposed the Secretary-General's neglect of fundamental administrative concerns during the Hammarskjöld era, that was not evident to the staff. However, in the last months of Hammarskjöld's life, some irrepressible manifestations of the interior situation apparently made themselves felt to him, and in a manner likely to engage his interest since it had direct repercussions on the quality of personnel available for his emergency political missions:

Naturally, however, the experiences have demonstrated also weaknesses in the organization of the Secretariat. It does not dispose of a sufficient number of highly qualified senior officials for all the tasks that now have to be met — in spite of the feeling sometimes voiced that the Organization is "top-heavy." There is, generally speaking, within the Secretariat not enough of a diplomatic tradition of staff with training in political and diplomatic field activities to meet the needs which have developed over the years.
— Dag Hammarskjöld,
Introduction to the Annual Report,
August 1960

It was precisely in "top-heaviness," in an administrative weight repressing natural energy and excluding the new, that the principal weakness lay and has continued to lie. The full text* of Hammarskjöld's last address to the staff, in September 1961, a few days before his death, strikes a new and significant

* As distinct from the abridged version that appears in the posthumously published selection of Hammarskjöld's speeches *Dag Hammarskjöld: Servant of Peace*, edited by Wilder Foote (New York, Harper & Row, 1963).

182

note — revealing a growing concern for the adverse consequences of the geographical appointments, and a far more acute
awareness than previously of the frustration among his personnel. An aspect of the Secretariat condition that came to
light, foreseeably enough, during the Hammarskjöld era was
that his political missions — in the Suez crisis, for example,
and in the Congo — tended in certain instances to suffer, in so
far as they were staffed by Headquarters personnel or other
veteran UN appointees, from a lack of talent and resourcefulness at the "heavy" top; while some of the lower orders
bloomed on finding themselves actively engaged at last. Two
examples may be given here, one briefly and one at length;
both of these, in differing degrees, reflect important — and one
might say fatal — flaws in United Nations administrative attitudes.

In the first instance, it should be said that official scorn is
poured on the acrimonious published memoirs of one of the
most senior appointees of the United Nations mission to the
Congo in 1960–1961, the emphatic assertion by UN officials
being that the man was in fact shorn of his responsibilities on
the mission when — like Samson — he lay in heavy sleep;
and bundled, befuddled, on to a departing United Nations air-
plane by his UN Delilahs. Even if one accepts the categorically
asserted UN position, three features of the episode remain un-
accounted for: this official, concerned with military aspects of
the mission, had come to the Congo from another post of high
UN authority; his assignment to the Congo would appear to
involve a most unsuitable appointment (again, if one accepts
the United Nations' view) to a sensitive and important political post; and, lastly, we have the baffling sequel — unmentioned in any UN account — of the reappointment of this same
official, after his Samsonian departure from the Congo, to
another top post, this time in charge of a United Nations mission in the Middle East, following a brief resumption of his
original, pre-Congo responsibilities.

This case, while a variation of a serious and familiar United

Nations theme and an illustration of UN administrative determination to have it both, or several, ways, may have some light overtones. The second example does not.

After the Hungarian uprising of 1956, a United Nations mission took evidence from over one hundred political refugees who had fled Hungary for Western Europe. The majority of these fugitives testified anonymously for fear that reprisals would otherwise be taken against their families and friends remaining in Hungary. The Deputy Secretary of this UN Special Committee on Hungary, a Dane named Povl Bang-Jensen, had been a senior official of the UN Secretariat since 1949, in the Department of Political and Security Council Affairs, and had been acquainted with Hammarskjöld before either of them came to the Organization.

Bang-Jensen criticized the official attitudes of colleagues on the Special Committee on Hungary and asserted in violent language that the Committee's report suppressed important facts and distorted others.

After his return to UN Headquarters, Bang-Jensen refused to relinquish to his UN superiors a list concerning the anonymous witnesses from Hungary, on the grounds that the documents might become accessible to Soviet staff members, with resulting recriminations in Hungary. (This, on the face of it, is a reasonable position; and Hammarskjöld's response that there had been no unauthorized access to confidential papers at the United Nations in twelve years seems inadequate. In fact, this seems a case where there *were* "secrets" at the United Nations.) Bang-Jensen insisted that he had received prior assurance that he would have exclusive knowledge of the identity of certain witnesses; his superiors denied that he had been authorized to be sole custodian of such papers, and contended that the documents were in jeopardy in Bang-Jensen's possession since he had no means of safeguarding them.

Bang-Jensen was suspended by the Secretary-General (who refused at the time to grant him an interview, declaring: "I do not know that there is any obligation on the part of the

Secretary-General to go into such matters personally"), while a committee headed by Ernest A. Gross, former State Department official and deputy United States representative to the United Nations, investigated Bang-Jensen's conduct and "the disposition of certain papers." The case attracted notice in the newspapers (to whom Bang-Jensen unburdened himself), and, possibly because of that pressure, sealed envelopes containing the disputed papers were burned — on the recommendation of the investigating committee and by Hammarskjöld's instructions — on top of the United Nations building in an unearthly ceremony officiated at by Bang-Jensen, his counsel Adolf A. Berle, Jr., the UN Under-Secretary for Political Affairs, and the ubiquitous UN security chief Begley.

"Security" now reenters the United Nations scene, and with peculiar irony. While the reviewing committee deliberated, Bang-Jensen's cause was taken up by the right-wing press and by the same fanatical McCarthyist elements whose opinions had carried such weight with the United Nations administration in the days of Trygve Lie — including, in particular, by Robert Morris, former counsel of the McCarran Subcommittee, who had been made welcome in the Secretary-General's office in 1952 and had shared in the administration's tributes to the Subcommittee's "courtesies" and "complete fairness." The deluded Bang-Jensen — who in fact appears to have been the victim of an anti-Bolshevik paranoia even more virulent than that which had previously afflicted certain of his United Nations superiors — accepted this "support" for his position. The iniquities of Bang-Jensen's reactionary allies, in their meretricious attacks on the United Nations administration, were vehemently condemned by the Secretariat's leading officials — some of whom might better have expressed their abhorrence of these elements and tactics in earlier years.

The investigating committee censured Bang-Jensen. Although allowing that circumstances "inevitably created pressures of time and confusion as to administrative arrangements," and withholding criticism of Bang-Jensen's concern for the safe custody of the papers, the committee members found the essence of the matter to lie "in the aberrant conduct of an individual" who was "not open to rational persuasion." Bang-Jensen was recommended to take a "medical examination." (The portion of the committee's report dealing exclusively with Bang-Jensen's conduct was not released; but its contents may be deduced from later and lengthy communications on the subject from Hammarskjöld himself.)

A Joint Disciplinary Committee of four Secretariat officials next reviewed Bang-Jensen's case to determine what action should be taken. This second group found Bang-Jensen guilty of "grave errors of judgment and serious acts of indiscipline" that made him unfit for continued service with the United Nations. The finding of this disciplinary committee (also released only in part) includes the crucial statement, referred to earlier in this book, of the administration's view of UN staff obligations: that the staff "should not only subordinate their personal views to the decisions of their responsible superiors in the Secretariat, but also understand and accept the overriding authority in all matters of substance of the bodies themselves." Finally — or so it seemed — in a long and terrible letter of 3 July 1958, which he released to the press, Hammarskjöld excoriated Bang-Jensen personally, morally, and professionally; and, not surprisingly, terminated his association with the United Nations. The position forcibly stated by senior UN officials concerned was, and has never ceased to be, that Bang-Jensen was seriously deranged: in the words of one member of the Secretary-General's staff, he was "completely unbalanced." It has likewise been consistently asserted that the case was handled throughout with compassion and restraint. Representative extracts from Hammarskjöld's letter of dismissal will be found in the notes at the back of this book.

Bang-Jensen was assigned indemnities of thirty thousand dollars by the United Nations. His appeal, somewhat confusedly presented, was rejected by the Administrative Tribunal in the year of his dismissal.

In November of the following year, Bang-Jensen's body was found in a Long Island park, a presumed suicide.

The papers available to me regarding the Bang-Jensen affair are those, as far as they may be scrutinized, of the United Nations administration, the official investigating committees, and the Administrative Tribunal. (A fictionalized version of Bang-Jensen's point of view is contained in a novel published some years after the event.*) Assuming the administration's opinion of Bang-Jensen's condition to be accurate, the official conduct of his case may be questioned throughout.

The first — the investigating — committee released its derogatory view of the defendant's conduct while the investigation was in progress. (Challenged on this point at a press conference, Hammarskjöld asserted that the committee "should be entitled to present its arguments and the basis on which it reaches its conclusions.") No representative of that disregarded body, the UN Staff Association, was included in the committee's composition — Hammarskjöld declaring, on this issue, that Bang-Jensen was himself a "staff representative," and Ernest Gross taking the position that the committee was not a formal group and therefore not bound by the usual rules of the Secretariat. Hammarskjöld showed a — perhaps natural — reluctance, and some hostility in discussing the matter at press conferences, on one occasion insulting a Danish reporter who questioned him closely.

The tone and premises of the second, disciplinary committee are such that one might wonder what likelihood there might be, in different circumstances, of a verdict *against* the administration; and it is made clear that submission was a parallel

---

* Edwin P. Hoyt, *A Matter of Conscience,* Duell, Sloan and Pearce (New York, 1966). Another book, *Betrayal at the UN: The Story of Paul Bang-Jensen,* by DeWitt Copp and Marshall Peck (New York: Devin-Adair, 1961), emanated from Bang-Jensen's rightist supporters: adopting an overwrought tone that gives little confidence, it nevertheless incorporates documents of interest exchanged between Bang-Jensen and his UN superiors.

— perhaps even the major — issue, quite distinct from Bang-Jensen's condition. The menace, of course, of taking and proclaiming such an authoritarian position lies not simply in its application to those few cases that may come to investigation and appeal, but — as with the security clearance procedures themselves — in the proscriptive and conformist atmosphere that it disseminates throughout the entire staff to which it is addressed.

The view of the Joint Disciplinary Committee on this matter was a direct reflection of the attitude of Hammarskjöld himself — who in dismissing Bang-Jensen informed him that when Bang-Jensen discovered in himself "moral reservations" in conflict with Secretariat policy, "it was your duty to resign from the service." It will be imagined how many moral reservations are likely to be aired in such an atmosphere.

Lastly, the devastating letter in which Hammarskjöld castigates Bang-Jensen in twelve pages of vengeful prose leaves room for doubt as to whether aberration was exclusively on Bang-Jensen's side. (The bureaucratic density of this communication suggests that Hammarskjöld himself may not have written it; if not, his signature is a curious endorsement of a drafter's savagery.) The public release of the letter, almost simultaneously with its dispatch, was said to have been "formally requested by a member state"; this surely could have been overcome in private, in the case of a paper annihilating to the recipient's self-esteem and highly prejudicial to any future employment he might seek; and must certainly have reflected Hammarskjöld's own desire, inflamed by Bang-Jensen's intractability and the public treatment of the affair.

If the administration and the investigating committee were, as it would appear, correct in judging Bang-Jensen unbalanced, the inhumanity of addressing such a letter (which even condemns his "childish" physical behavior, accusing him of "shouting very loudly" and of "physical interference" — the latter apparently consisting of nothing more than having grasped an irate official "firmly by both arms," a circumstance that scarcely seems to have merited reporting and reiterating among grown men) to a person in his state, and making it public, must be heavily judged. It is not a communication that would leave untouched the equilibrium of even a rational recipient.

It is precisely the official contention that Bang-Jensen was mentally unhinged that puts the worst construction on the handling of the affair. It was stated by the reviewers of this case that Bang-Jensen had done harm to the United Nations, and had attracted to himself "undeserved sympathy." However this may have been in the initial stages, it will be seen in retrospect that harm and sympathy were equally transient; and that the Bang-Jensen tragedy is periodically revived because it is a moment of nakedness on both sides.

This bizarre episode has been related in some detail both for its own significance and for the light it casts into what might be called the heart of UN administrative darkness. As in so many United Nations matters, the central question of the Bang-Jensen case appears to have been completely ignored in the innumerable siftings and pronouncements concerning it. Let us, again, assume that the United Nations' view is correct and that Bang-Jensen was "not open to rational persuasion." *Unless we accept the notion that he became "completely unbalanced" on the plane that bore him to his assignment for the Special Committee on Hungary, we must believe that a deeply disturbed personality was sent on one of the most urgent and delicate political missions ever undertaken by the United Nations.* At the time of his dismissal Bang-Jensen had held a senior position in the UN Secretariat for nine years. During that period, his staff had presumably, under the Eichmannesque doctrine promulgated by the Joint Disciplinary Committee, been required to "subordinate their personal views" to him as their "responsible superior." Neither of the examining committees, nor even the Administrative Tribunal, seem to have concerned themselves with this aspect of the problem or to have contemplated the censure or reform of the procedures that created it.

> Astray in his conceptions, entangled in words, man loses the flair for
> truth, the taste for nature. What a powerful intellect must you pos-
> sess, to be suspicious of this moral carbon monoxide and, with your
> head already swimming, to hurl yourself out of it into the fresh air
> with which, into the bargain, everyone round is trying to scare you.
> — Alexander Herzen,
> *My Past and Thoughts*

As early as 1951, Trygve Lie was already referring to "the vast mass" of United Nations records. During the Hammarskjöld term, through negligence and the misinvestiture of authority with resultant *"trop de zèle,"* the Secretariat contribution to UN paper production burgeoned into nightmarish proportions.

The monstrous volume of United Nations documentation, much of it useless in two or three languages, has to be experienced to be believed. Even with the merciful intervention of microfilm, warehouses are maintained for its retention. UN Headquarters alone prints over half a billion pages of documentation annually: a UN press release tells us that "laid end to end, these would stretch nearly 100,000 miles, or four times around the Earth at the Equator." The United Nations holds about seven thousand major meetings annually, all replete with working papers, proposals, counterproposals, records and reports. Mr. Lester Pearson describes the Organization as "drowning in its own words and suffocating in its own documents."

Even documents that might be of use and interest naturally grow meaningless or are passed over in the self-defeating inundation. Many, many of the papers circulated in the Secretariat and the conference rooms go into wastebaskets unread; it is perhaps only thanks to this instinct of survival that the United Nations can continue at all. (Documentation for one forthcoming conference was recently reduced from a proposed 6,500 pages to 1,600 in favor of "a more substantial investment in brainpower.") Many of the prolix Secretariat reports to the General Assembly or other UN councils have, moreover, developed to a phenomenal degree the bureaucratic talent for transfiguring actual chaos into a paper order.

It is the unbridled nature of United Nations governing bodies to exude paper; and Secretariat spokesmen unhesitatingly put the blame for the documental extravaganza squarely on the shoulders of governments — where it by no means exclusively belongs. Repeated General Assembly directives to reduce documentation* (pages are being feverishly counted up, as of this writing, in pursuance of another such admonition) might have been gratefully seized upon as a mandate for radical reform, had there been a Secretariat will for change. Any person who has worked in the Secretariat knows that the paper increase is the jealously defended justification for many a redundant post on the manning-table, and that "productivity" is more often than not assessed in wordage. It is not a matter of reducing or eliminating surplus documentation in order to facilitate a basic operation: in many cases, the basic operation *is* the paper-production, without which there would be no underlying job. It is because of this artificiality that the paper procedures must be defended and multiplied by their progenitors, since they are not based on a reality that might be more efficiently served in other ways.

A refreshingly frank treatment of the Secretariat role in United Nations documentation appeared in 1971 in a survey by Mr. Robert M. Macy, a member of the UN Joint Inspection Unit.

On the governmental side, it need perhaps merely be said that a thirty-one-nation Special Committee on the Rationaliza-

---

* The UN Joint Inspection Unit estimated, in 1971, that a fifteen per cent reduction in total documentation might be expected to yield an annual saving of $4.5 million. The annual documents budget of the United Nations runs at approximately $30 million, although a 1971 report on documentation informed the General Assembly that "the trend of printing costs indicated in the United Nations Budget is not only misleading, but is 'only the top of the iceberg.'"

tion of the Procedures and Organization of the General Assembly, appointed in 1970 to grapple with problems of excessive documentation and procedural hindrance in United Nations deliberations, spawned a variety of working groups and drafting subcommittees, conducted forty-five closed sessions over a period of a year, and produced a 219-page report that reads like a parody of bureaucratic inconclusiveness. (Of this document, the New York *Times* remarked, in November 1971: "The report takes the bull by the horns and, 219 pages later, is hopelessly impaled.")

There are contingent menaces, beyond the Parkinsonian, in the maniacal paper-pushing of the United Nations. One is the illusion it apparently creates among delegates and senior UN officials alike that something is being accomplished. All manner of obscure analyses and obsolete resolutions will be cited by UN officials as evidence of United Nations "activity" on vital issues. The ludicrous and tragic extremes to which this documental obsession can go may be illustrated with the reminder that, while the Security Council was finding itself unable first to discuss, then to deal with, the war between India and Pakistan in November and December of 1971, the Legal Committee of the General Assembly was struggling, as it has for decades, with the semantics of defining "aggression." (In late December 1971, the Security Council finally agreed on the wording of a resolution "endorsing" the cease-fire already in operation between India and Pakistan.)

A recent documentary film on the United Nations* shows, among other disheartening episodes, the following scene, as described by the New York *Times:* "In one sequence the viewer sees Nigerian soldiers clubbing Biafrans while in the ad hoc committee on periodic reports on human rights he hears a British delegate at the UN quibble over the grammar of a document doomed to the dustbin. The UN never found itself able to intervene or mediate in the Biafra holocaust."

* Assembled in 1969 by Mr. Arthur Zegart for United States National Educational Television.

These are but single instances of an abstracted way of thought and conduct: it is Academism over Life, and with a vengeance.

The worst danger is in the linguistic inhumanity. In his introduction to *The Pentagon Papers*, Neil Sheehan comments on the fact that "there is an absence of emotional anguish or moral questioning of action in the memorandums and cablegrams and records of the high-level policy discussions." Similarly, one may pick up almost any United Nations document and read an account of some UN enterprise from beginning to end without ever discovering that these are actions or intentions emanating from diverse, fallible human beings and having consequences for their — likewise diverse and fallible — fellows. (The rare instances where this is not the case — for example, the 1971 FICSA summary, or Sir Robert Jackson's 1969 Study of the Capacity of the UN Development System — produce a shock of relief and meaning by contrast.) The polysyllabic jargon in which many UN papers are written could reduce the most profound reflections to absurdity, if profound reflections were in the habit of appearing in their pages.

The implications go far beyond the merely ridiculous. At best, they partake of the delusion that comment on human affairs is more "professional" if rendered in a series of sociological abstractions having no conceivable reference to individual lives. At worst, and more generally, they represent a dehumanizing and, in a deep sense, illiterate form of modern "official" expression of which world leaders have themselves become indefatigable exponents. Professor Hugh Trevor-Roper has written of this menace in the following terms:

Language is not only a store of images or a reflexion of social forms: it is also an instrument of thought which, if perverted, can be a means of hypnosis or deception. Nowhere has the academic perversion of language been carried further than in the German universities whence so much muddy philosophy has flowed over the Western world. . . . If German society so passively accepted the horrors perpetrated in its name, part of the reason lay not in an atavistic polytheism belatedly revolting against the inflexible command of Moses in the oasis of Kadesh, but in the cosy anesthesia more recently introduced into inattentive minds by pretentious jargon.

Hammarskjöld, self-sufficient in his abilities and his high office, allowed the paper snowstorm to bank up remorselessly beneath him, and left the staff to shovel it all about as best they might. Despite the occasional directive to "reduce," United Nations documentation increased immeasurably during his term. Networks of intricate and unreasonable procedures were also permitted to festoon the simplest undertaking, complacently enforced by those who habitually enforce such systems with complacency, and ensuring maximum inhibition of any useful intention. Those who did attempt simplifications of the system only created further chaos, grappling yet again with outward forms only and trying to introduce inflections into rigidity.

At a 1959 press conference Hammarskjöld remarked, of his own productive negotiations with governments, that "simpler and smoother methods have been initiated to arrive at solutions — partly through bypassing regular procedures." In a sense he seems to have bypassed the Secretariat and much of its unwieldy, disregarded machinery; and, where he did avail himself of Secretariat procedures, he tried to wring from them their long-lost and perhaps never seriously intended meaning.

The Secretariat itself emerged from the Hammarskjöld years more bureaucratized and with less identity than ever. They were, in effect, the same staff left behind by Trygve Lie, embittered by the passage of a further seven years with still no Rachel in sight: a body of persons who knew they were not respected, were under surveillance, would be neither asked for their views nor encouraged to display their capacities. More than ever, "administration" was divided from staff; and "authority" had now soared into the astral reaches. Personnel chiefs came and went without the staff in general even knowing

what they looked like. A distraction from some of these grievances had been provided by the comet of Dag Hammarskjöld's
career, shedding vicarious glory and even some sporadic activity in the staff's direction. But the misfortunes of United
Nations personnel as a working body, founded on the formative policies of Trygve Lie, had consolidated and multiplied in
the Hammarskjöld era. Triviality and timidity in all forms had
been allowed to flow unchecked throughout the Secretariat
and, as soon as the prodigy of Hammarskjöld's leadership was
extinguished, they were to be publicly assumed as the Organization's character before the world.

Six.

"'Collapse' Would Be Better"

Matter rather than forms should be the object of our attention, its configurations and changes of configuration, and simple action, and law of action or motion; for forms are figments of the human mind, unless you will call those laws of action forms.
— FRANCIS BACON, *Novum Organum.*

With the death of Dag Hammarskjöld, the United Nations entered politically into a kind of vaunted inertia. The Secretariat over which U Thant assumed leadership was virtually the same, in structure, personality, and personalities, as that from which Trygve Lie had departed eight years before, its further debilitation only partially and temporarily obscured by the public initiatives of the Hammarskjöld era. Although, with the influx of many "new" member nations and consequent manifold pressures for Secretariat appointments, the staff was now to increase, new recruits accepted the United Nations Secretariat on a basis of mutual, and thus intensified, restrictiveness — limiting their significance to the geographical — rather than bringing growth and diversification to it. Negativism, burgeoning with the death of Hammarskjöld from a latent into the most manifest of United Nations attributes, now became an actual source of pride in the upper echelons of the Organization. The "inside story" from now on was all too often to be the chronicle of the In reasons why such-and-such could not conceivably take place, as United Nations officials and delegates alike acquired a sort of proprietary right of first refusal in world emergencies and an encyclopedic expertise in proscription and retreat.

Timorousness is not necessarily coupled with humility; and the curious turning of timidity into cause for a public show of self-satisfaction is a modern phenomenon — the product, in part, of vast bureaucracies of the mind bred by an overpopulated world. The United Nations, in its relative newness and self-containment, again provides a critical specimen — its defection, as always, making a supreme and tragic contrast with its founding principles and professed objectives.

The emergence of this new position may now be followed from without — in the public statements of United Nations leaders over the past decade; in the public attitudes evoked in response; and of course in the present condition of the United Nations. Examples in this connection are endless, and the reader should not be wearied with them: even from the selection given here, it will be seen that an important, if unconscious, point of view is developed, and that the basis of that point of view is lack of conviction. *The United Nations' own argument may be summarized as the contention that the mere existence of the present Organization contributes to world peace, that its political passivity is an integral part of its usefulness, and that only an irresponsible and uninformed person would expect it to do better.* This was the position persistently and, one might say, aggressively stated by Secretariat leaders throughout the decade of U Thant's tenure.

A recent cartoon in an American magazine shows the United Nations gloomily adrift on a life raft, with the caption, "I may not be getting anywhere — but I'm afloat." The fact that nominal survival — or at least not official discontinuance — is put forward as a measure of fulfillment is the best indication one can give of the personal and official spirit emanating from United Nations leadership for ten years.

Contrasting the Thant approach with that of Hammarskjöld,

the New York *Times* felt that "Mr. Thant, undramatic and low-keyed, uses an approach that is entirely different. He seems to have decided once and for all that the office of the Secretary-General and the United Nations as a whole have no power of their own, but must wait for action to be initiated and sanctioned by members."

In a lengthy and very favorably disposed interview, in 1967, with the *Sunday Times* of London, entitled "U Thant: or the Rise of Mr. Nobody," Mr. Thant was praised in the following terms:

Considering how much America gives the UN financially and that its Headquarters are in New York, his stand [on Vietnam] has been very brave. . . . He had been criticized for not being imaginative enough, for not trying out new policies or methods. This might be true. But it was in bulldozing their personalities through that his two predecessors ran into opposition.

And the interviewer, having mentioned that the 1960 Khrushchev proposal of the "troika system with three men doing the job of Secretary-General" was put forward as a brake on Hammarskjöld's strong personality, naïvely comments in approval of U Thant: "The troika idea wasn't even mentioned when last December he was unanimously re-elected for another five years." In the same article Lord Caradon, then United Kingdom representative at the United Nations, sighs with relief: "It is restful to be sure of one man's integrity." Nothing could have been more indubitable, or less restful, than the internationalist integrity of Dag Hammarskjöld.

The same 1967 interview contains the following scene from 38th-floor life at the United Nations:

"About this *débâcle* in the Middle East," said the Indian editor of the UN official reports, coming into [his directorial colleague's] office.
"What about it?"
"Don't you think the word *débâcle* is a bit strong?" said the edi-

tor, handing over the draft of a report. "It does imply a certain amount of comment. I think 'collapse' would be better."

"I don't think so, but let's see what the dictionary says."

They got out the larger Oxford Dictionary and looked it up.

"Perhaps you're right. But you'd better see Bunche before you change it. He wrote that bit."

As in the delegates' lounge and in the Press boxes, the big excitements at the UN take place over words. But at least it is some sort of excitement.

And a few lines later U Thant himself is recorded as stating, "I can tolerate criticism when it's fair. And even when it's based on false facts. But not when it's malicious."

"Malicious" in such a context is often a synonym for "to the point," or "painful." And criticism based on erroneous information is certainly the most bearable variety, being easily refutable. Given the United Nations' circumstances in 1967, or at any moment since, the only conceivable consideration for U Thant or his successor in weighing criticism should be whether or not it is true.

The public, with whom the meaning or failure of the United Nations must lie, pathetically falls in with the "strength through weakness" posture. The United Nations is "a safety valve," declares *The Times* of London, adding: "many crises would have been worse if the two sides had not been able to 'take it to the United Nations' and proclaim their grievances to the world. Some of the dangerous pressures were released in the process, even if in the end the United Nations did nothing positive." As long, in other words, as they keep talking.

An American correspondent at the United Nations tells us, in an article entitled "Signs of UN Maturity," that "the best thing that can be said about the UN's silver anniversary is that it did not do much harm. In fact, it even did some good — if one has the courage to dig for gold in the welter of endless and often silly speeches, inane backroom maneuvering over meaningless amendments to inconsequential resolutions, and revolting examples of the lack of understanding among nations. . . . Much of the shouting in the UN halls is done out of pure frustration and quite often the shouting is a substitute for the shooting — an inglorious but not ineffective way to preserve the world's shaky peace." As long as they keep shouting.

(By 1972 the pitch had risen, and "a long-time member of the Secretariat, much of whose effectiveness depends on anonymity" was reported in the New York press as stating, "After all, it is better screaming at each other at the conference table than carrying on dark maneuvers along the border" — as ever, without reference to the crucial fact that United Nations conferences have had less and less deterrent effect on dark maneuvers.)

In 1969, James Reston, writing in the New York *Times*, felt that the "United Nations, whatever else it does, provides an excuse to get the informed representatives of the nations together. . . . Usually, the foreign ministers make the usual statements at the airport and speeches on the UN podium, go to the good New York restaurants and then go home, leaving all the problems about as they were. . . . The 24th General Assembly . . . will probably do very little about these problems in public. It may even make them worse. But privately, there is a chance for serious talk."

Despite the outcome of that year's Assembly, Mr. Reston retained his optimism into the following year. In preparation for the 1970 anniversary celebrations he wrote:

While the generals have been the dominant force in recent years, the United Nations has seemed almost like an impotent mausoleum on the bank of the East River. But it may have its uses now. What started as a rather melancholy twenty-fifth anniversary, to weep for lost causes, now provides a chance to bring the world leaders together at a moment when private talks may be helpful and even significant. For example, both the United States and the Soviet Union have reserved time for their leaders to address the General Assembly during this autumn's session. . . . This is still one of the great services of the United Nations. It provides an excuse to talk, not only openly but privately.

The leaders mentioned did not attend. It should be recalled that, throughout these years, the war in Vietnam was never discussed in the United Nations* or, with any constructive effect, among the world's leaders. The talk in United Nations councils has not been, as claimed, a substitute for strife but a disregarded accompaniment to it.

Again, *The Times* of London, in a 1970 anniversary tribute to U Thant:

Undoubtedly Viet Nam has dominated his term of office and depressed him both because he saw the war as "barbarous" — a word he used in an unguarded moment at a press lunch — and because he found his own initiatives bore no fruit. . . . The Middle East has probably never engaged his emotions as deeply as Viet Nam. Perhaps that is why he was slow to react to it. . . . The blunt answer is that the great powers were happy to use the United Nations but never remotely willing to make concessions at its urging. In such circumstances U Thant's failings can be seen as an aspect of his virtues. The moderate, conciliatory public servant has not been able to make the United Nations a force in the world when no current was fed in by any of the great powers. Nor is he the driving administrator who can create loyalties and dedication that could make his own headquarters a force in its own right — the complicated national components make it a cumbersome machine at best. There have been times when the Buddhist detachment has served admirably, as in U Thant's refusal to get mixed up in the Nigeria–Biafra quarrel. . . . Whatever the future the United Nations may carve out for itself in the world U Thant will have contributed an essential ingredient of devoted peacemaking.

* The Vietnam issue had been brought before the United Nations in 1959 on the initiative of Laos. In 1964 the Security Council debated the Tonkin Gulf incident, Adlai Stevenson denying that those hostilities were the result of provocative action by the United States ("This allegation is false. No United States ships intruded into the territorial waters as alleged, nor did United States ships shell the island referred to. . . . There was only one conclusion to be drawn: the attack constituted a planned, a calculated, a deliberate act of military aggression against the United States. . . . The United States Government had no choice but to reply.") The Vietnam conflict surfaced again on the Security Council agenda in 1966, but the Council declined to deal with it.

This time the message seems to be: "We may be passive, but that's our most constructive function." The above-described attitudes of the Secretary-General, and public acquiescence in them as expressed by the press, may be contrasted with Hammarskjöld's urging that the United Nations become "an instrument for negotiation of settlements, as distinct from the mere debate of issues," and his assertion that "what has been lost in power can be made up by leadership."

On U Thant's departure from the United Nations, at the end of 1971, an editorial and articles in the New York *Times* praised his "exceptional diligence and devotion . . . his commitment to the UN Charter, his perception of the problems of an interdependent world and his eloquence in articulating the cause of international cooperation. . . . His critics forget that while the Secretary-General is entrusted with broad responsibilities, he has virtually no power. His effectiveness depends [here we go again] on the cooperation of member states, particularly the big powers." A companion article tells us:

One of the criticisms against him is that he had not been able to rescue the world organization from the threat of bankruptcy. The United Nations moreover has lost prestige and public support in many countries. There are those who say that a more dynamic personality could have given it the dramatic image that would have kept interest in it high. . . . Men who have been watching the workings of the United Nations Secretariat and the specialized agencies say that Mr. Thant's biggest failing was his "hopelessness as an administrator." Some diplomats say he lacks the toughness that it would have taken to dismiss incompetent aides. As far as is known he never challenged a member government when it nominated an ill-equipped man to a position on the staff, one diplomat said.

Yet the same correspondent agrees that "the Secretary-General . . . has a great deal of power if he seeks it. . . . [However,] it is easy to imagine what would have happened to United States–United Nations relations if Mr. Thant had insisted on giving the world organization an active role in Vietnam, the Dominican Republic or even Biafra."

It will be recalled that Mr. Egon Ranshofen-Wertheimer, writing nearly thirty years ago about the demise of the League of Nations, reminded us that the Secretary-General of the League "would have been clearly within his authority" to stand firm against destructive national pressures. "But . . . the Secretary-General of the League would have been pitted against a big power, and the outcome would have been a defeat for the Secretary-General." *It will also be recalled what was the ultimate outcome for the League of Nations.*

In another salute to the retiring Secretary-General, *The Times* of London felt that

Dag Hammarskjöld was an activist, it is said, and thereby made the United Nations a potent influence on the international scene. U Thant took a more passive line; while regarding himself, quite rightly, as the servant of the member governments he was inclined (it is claimed) to wait too long for instructions that never came or, as over the removal of United Nations forces from Sinai in 1967, to act too precipitately on instructions with which he might well have argued. . . . U Thant achieved a good deal; if he seemed to be of little account in the big crises the fault was very far from being his alone. The first place where Dr. Waldheim will have to display his talents is in the United Nations itself. The organization is in bad shape. Its structure is flabby, and the morale of its staff is low. The situation cries out for an administrator who is prepared to be tough — to rationalize procedures, to promote merit and to dispense with incompetents. If this was done there would be a much better chance of producing a machine which could be called on with some confidence in a crisis.

What is cumulatively evident from a reading of these and many, many other public pronouncements of the past decade on the United Nations is a shrinking from logical conclusions — a journalistic clutching at straws, for apparent lack of anything else to clutch at, and from the well-intentioned desire to find something positive in an inundation of circumstances which, when enumerated, turn out to be almost exclusively negative. If the "impotent mausoleum" of the United Nations "does nothing positive" about the world's problems and "may even make them worse"; if a passive Secretary-General's "exceptional diligence and devotion" result in an organization that has "lost prestige and public support"; and, while his "failings are an aspect of his virtues," his "biggest failing" is his "hopelessness as an administrator," just what are we being asked to console ourselves with? The promptings — "admirably," "quite rightly" — to our indulgence, and urgings that we refrain from criticism — "his critics forget," etc. — have increasingly the ring of desperation. Here again we have the well-meant, fatal disinclination to subject the Organization to proper standards: and persistence in this in the face of a mass of evidence irresistibly adduced by the well-wishers themselves. The insistent reluctance, as it were, to grapple with the obvious by now stems not from belief that the Organization can somehow prevail, but from agonized refusal to face the fact of its failure; *and from lack of realization that it is only through that admission that the United Nations concept can be re-created in an active form.*

On the United Nations' side, the celebration of default might also be illustrated indefinitely. Many are the "admirable" refusals to get mixed up in the world's troubles; many the failings that, with the required perspective, can be seen as virtues. "Even the *frustrations* are stimulating," said Ralph Bunche. "The duller the debate in our meetings, and the more boring, the better." And he added — that was in 1967 — that the United Nations "is not giving up on Viet Nam." Many the dull meetings that are all for the best, no doubt demonstrating that progress must of necessity be boring.

(The United Nations has traditionally taken a certain pride in tedium. More than once, for example, in his memoirs, Lord Gladwyn comments on the dullness of his own speeches with what one can only feel is a measure of satisfaction. Reporting that an intelligent member of his audience wrote entreating him, for the sake of the United Nations, to cultivate a less pedantic and pompous delivery — telling him that "many people gave up attempting to follow or hear and went to sleep. They were also deeply disappointed at the content of the speech" — he concludes: "She was dead right. But I repeat that I really was out to bore this particular audience.")

A statement of U Thant's own view of the nature, requirements, and limitations of his office is contained in an address made by him, in September 1971, to the United Nations Correspondents Association. Referring to the "persistent illusion that the Secretary-General's position is in some way comparable to that of the head of a Government, and that clearcut and decisive action can, and should, be taken by him," he nevertheless advocates Secretariat initiatives "no matter what the consequences" to the Secretary-General personally or to his office if "it might mean the difference between peace and war." His address is in part concerned with the obstacles he himself encountered to any such bold course.

Delegates themselves express warm support for the non-enforcement procedures. A former United States Deputy Representative to the United Nations, Mr. Francis Plimpton, is quoted in a capsule biography as holding that "you can't have a strong Secretary-General. Trygve Lie and Dag Hammarskjöld alienated the Russians and became powerless"; yet the same article gives the view that the space treaty produced by a United Nations committee of which Plimpton was a member was "one of the few solid U.N. accomplishments of the sixties." One may contrast those lean 1960's with the United Nations' most productive period — the Hammarskjöld years of the 1950's. Many are the delegational expressions of preference for form over matter: none other than the Foreign Secretary of Greece, at the 1970 General Assembly, paid tribute to what has apparently come to be regarded as the empty show of legitimacy required by the United Nations Charter, saying that where aggression existed it at least "feels the need to wear a mask."

Who would think, from all this, that the United Nations' peace-keeping machinery had ever known a dynamic period of action and intervention? Who would imagine that, if Secretaries-General had kept coming forward who were implacably bent on implementing the United Nations Charter, on making themselves useful even if usefulness meant that tenure would not be renewed, and on belaying the climb of their successors, member states would have had to reckon with an office, and ultimately with an instrument, which they must either compromise with or adapt to — or liquidate, as in any case they have virtually managed to do? Of the arduous, vital furnishing of positive precedent, Hammarskjöld once said:

If a mountain wall is once climbed, later failures do not undo the fact that it *can* be climbed. In this sense, every step forward in the pioneer effort of this Organization inevitably widens the scope for the fight for peace.

What has evolved, instead, at the United Nations is a new species of pusillanimity whose tenacity, energies, and inventiveness are concerted not only towards inaction but to pugnacious defense of the procedural righteousness of inaction — all the while, it must be remembered, laying claim to a positive role in human affairs and exhorting others to risk, activity, and sacrifice. It is within this context, and against these inherited handicaps, that the efforts of Mr. Waldheim to reactivate the Secretariat role have had to take place.

Everyone realizes that United Nations officials may not allow themselves expressions of private opinion in their public capacity. But the extreme paradox has arisen — surely unforeseen at the Organization's launching — whereby this restraint on "private opinion" is equated with a prohibition against making a public stand for principle or a courageous public espousal of right over wrong. It cannot have been intended that United Nations Secretariat leaders should have *less* public courage and conscience than other mortals, or give less moral leadership than other public figures.

Advocating his dismissal and security clearance policies be-for the General Assembly in 1953, Trygve Lie — whose sense of internationalist discretion had not inhibited him from conspiring to violate the Charter, or from bullying his staff into compliance with his course — referred obliquely to the "political climate in which the United Nations Secretariat has had to carry on its work here," and stated:

It is not for me to express my opinion of some of the things that have been said and some of the things that have occurred.

To whom, then, would such a responsibility fall, if not to the United Nations Secretary-General? ("Out of office," Lie informs us in a footnote, "I am free to do so at last." Which is to say, when the power and duty to stand on principle had passed from him.)

During the 1960's, the United Nations Secretary-General, specifically charged under the Charter with bringing mortal conflicts to the world's attention, was commended for denouncing the holocaust of the Vietnam war "in an unguarded moment," and for unproductive private efforts that involved him in a minimal public commitment and provided no point of convergence or center of expression for the moral indignation aroused throughout the world.

In 1971, Gunnar Jarring, the United Nations mediator in the Middle East who is also the Swedish Ambassador to the Soviet Union, declined to present the Nobel Prize medal to Aleksandr Solzhenitsyn except in an unwitnessed meeting. Interviewed on his eightieth birthday, the then chief administrator of United Nations economic development programs, Paul Hoffman, declared that he had "his own strong views" in opposition to the Vietnam war but must refrain from expressing them publicly.*

---

* This kind of Pilatic abstention was not required from United Nations officials originally: when H. L. Keenleyside, a first chief of UN economic assistance programs, refused at an official reception in postwar Indonesia to shake hands with Hjalmar Schacht — the former finance minister of Hitler then advising the new Indonesian nation on its economy — and announced that nothing would induce him to do so, he was completely

No system of impartiality directed to peace and justice is conceivably served by indicating one's opinions but declining to articulate them, or by refusing to honor the champions of principle, or by reserving one's stand on moral issues until such time as it will have ceased to have influence. The strange, and monstrous, turn to such attitudes in United Nations circles is that they are rationalized as being "in the best interests of the Organization" and as in some way contributing to the standing and effectuality of a body whose constitution preaches a precisely contrary standard of behavior. It is as if these leaders imagined they were to have some second life in which to act upon the principles they have laid down in this one.

When the more glaring of such apostasies have been criticized in United Nations leaders, the response has been the conditioned reflex of categorical justification, or at most the admission that the official concerned "is in a difficult position." Any significant choice between right or wrong will place the exerciser of it "in a difficult position"; and, since the United Nations instance is a peculiarly complex one, it is worth dwelling a little on the presumed *constructive purposes* of impartiality rather than treating impartiality as a noncommital end in itself or, as Hammarskjöld warned, as "a negative neutrality."

In his long preoccupation with an internationalist objectivity, Hammarskjöld approached impartiality not as a votive shrine, another useless "refuge," but as a source of strength and a basis for action. He understood that, if it were to have meaning

---

upheld by the United Nations. UN Secretariat leaders have, in fact, from time to time expressed and published their personal opinions without arousing public controversy and even, apparently, without incurring the official disapproval visited by the Organization on subordinate staff for indiscretions of the kind (illustrated in a recent administrative circular enjoining Secretariat staff against criticizing member states under any provocation and reporting that an employee has been reprimanded on this score). Paul Hoffman himself, in his first years at the United Nations, regularly included, in his public addresses and interviews in support of UN development programs, the injunction "How many Cubas do you want?" — a curious justification, surely, for an internationally staffed humanitarian enterprise to which the Soviet bloc has substantially contributed in funds, experts, and equipment.

and moral influence, impartiality must be seen *to rise above* the commitments of partiality, rather than to sink below them or to detach itself from commitment entirely: that is, to transcend the passing engagements of prejudice in favor of large, bold and constant principles. Instead of seeking, under a cloak of impartiality, to evade any open choice between right and wrong — and therefore to espouse wrong by default and destroy credence in the reality of international standards — Hammarskjöld strove to reserve and fortify the authority to stand for right. A United Nations Secretariat that could never, individually or collectively, face a challenge to its own pledges would, as he foresaw, become bound in shallows and in miseries, incapable of distinguishing between discretion and faintheartedness or of greeting truth.

Hammarskjöld's own stature — and his unique *persona* which could direct itself with passion, and even obsession, to this problem of dispassionateness — were too exceptional to provide an exact and individual model for others. (There are times, too, when his magisterial conviction of his own virtue in this regard veers perilously towards a Doctrine of Infallibility.) Rather, he demonstrated that a reality of constructive impartialness could exist and develop, and that there could be active exponents of it; and, above all, that it could be the very basis of intervention and the very justification for action, rather than a plea for abstention.

What has happened, instead, is that "impartiality" has in large measure come to be considered a self-fulfilling condition, and a void.

The following statement, included in Hammarskjöld's reply to the Soviet allegations against his integrity during the Congo crisis of 1960, serves to illustrate the strength of his belief in the active instrument of impartiality, and the lengths to which he was by then prepared to go in its defense:

Thus, if the office of the Secretary-General becomes a stumbling block for anyone, be it an individual, a group or a government, because the incumbent stands by the basic principle which must guide his whole activity, and if, for that reason, he comes under criticism, such criticism strikes at the very office and the concepts on which it is based. I would rather see that office break on strict adherence to the principle of independence, impartiality and objectivity than drift on the basis of compromise.

No assertion could be more greatly at variance with Secretariat attitudes of "impartiality" during the past decade than that made in the last sentence. Most certainly, its utterance by Trygve Lie in the face of the evils of twenty years ago would have changed the history of the United Nations: is there anyone who doubts that such change would have been immeasurably for the better?

Along with the self-justifying paralysis there naturally flows an ever-intensifying hostility to criticism (especially to that *not* "based on false facts"), a craving for complaisant approval, and consequently the ever-contracting insularity. It is a fact of life that institutions, like human beings, will readily admit the general likelihood of imperfections, but deeply resent having any particular fault pointed out — especially if that is done with a view to its correction. When the United Nations collectively laments its own shortcomings at the General Assembly each year, it is not intended that anyone else should join in. There is always a "good reason," or a plethora of good reasons, for any specific form of United Nations inaction, and it is never traceable, even partially, to attitudes or persons inside the Organization. The big powers scuttle it on large issues; and it does not have the authority to deal with smaller ones. One feels that Armageddon itself will (and "quite rightly"!) pass unnoticed at the United Nations because "no one put it on the agenda."

Public pronouncements, such as those made both in 1969 by U Thant and in 1970 by Lester Pearson to the effect that "the United Nations has only ten more years to live unless radically reformed" appear to be perfectly acceptable; it is the imposition of the radical reforms that will be resisted literally to the death. (It may be noted that anything approaching the frankness of the penetrating reports produced in recent years on the Organization's internal deterioration had been evaded and delayed for decades — to the point where there is real doubt as to the possibility that the situation can now be significantly redressed; and that these reports themselves repeatedly comment on the fact that adverse conditions that were manifest or foreseeable were allowed to develop undisciplined by governing bodies or by the Secretariat itself.)

"Criticism of the United Nations' weaknesses can be a useful service," remarked the President of the 1970 General Assembly; but he objected to "one-sided pessimism that leads easily to defeatism." The only true pessimism is to believe that we must accept the Organization in its present form, or that it is doing its best.

"Men are so happily absorbed in their own affairs, and indulge in such self-deception," wrote Machiavelli. The contracting island of United Nations attitudes makes cramped spiritual quarters these days, for staff and delegates alike. The outgoing President of the 1968 General Assembly stated in his concluding address: "It often happens that the major topics are not on our agenda." (He mentioned Vietnam, Czechoslovakia, the incident of the United States intelligence ship *Pueblo*, civil war and starvation in Biafra, and the Middle East problem, which in 1968 was passed over for another year.) The President of the subsequent Assembly, in her departure speech, contrasted "the parochialism and the lack of a sense of reality with which [UN] business is often conducted" with present-day life in the real world. Ralph Bunche remarked, of the massive security measures taken during the 1970 anniversary session of the General Assembly, "It is like entering the war zone or a prison." On the same theme, a Middle Eastern delegate observed, "We are in a beleaguered fortress. The world organization is cut off from the world." "They are an elite, talking to themselves," was the judgment of youthful participants in a 1970 United Nations environment symposium: "Their jargon is just evasion."

A sad little comment on the level at which the Organization has come to be regarded by heads of state nowadays was provided by the Rumanian President Ceausescu on his trip to the United States during the 1970 General Assembly: "I'm happy I was able to take advantage of my visit to the United Nations to visit Disneyland too." A year later, at the 1971 Assembly, the United Nations was designated by the Foreign Minister of Turkey as "the house of illusion": the first illusion, he said "is that anything happens here; the second, that anything could." And an article in the New York *Times* giving guidance to tourists visiting UN Headquarters innocently advises us, "Do go to some meeting even if the subject sounds dull. At least you'll be able to put on the earphones and listen to one after another of the simultaneous translations into the U.N.'s five official languages." Those for whom the linguistic novelties have palled may be less sanguine over the quality of discussion in what is fast becoming a theater of the absurd.

Nobody need be cut off from "the real world" unless he chooses to be. "We are no Vatican, we are no republic," wrote Dag Hammarskjöld*; "we are not outside the world — we are very much in the world." The impossibility, as it has come to be, of evoking a heartfelt response from United Nations officials with regard to the jeopardy in which their institution stands; the certainty, instead, that any possibility of error or improvement will be angrily or smugly rejected — and that this is in fact the single area in which the United Nations can be galvanized into instant and concerted action — what are all these but the frantic signals of culpability and distress?

"The United Nations," said Hammarskjöld, "is, and should

---

* Although W. H. Auden, in his foreword to *Markings*, reports of Hammarskjöld: "To be Secretary-General of the U.N., he once jokingly told me, is like being a secular Pope, and the Papal throne is a lonely eminence."

be, a living, evolving, experimental institution. If it should ever cease to be so it should be revolutionized or swept aside for a new approach."

There was, until recently, a worldwide view that conflicts not "sanctioned" by the big powers could quickly be brought into line — by threats of "decreased appropriations," or simply by suspension of fuel, armaments, and supplies to the transgressors from the centers of influence. (It is a measure of our current situation that such assumptions, together with the "balance of terror," have been thought to constitute our security.) Deploring the United Nations' failure to forestall an outbreak of hostilities between India and Pakistan, in 1965, James Reston, writing in the New York *Times*, gave his opinion that — because of the disputants' economic dependence on the great powers — "this kind of war cannot continue long enough to compel surrender by either side. . . . There is something infinitely sad and old-fashioned about this test of strength in India. Both sides were spoiling for a fight, like pugnacious delinquents [but] . . . Washington and Moscow alone can probably bring enough pressure to bear on them to get the dispute back to the conference table."

In the prolonged emergency of East Pakistan, in 1970–1971, there was in fact no conference table to get back to. The impotence of the international political community — starting with immobility over the military crackdown from Karachi in March 1971 and culminating in the excruciating performance of the United Nations Security Council in November and December of that year — to promote any kind of settlement of the crisis was accompanied by a self-destructive and blatant reluctance to face a situation whose outcome was increasingly apparent to the entire world.

U Thant, who in June 1971 was "confident that substantial relief would be organized in East Pakistan in a very short time," finally got a United Nations observer mission together in August, after pressure from the United States government was reinforced by a "secret" World Bank report on the emergency. Notwithstanding the fact that the World Bank report challenged the United States policy of heavily favoring the Pakistani regime, the UN mission was patently sponsored by the United States and directed towards consolidation of Karachi's military control in East Pakistan.

United Nations representation and relief undertakings were, of course, subsequently withdrawn on the outbreak of war between India and Pakistan; and reassembled towards the resettlement of the refugees in their new state of Bangladesh in 1971, without a backward glance at UN official attitudes and pronouncements. The systematic amnesia was apparently not shared by the Bangladesh authorities, and the New York *Times* reported that UNICEF officials "initially found Government representatives in Bangladesh . . . expressing lingering bitterness about the United Nations failure to come to their aid. . . . There was at first some inclination to refuse United Nations help, but their approval and cooperation were finally pledged to UNICEF."

Humanitarian assistance from the United Nations was, as a UNICEF official foresaw at the outset, "severely hampered by military and political considerations." Yet the Organization had had twenty-five years in which to equip itself towards the prompt alleviation of physical disasters in the world and to link its own efforts closely to those of other international relief bodies. An agency for this purpose was not the subject of any forceful agitation on the part of U Thant during his term of office, and was — as may be recalled — only approved in principle in 1971, largely as a result of the succession of catastrophes in Pakistan. The efforts of UNICEF — first in the cyclone emergency in East Pakistan in 1970, and subsequently on behalf of the Bengali refugees — would have profited immensely from the existence of just such a body, which might have had years of experience in overcoming bureaucratic and logistical impediments to the procurement, unloading, and distribution of relief supplies on the scale required, the forecasting of transportation problems, and the marshaling of experienced personnel; to say nothing of a crucial fund of experience in disengaging itself from the stranglehold of political fluctuation and dispelling wasteful rivalries among individual relief agencies.

No one can believe that, throughout the frantic indications of a year, no opportunity presented itself for a United Nations Secretary-General's initiatives. Typically, when the Security Council found itself unable to take up the crisis between India and Pakistan in November 1971, U Thant, according to the New York *Times*, "was said to have no intention of calling for a Council meeting, even though he had the power to do so under the Charter. Officials said that it would be the 'height of irresponsibility' for him to do so in the knowledge that the principal members were deadlocked on the subject." Again the self-righteous and belligerent tone, the eternal chip on the shoulder; and one is left to wonder whether these same officials accordingly regard Secretariat immobility on its Charter obligations, throughout a decade of world emergencies, as the height of *responsibility*. Hammarskjöld, it will be remembered, felt that, while a Secretary-General should look for guidance to the main organs of the United Nations, he "should be expected to act also without such guidance should this appear to him necessary in order to help in filling any vacuum that may appear in the systems which the Charter and traditional diplomacy provide for the safeguarding of peace and security."

Dag Hammarskjöld likened the office of United Nations Secretary-General to that of "a chief executive officer who is not simply subordinated to the legislative organs but who is constitutionally responsible alone for the execution of legislation and in some respects for carrying out the authority derived from the constitutional instrument directly." The Secretary-General, as Brian Urquhart wrote in 1964, "has unrivalled possibilities for constructive and conciliatory action." "The Secretary-General," as the New York *Times* reminded us in 1971, "has a great deal of power if he seeks it."

In 1972, following the installation of the new Secretary-

General, Ernest A. Gross, United States Assistant Secretary of State under Dean Acheson and former deputy representative to the United Nations, published an appeal in the New York *Times* for a show of independence and initiative from the United Nations Secretariat. Referring to the "large and latent assets" and "largely untapped resources" of the Secretary-General's office, Mr. Gross noted that "the secretariat's potential for peace has been neglected by the members of the United Nations generally, and by the major powers in particular." He went on to draw attention to the scrupulous independence from national pressures pledged by Secretariat officials under the United Nations Charter, and to point out:

Such a pledge can be translated into practice only with unreserved acceptance of the principle by member states.

The reluctance of members to support a vigorously functioning and independent secretariat provides the acid test of their attitude toward the United Nations as an effective instrument for a stable and just international order. As is true of most other aspects of the organization, the tools are at hand. The fault lies in failure of use.

No one with knowledge of the forging of the pattern of Secretariat subservience, and of the United States' role in that degeneration, can read such a statement without the sense of a momentous full circle, of a terrible harvest that has been reaped from what was wantonly sown more than twenty years ago. "What voice has been raised," Telford Taylor was asking in 1952, "to say that the United Nations is the creature and vehicle of all the nations . . . to point out that the notion of political conformity within this staff can, and surely will, be applied to the grave disadvantage of the democratic cause?"

Seven.

The Whole of Life

The Gust from the Sea

The economic and social programs of the United Nations, directed at the development of poor countries, are the activities to which most people, both inside and outside the Organization, now naturally turn with relief when discussing United Nations affairs: "Now there is the real work of the United Nations"; "This is what will last" — thus it goes. The United Nations itself presents these expanding operations as an imperative and productive enterprise in which the resources of the Organization and its agencies are concerted against world poverty. And that is undoubtedly the intended objective.

No one should form an opinion on the efficacy and character of United Nations assistance programs without studying the vast and remarkable report, possibly the most thoughtful document ever to come out of the United Nations, entitled *A Study of the Capacity of the United Nations Development System,** produced in 1969 as the result of an exhaustive survey by the

---

* This report, combined with the Report of the Joint Inspection Unit on Personnel Problems in the United Nations (A/8454, Parts I and II) and the FICSA statements of 1971 and 1972 (SCB/267, SCB/303 and A/AC.150/R.4), provides a definitive picture of the United Nations' internal administrative condition at the time of this writing.

217

Australian managerial expert Sir Robert Jackson. This Capacity Study, undertaken over eighteen months and at a cost of half a million dollars, is so far as I know the first attempt by a commission appointed by the United Nations to grapple with the whole great confusion of human factors which, unacknowledged and undirected, have brought the Organization to its present pass; and with the contingent, all-permeating issue of quality and its eternal shadings in the spectrum of United Nations affairs.

The Jackson Capacity Study changed the tone, not — alas — of United Nations administrative practices, but of certain crucial official reporting upon them: it is the precursor of all the more realistic reports of the 1970's that have been discussed in these pages.

The major theme of Jackson's inquiry is stated in one of the study's opening passages:

For many years, I have looked for the "brain" which guides the policies and operations of the UN development system. The search has been in vain. . . . There is no group (or "Brains Trust") which is constantly monitoring the present operation, learning from experience, grasping at all that science and technology has to offer, launching new ideas and methods, challenging established practices, and provoking thought inside and outside the system. . . . The UN development system has tried to wage a war on want for many years with very little organized "brain" to guide it. Its absence may well be the greatest constraint of all on capacity.

Here is the crux of the matter, and of all United Nations business. The Jackson Study goes, as it must, far beyond a specific consideration of economic and social activities in the United Nations, and sheds light into all the dim interior of Secretariat affairs, raking the administrative cavity in a vain search for the missing encephalon.

In a United Nations publicity brochure describing the development program, the Jackson Study's arrival on the scene is recounted as follows:

218

Sir Robert's report, commissioned as it was from within the UN family, marks a contrast, in directness of approach and in personal style, with the evasions and qualifications of much Secretariat writing. Some momentarily caught their breath, as if a sudden gust had blown in from the sea.

At last, in this study, we have a United Nations document that discusses the Organization's operations and procedures as though they stem from persons, rather than from bureaucratic and theoretical abstractions, and assumes that the forms and level of performance are not only related to but indistinguishable from the human quality, individual and collective, in which they originate. The paramount issue of *discrepancy* in United Nations matters is tackled head-on: discrepancy between professed goals and standards and the measures taken towards their attainment (and it may be said that, in the case of the UN development programs, the confusion in the public mind — and to a formidable extent in the official one — in this respect appears to be total); discrepancy between theory and practice, between principle and conduct; and, above all, between potential and delivery. One of the features that most distinguishes — in every sense of the word — the Jackson report from other official surveys of United Nations performance is that *it describes conditions and operations recognizable at every level to the entire staff engaged in them,* rather than transmuting these into fictions or abstractions comforting, or at least tolerable, to a small minority of leaders.

A measure of the humane and imaginative approach of the Jackson Study — and of its reverse complement, the situation with which it is concerned — may be given by citing another introductory remark: "In its efforts to look towards the end of this century, the Study asked everyone, both inside and outside the system, to advance unorthodox and heretical proposals for new actions. The response was disappointing. . . . It is difficult to escape the conclusion that those who command this kind of knowledge are unaware of the need, while those who stand in need have no access to the knowledge." One is tempted to quote repeatedly from the Jackson report, whose large object is never for a moment forgotten by its author — to bring productive order out of wasteful chaos. It is in this document that the results of negligent, top-heavy, and misdirected administration of major United Nations operations come implacably forward. "Objectively regarded," says Jackson, "the United Nations development 'system' exists only in name."*

If the reader cannot summon up for himself a mental picture of the "administrative jungle," as Jackson calls it, that governs United Nations economic and social assistance, then the foregoing pages have been to little purpose. Deploring "the great inertia of this elaborate administrative structure which no one, it seems, can change," Jackson finds:

At the headquarters level, there is no real "Headpiece" — no central co-ordinating organization — which could exercise effective control. Below headquarters, the administrative tentacles thrust downwards into an extraordinary complex of regional and sub-regional offices, and finally extend into field offices in over ninety developing countries. This "Machine" now has a marked identity of its own and its power is so great that the question must be asked "Who controls this Machine?" So far, the evidence suggests that governments do not, and also that the machine is incapable of intelligently controlling itself. . . . As a result, it is becoming slower and more unwieldy, like some prehistoric monster.

The United Nations' administrative nightmare, in all its guilty past and disordered present, is here unbridled — with

* It should be said here that, while the development programs of the United Nations specialized agencies, as well as those of Headquarters, are a direct concern of the Jackson Study, the activities of UNICEF are outside its scope and that these have always been distinct from other UN assistance programs. However, it may be added that every department and agency of the United Nations may consider itself surveyed in the Jackson report in so far as its administrative pattern derives from the UN system.

the good cause obscuring, and being used to obscure, fundamental disabilities: put up as a shield to deflect self-knowledge, and, in some cases, as a bludgeon against inquiry. Inescapably, it returns to human potential — to the refusal of some, from limitation, inflexibility, or *amour propre*, to question deeply what they see, and of others to speak their inward question; to pettiness disguised as method, and assertiveness dignified as stature; unwillingness at the top to entertain painful possibilities or lessons of experience, and reluctance in the ranks to press for realization. Much of what is truly achieved in the underdeveloped countries similarly rests with the individual caliber of the expert or representative who can *outwit the system* and make himself useful in spite of it. At Headquarters, the system's omnipresence, and its toll of human energy and talent, makes its outwittal virtually impossible among subordinates, while leaders naïvely imagine themselves above it. At no point in United Nations operations is the nullifying effect of ingrown, self-propagating bureaucracy more devastatingly apparent.

As with other organizations and professions of benevolent intention, a system of what might be called moral class consciousness, a certainty of good intentions, tends to insulate the very persons who should be most open to contrasting and dissident views on performance. Here again — and more than ever — criticism will be abused as "damaging" or "distorted" even when it is known to be aimed at a higher level of performance. Gunnar Myrdal, a veteran of United Nations programs, observes that *"there is a tendency for all knowledge, like all ignorance, to deviate from truth in an opportunistic direction,"* and goes on to point out:

From the point of view of the student, *optimism, like pessimism, means nothing but a biased view.* What he should seek is realism, even if he then conflicts with prevailing ideas within his own profession. And if he has carried out his work sincerely and effectively, he has the right to protest if his more realistic views are simply labeled pessimistic.

It may be added that any authentic form of optimism will be based on the closest possible scrutiny of truth; and that a show of knowledge, judgment and inquiry in itself gives rise to optimism, especially when directed at the elimination of concealed defects. This is the great strength of Sir Robert Jackson's Capacity Study.

Another, related weapon employed to silence critics of multilateral aid programs is the claim that adverse comment may result in diminished allocation of funds and their diversion, instead, to self-serving bilateral operations. These charges were of course leveled against the Jackson Study at the time of its publication, when its findings attracted certain (though, considering their importance, minimal) attention in the press — as illustrated in the following passage from an editorial in *Life* magazine:

The UN development system, through rapid growth and administrative neglect, has become a tangled, monstrous nonsystem. It groups 30 politically competitive governing boards which lack any effective coordination, agreed priorities or sound evaluation procedures, and 90 client states scrambling to commandeer easy credit for often imprudent prestige projects. The US and other donor nations simply will not be willing to channel more funds through the UN until this snakepit of a development system is cleaned out.

In point of fact, the vicissitudes encountered by the United Nations budget in recent years have been related to extraneous and mainly political events, and seem to have had little reference to the fundamental questions of competence raised in the Jackson report. The press, after its brief show of concern over the interior condition of the aid operations, soon reverted to its former practice of administering occasional absentminded pats on the back. However — as in so many fields of social endeavor today — the sanctity of fund-raising and expansion, and the obligation at all costs not to rock the financial boat, have been given precedence over other objectives and standards and the means of attaining these.

Summarizing his impressions upon completing his study, Sir Robert Jackson tells us: "The first one is positive. I am convinced that technical co-operation and pre-investment are one of the most effective ways of assisting the developing countries in achieving economic and social progress. I believe the United Nations, despite its present limitations, has demonstrated conclusively that it is the ideal instrument for the job." The present author has no competence whatever to discuss the merits of technical cooperation in such terms; nor to reiterate and try to assess the enormous array of past and present United Nations undertakings of the kind, regarding which a large variety of reports, publicity releases, articles and books has, over years, reached an audience of millions. The object, in touching on the complex issue of development here, is to relate this activity — which is now, in expenditures and volume, the largest of all United Nations regular operations — to the administrative policies discussed, to direct attention to the basis from which it emanates, and to suggest that the value and potential of what is produced must necessarily be — as Sir Robert Jackson illustrates in detail and at length — a direct reflection of the condition of the machine.

The great difficulty in making any such attempt is to focus full attention, even briefly, on the underlying administrative condition of the operations. I myself long ago gave up any such attempt in conversation with United Nations officials, finding that the unwelcome administrative shortcomings of the machine were invariably submerged in "retaliatory" and often hostile recitations of praiseworthy operational enterprises. (When I recently addressed a university seminar on this basic theme, for example, I was immediately challenged by a United Nations official present as to why I had not mentioned commendable UN projects such as those in water resources development, and attention was consequently diverted from the unflattering but all-affecting essentials of Headquarters quality.) Unconscious diversionary action of this kind is often, in my experience, *the sole response* when these administrative questions are raised in connection with development operations.

The term "constructive criticism" is another serious menace of the bureaucratic lexicon, frequently being employed as a demand that criticism be interlarded with sufficient compliments to dispel meaning and facilitate oblivion. This process is also known as "giving a balanced picture." It is, however, hard to believe in a plea for "a balanced picture" in which background is obliterated, perspective distorted, and execution disregarded.

Although few would deny that even the most demonstrable achievements of United Nations development operations might be more imaginatively conceived and effectively carried out, the question is not simply whether these things might have been better done; but, beyond that consideration, whether other, farsighted goals might have been set and different courses followed.

"The maximum interchange of knowledge"

In his book *The American University*, Jacques Barzun cautions against promiscuous and platitudinous calls for "leadership," "innovation," and such perennials as "bold answers to the challenge of our times" — phrases which not only lead nowhere in themselves but give the utterer the illusion that he at least has done his bit in facing up to the situation. Nevertheless, the United Nations idea has in the past, as we have seen, responded to leadership (in part because the Organization is *not*, as claimed by Barzun in the case of the universities he discusses, "staffed by highly independent individuals"); and there was never, ideally, a more fertile ground for the exploration of innovatory ideas and techniques, *particularly if innovation is regarded as being, in an ultimate sense, the ability to learn from experience.*

Lewis Mumford has written of "a still unborn United Nations organization that could be assembled to provide the maximum interchange of knowledge or of energy, and, eventually, to exercise moralized control over the de-moralized, premature applications of scientific knowledge." Such a service, which would be one of professional and intellectual excellence, would lead away from the dominance of financial considerations and the quantitative show of activity, into the realm of quality.

Administrators of the present United Nations might well, from their advantageous multilateral position, have been originators of fresh thinking and enlightened action in the development field: the network of United Nations agencies in multiple fields, cultural and agricultural, social as well as technical, would appear to provide an ideal basis for the consideration and practice of "development" in all its interrelated complexities and potentialities. The United Nations aid agencies, as Sir Robert Jackson says, "are, or should be, world authorities in their respective spheres." A supreme opportunity, in which the United Nations might have led the world, to study and — in the most profound sense — profit from past mistakes and new discoveries has been cast away in favor of savage parochial rivalry, dated thought, and a well-meant but often superficial and self-gratifying concept of doing good.

Thinking, especially fresh thinking, can only be done by thinkers. And it must be remembered that the United Nations, reinforced by security clearances and geographical distribution, has resolutely set its face against the exceptional and cerebral, and has itself decreed that those who find its established attitudes unacceptable "must leave the service." So much for ideas, particularly new ideas: short of actual oppression, there can be few climates as little likely to nurture productive trains of individual thought as that prevailing within the present United Nations Organization.

Jurisdictional jealousy among the many United Nations agencies engaged in economic and social development, and even among departments in the secretariats of those agencies, is and has always been one of the strongest single influences brought to bear on the initiation and allocation of UN aid projects. Untold energies of senior officials are expended in wresting projects from FAO or WHO or UNESCO on behalf of United Nations Headquarters; while FAO, WHO, UNESCO, and all their brethren are equally assiduous on their own behalf. The self-defeating lengths to which this infantile rivalry can go may be illustrated by the fact that, in the years during which this author worked in the United Nations development program, numbers of proposals known to be worthless were set aside by the United Nations and other agencies for possible approval at the end of the fiscal period, rather than turn any unspent funds back to the common pool as was the regulation. The Jackson Study shows that such practices have intensified, as has the acrimony that accompanies them.

Jackson estimates that projects of no value — "deadwood" — account for approximately twenty per cent of current UN aid operations, representing, in 1969, "an expenditure of roughly US$36 million per annum." Jackson also points out that "in the category of non-worthwhile projects . . . 75 per cent of the causes lay in the origins of the project and should have been foreseeable at the time."

In an endless attempt to cut the developmental ground from under one another, spokesmen for the agencies constantly tour the underdeveloped lands, like so many brush salesmen, urging their particular line of "progress" over their UN rival's. Jackson, condemning "the element of salesmanship, particularly at programming time, which local officials find confusing and Resident Representatives embarrassing," reports that the number of officials visiting underdeveloped countries often "exceeded — sometimes by a considerable margin — the total number of UN experts already serving in the country. In absolute terms, the figures often signified two or three visitors per working day."

The possibilities for useful cooperation among a set of budgetarily antagonistic organizations, some of them having headquarters on different continents and all of them operating on the United Nations administrative pattern, have therefore been drastically and quite unnecessarily limited throughout a period when the world itself grew increasingly aware of the interaction of all aspects of "development" and of the need to relate them to one another.

That this jurisdictional malady, along with other infirmities diagnosed by Jackson, is far from being remedied is confirmed in a recent Report of the Secretary-General on Restructuring the Department of Economic and Social Affairs (where we are told, in a splurge of lingo, "A questionable amount of competitive promotional work exists among elements of the Secretariat and with some other United Nations organizations and agencies, often resulting in suboptimal allocation of resources"). Lack of courage and willpower to redress the grotesque situation, and to stem the complementary tide in the recipient governments that are accessories to it, is reinforced by what can only be called a competitive reveling in it. Reading and listening to the sober reflections of United Nations administrators on this problem, who would imagine that these very personages have played a leading role in its creation?

That governments themselves indulge in and encourage these practices in no way detracts from Secretariat responsibility, but further distorts the complex question of multilateral development aid. If official postmortems on the periodic sessions of the United Nations Conference on Trade and Development are an indication, these huge and costly assemblies, held at intervals around the globe, center in large part upon disputes between "wealthy" and "poor" governments over expenditures on — rather than quality of — development;* feuds between Third World denizens over institutional forms and prerogatives; and

* The mammoth 1968 UN Conference on Trade and Development held at New Delhi was directed at securing from "wealthy" nations the pledge of providing aid equivalent to one per cent of their gross national income to the poorer countries. Of this arbitrary objective, Samuel P. Huntington, Professor of Government at Harvard, has written: "There is something clearly wrong with a program when its goal has to be expressed in terms of how much should be spent on it rather than what should be achieved by it. . . . It is . . . a simplistic slogan symbolizing a backward-looking approach to the critical demands of development."

power squabbles among United Nations governing bodies and Secretariat departments over their respective exercise of authority.

Conscious, self-justifying waste of this kind is of course a factor in all corporate and bureaucratic appetites for power. As ever, what makes the example more poignant here is that it is occurring within the organs of the United Nations, and at the expense of what might have been a unique collaboration for the benefit not only of the underdeveloped lands but of the world community.

Not only is every modern experience of bilateral or multilateral development necessarily a recent and incomplete one, but the conditions to which development is being applied are in a continual and complex state of change. Any such process, if applied at all (and there are many shades of opinion on that fundamental question), must constantly adapt and even reverse itself in the light of its own discoveries. It must also be highly accessible to the promptings not only of its own experience but that of others, and ambitious to maintain, as it were, an intelligence service among all thinking that bears on its operations. The United Nations cannot operate on these terms until such time as its present administrative pattern is overthrown.

As the world has drawn involuntary as well as informed lessons from the accelerating technological chaos of the postwar decades, the United Nations, on the contrary, turned inwards and, as Sir Robert Jackson puts it, "learnt to resist change." That inversion was an integral part of all other United Nations withdrawal from the scenes of innovation, accessibility, and imagination. "Twenty years on," says Jackson, "we are still trying to bake the cake in basically the same way as we did in the 1940's." Radical new concepts would have meant not only temporary loss of face, both institutional and individual, but an agonizing reappraisal of, and departure from, the entire basis of the Organization's operations.

I do not mean that this rejection was a reasoned process (by definition, it could hardly be that), or even a fully conscious one — though there have been many conscious and truculent refusals to entertain contrasting ideas, the execrable "procedures" being allowed full rein in UN aid operations with new approaches consequently mummified in windings of red tape that would doubtless "stretch four times around the Earth at the Equator." It has been, rather, a gradual freezing, through professional and personal commitment to past practices that were still, through United Nations insularity, imagined to be current and forceful.

Referring to the resistance that his proposals for reform will encounter, Jackson observes: "I do not imply any deliberate obstruction but rather refer to those whose official positions require them to sustain the *status quo*. . . . Many senior officials, whilst readily acknowledging that change is essential, would be impelled to resist it. They would do this on the understandable grounds that they are so heavily committed to the present operation that they could not physically find time to introduce a major reorganization. I sympathize, but it is a situation which cannot be accepted for progress would on these terms be impossible."

While wishing at all costs to dissociate oneself from the semanticists who pass their days defining "aggression" while slaughters multiply, even one unblessed with expert qualifications may still raise the eternal question: *What is development?* Not only are the definition, application and prospects of development not agreed among developers themselves, but impediments and fallacies in past theories are being daily and almost hourly exposed; and the interdependence, previously discounted, of its multiple factors is increasingly recognized.

"In reality," says Gunnar Myrdal, "there are no 'economic' problems; there are simply problems, and they are complex."

Mr. Denis Goulet, in his book on development, *The Cruel Choice*, observes that "many experts continue to speak of development as if it occurred independently of the larger processes which constitute its very matrix. The truth is, however, that development has no meaning apart from the ecological and symbolic transformations which envelop it." The terms "development" and "underdevelopment" have come, in fact, to encompass the whole of life: those who comprehend development — and, as Jackson says, "there are very few of them either within the system or outside" — are necessarily those with a large, profound, and intuitive view of life itself.

Development, as it has been practiced by such programs as those of the United Nations, is not a series of individual humanitarian alleviations over which a country may retain the sovereignty of its identity, nor is it even limited to an exchange of useful skills, or to the increase of crops or the introduction of electrification. Cumulatively, it represents the imposition of transfiguring and often alien new concepts that may well exterminate national and regional character within a generation. The responsibility of even a minor developer, in such a situation, is an enormous one. "Superstition or poor hygiene must not be preserved," says Denis Goulet, "simply because they are picturesque. . . . On the other hand, Third World societies are now being subjected to the attacks of a technoculture which disdains their most cherished self-images as puerile and obsolete. . . . It is because some of the fruits of progress — lower death rates, better food and housing — are genuine benefits that the problem exists. The solution therefore is not to reject modernization, but to introduce discernment and creativity in impact strategies used to induce change."

As thought can only come from thinkers, so must discernment and creativity come from the perceptive and creative. A United Nations development expert has pointed out that "one basic reason for shortcomings in achievement has been the inevitable [sic] tendency of experts simply to transplant to developing countries techniques and procedures used in developed countries." Why should this, of all processes, have been regarded as inevitable? The United Nations and its agencies might, *from the beginning*, have sought wisdom in the lessons before their very eyes, and drawn on a fund of outside knowledge of this complicated issue in order to educate their experts and enrich their programs.

Here again there seems to be outright conflict between economic developers and those engaged in projects of social assistance, and one United Nations aid authority writes: "From the standpoint of economic development, the problem is that social programmes . . . are not always properly adjusted to the economic realities of the countries. . . . Ideal goals of great social value are established, but they may contribute very little to the economic development without which they cannot be financed, and they may actually hamper growth."

The same official continues: "The economist foresees that a social obstacle to industrialization will be the excessive individualism characteristic of both labourer and entrepreneur [in the underdeveloped lands being discussed]. Although collective discipline may seem neither desirable nor pleasant from other points of view, industrialization requires large groupings of workers willing to accept it."

"Developing" populations may well echo the question once posed by Vice Admiral Hyman Rickover: "Does the economy exist for us, or we for the economy?"

Development, in such terms, would appear to be more or less frankly directed at little more than survival. Yet — although all authorities emphasize the near-exhaustion of the natural and food resources of the world — few developers have been inhibited by comparative demographic statistics in which an immediate, and counteracting, consequence of development is shown to be population increase; or have felt, until recently, the imperative need for programs of population control to be encouraged and built in, wherever possible, to the development process. Fewer still have distressed themselves over the wanton introduction of lethal or disabling industrial and nervous diseases. Development has in general been regarded as some form of package deal, in which countries are condemned by their reduced and supplicant condition to take what we know to be the bad along with what we hope may be the good.

No rational being will withhold from his fellows the modern

means of saving and preserving life. If, on the other hand, the true object of development is not mere survival but is — as it is declared and ought to be — the increased opportunity for a full life, it is hard to see how this can be conveyed from an industrialized source in a crisis of personal and collective unfulfillment. "Notwithstanding impressive mastery over nature and inanimate objects," says Denis Goulet, the developed societies "have in the main failed to bring wisdom to their social structures and human relationships." And an American philosopher, Sebastian de Grazia, reminds us that "the wisdom of the world was madness if, in teaching men how to subdue nature and transform the earth, it made them turn their back on life." Even a poor country — and even a developed country — has a spiritual capital as well as a gross national product.

Taking issue with the view that development is a progression starting from bodily satisfaction and leading through productivity to "higher purposes," and that civilizing attributes can be expressed or attended to only after animal requirements are met, Goulet observes: "Every human society, no matter how poor, ill-fed, badly clad, devotes a portion of its meager resources to the satisfaction of non-utilitarian needs: celebration, ritual, artistic expression, and playful activities. On grounds of common human experience, if no other, we must surely conclude that men's primary needs extend far beyond mere life-sustenance." One may go further, and point out that many in the materially productive, developed lands never attain to celebration and the higher uses of leisure, and that a turning away from continuity and contemplation is *characteristic* of the technological society. Incomprehension of and incapacity for leisure in an industrialized society is the theme of Mr. de Grazia's admirable book.

Of attitudes on the part of the "developed" state in such matters, we need but consider the disproportion of government spending towards such ends — the lack of beauty and amenity in modern cities, the salaries of teachers and the situation of schools, the destitution and enforced closing of public libraries, the surrender of a tradition (which in England dated back to the eighteenth century) of free entry to public museums; and the adoption, in times of peak economic production and developmental prosperity, of a depression-minded dole system whereby "relief" is paid to unemployed and unemployable millions and the very word "welfare" has come to be synonymous with hopelessness.

The United Nations programs of technical aid were initiated, though not of course in their present volume, in 1950, on the basis of a principle embodied in the UN Charter and implemented by the Organization, from 1946 onwards, in more specific and limited ventures. *The first full-scale United Nations conference concerned with world environmental problems convened at Stockholm in June 1972*, a generation later; and it should be noted that this conference was called "to prevent universal destruction of man's environment through technological progress." (Several "poor" governments expressed suspicion of the conference as "an attempt to impose pollution controls that will stifle our development" — indicating that developers have made fanatical converts. The head of the Swedish delegation to the United Nations has observed that the attitude of the developing governments in these questions is: "We've got lots of clean air; what we want is more smokestacks.")

Pollution is not a new problem. ("The fish," wrote Horace, "feel the ocean diminish from the rubble flung in its depths.") What is new is the shortage of places left to pollute, and the "development" of more virulent forms of waste. If the United Nations structure was ideally adapted to anything, it was to the early pursuit and use of knowledge in such a vital matter for the guidance of its members: to constitute, in fact, just such an agency as that envisaged by Mr. Mumford in his "still unborn United Nations"; or proposed by Mr. George F. Kennan ("an International Environmental Agency staffed primarily by scientists and engineers who would be true international civil servants . . . an entity which has at heart the interest of no nation . . . but simply of mankind generally, together — and this is important — with man's animal and vegetable companions, who have no other advocate"); or the "Environmental Monitoring System," now spoken of at last at the Organization itself, which might have been launched twenty years ago by a different and farsighted United Nations.

The United Nations Conference on the Human Environment, held at Stockholm in 1972, recommended the establishment of a United Nations agency to study environmental problems and coordinate measures for their alleviation and solution. If this new arm of the United Nations octopus is to produce positive, universal results, rather than verbal sedatives, it will have to confront great social, economic, and industrial forces on a scale and in a manner totally at variance with present and ordained United Nations practices. It will also find itself in conflict at many points with the United Nations' own development programs and with the agencies administering these. Its chance for active intervention in the world's ecological crisis lies in its own composition — that is, in repudiation of the classic pattern of United Nations bureaucratization, and in limitation of its appointments to persons of "integrity, conviction, courage, imagination, drive, and technical grasp."

These — and other brains trust functions now belatedly urged at the United Nations — could only have originated in, and could only be exercised by, a high-caliber Secretariat enjoying a good measure of public confidence. For the creation of a brains trust one must first have brains and trust. Before the United Nations Organization can usefully extend into new activities of this kind, it must retrench into quality.

The invasion of technological theory and practice by environmental events in recent years, and the burgeoning public awareness and influence in that crisis, need no additional comment here. The prescient warnings of independent thinkers on these matters, and their early advocacy of industrial constraints and conservation policies, antedate the present emergency by decades. The question as to why United Nations officials should have been among the last, instead of the first, to call emphatically for ecologically minded restraints and innovations — which they, from their international advantage, were in a particularly favorable position to propose — is yet again related to stature and initiative, and accessibility to "the real world." Many of the world's present environmental problems were in fact predicted and predictable, and might have been alleviated not only by preventive scientific techniques but by a wider invocation of imagination, knowledge, and common sense.

In his opening address, the President of the 1971 United Nations General Assembly warned the members of the United Nations: "Now a stage is being reached where a runaway technology threatens to degrade the very quality of human life and even to alter the biological nature of man himself." Pointing out that world population may have doubled in the next thirty years, he went on: "There can be no workable international order unless a sensible balance is struck between world population and world resources, and unless developmental goals are linked with environmental objectives."

Yet, despite increasing lip service to the global emergency, much development, whether bilateral or multilateral, continues to be presented, and accepted, in statistics of productivity and per capita income — of "output" and "growth" — with its ultimate human and ecological consequences being pondered and ministered to only within the confines leading to those goals. An interview published in 1972 in *Time* magazine, on the occasion of Mr. Paul Hoffman's retirement from a thirteen-year chieftainship of United Nations development programs, contained the following passage:

At the age of 80, Paul Gray Hoffman still radiates the optimism of the '50s, when many Americans believed that all it took to make a better world was a little more generosity. "All you have to do is focus on improving people's personal incomes," he says, "and you can't go wrong."

Some readers may feel, with this author, that such a view takes little account of the accelerating crises of overpopulation, environmental disturbance, and depletion of world resources. One of the purposes of the UN-sponsored Stockholm Conference was to link United Nations development programs to an active consciousness of environmental problems: again, this objective can only be achieved if fundamental administrative and jurisdictional handicaps to the cooperative potential of United Nations operations are eradicated.

With regard to the absence of a forceful United Nations program in population control, awareness of the deficiency has been uneasily present in UN administrators from the first. Government pressures again dominated: this time largely by creating Secretariat misgivings towards the political and material repercussions, among Roman Catholic countries in particular, likely to result from United Nations assistance funds being used to supply birth control advice — to a country such as India, for example — except in the ineffectual forms acceptable to the Vatican. (The Roman Catholic Church did not of course have any jurisdiction over the assistance India might request from the United Nations, but political objections were foreseen from other participants and donors in the program — the Latin American countries, for example; and during the first decade at least, Russia and the United States — to the channeling of international funds in this direction, and the United Nations let it be known that applications for such assistance could not be considered.)

The first full-scale United Nations conference on the population problem will be held in 1974.

As it was, the General Assembly signified consent by calling for United Nations "research" into population problems only in 1966, and the United Nations had no coherent program in birth control until 1970, when $15 million was requested for the purpose — a tiny fraction of what is contributed by governments annually for UN technical aid. Half of this sum was provided by the United States, following the recommendation of a panel of population specialists, headed by John D. Rockefeller III. The report of this expert group makes clear, once again, that responsibility for United Nations initiatives and operations does not rest exclusively with member states; and that the present United Nations system, while theoretically providing an excellent instrument for beneficial multilateral action, functions in an unsound context to which governments are less and less likely to turn. A portion of the panel's findings may be quoted, as follows:

The question of mandates, of which agency should undertake what activity, has been used as a classic delaying tactic by a United Nations system which, taken as a whole, is reluctant to make a more impressive commitment. . . . Despite all the words . . . the amount of United Nations assistance . . . is still inadequate in terms of its potential. Even those operations which have been undertaken have not escaped the procedural hazards which, more generally, affect most multilateral activity. The principle of geographical selection and distribution of staff, for example, however desirable in itself, can lead to incompetence and inefficiency if it is applied uncritically at each level of command right down to the individual mission. Administrative bottlenecks and complex financing formulae can delay a project for months and even years. Quite apart from the question of mandates, internecine rivalries between the agencies may call for protracted clearance and consultation procedures.

This, then, is the historical record of United Nations involvement with population; these are some of the difficulties which the UN system faces. They cannot, and should not, be ignored. . . .

This new field of operational assistance requires an unprecedented scale of commitment by the United Nations system and a radical revision of priorities. A spirit of cautious experimentation and bureaucratic compromise, however appropriate in other spheres, is not appropriate here. There is not enough time.

As the UN population venture went into operation, the New York *Times* commented: "Unless the United Nations conquers its internal weaknesses and takes some action soon, its most strenuous efforts in economic development and in peace-keeping are likely to be of little avail." If the program prospers, it could become the most significant of all United Nations aids to "development."

H. L. Keenleyside, one of the first administrators of United Nations technical assistance, wrote in 1966:

With the exception of work for the maintenance of peace — with which it is closely associated — it is clear that in the world today the most important contribution that can be made by governments, by public or private agencies, and by individuals, to the general welfare of the human race is to be found in working towards a solution — through scientific research, education, propaganda, and through raising living standards where that is possible — of the population problem.

But Mr. Keenleyside passes over two decades of United Nations absence from this vital field with the single comment that UN action "is, for the present at least, politically impracticable." The fact that United Nations entry into the field of population control was authorized by the General Assembly in the very year that Mr. Keenleyside's statement was published demonstrates how accessible governments already were to some concerted show of Secretariat urgency over the problem.

"There is widespread criticism," says the Jackson Study, "that those concerned with the operation are all too often ignorant of the subtleties of the development process, and insensitive to the needs of the developing countries." The capacity to govern such a program as that of United Nations development, in which selection and management of projects and of the thousands of "outside" experts dispatched to needy countries devolves on the headquarters establishments, is of course a direct projection of the conditions and policies prevailing in those sites of authority. The personnel of the United Nations aid departments is not only in no way distinct from any other segment of the Secretariat, *it comprises the majority* of the staff whose vicissitudes have been discussed in this work, and labors under the debilitating procedures and systems here described.

It will be recalled that, although Mr. C. W. Jenks placed "technical grasp" after "integrity, conviction, courage, imagination, drive" and at the end of his list of requirements for an effective international civil servant, this attribute was nevertheless among the essentials. Leaders of the United Nations development program have not in general been chosen for specific technical competence; and, although economists and sociologists are involved in the operations, there is no suggestion that they govern the machine.

In the Report of the Joint Inspection Unit on Personnel Problems in the United Nations, we discover that "a Professional staff member may move from Political Affairs to the Office of the Controller or vice versa, from Human Rights to Personnel, or even from the secretariat of a political committee to the study of economic or social problems," and that a huge, top-heavy staff of "administrative generalists" supervises projects in hundreds of economic, industrial, and social fields, with specific technical competence required in rare instances only.* At the same time, the Joint Inspection Unit makes a plea for standards of overall culture, general information, and abilities of self-expression at present lacking in the Secretariat. While being denied, therefore, the use of those qualities given first priority by Mr. Jenks, and not necessarily required to fill the favorable definition of the term "generalist," United Nations staff does not function under any compensating prerequisite of technical qualification.

With respect to the work being done in the underdeveloped countries themselves, the Jackson Study tells us:

---

* It may be recalled here that the United Nations, one of the world's worst-administered institutions, gives worldwide counsel in administration: an eloquent expression, surely, of the Taoist axiom "All strive to comprehend what they do not yet know, none strives to comprehend what he knows." A recent UN survey describes "rusty headquarters officials" delivering field advice in "developing" countries to national administrators more advanced than themselves.

As far as the *quality* of the services being delivered by the UN system are concerned, the main criticism appears to bear on experts. . . . There was agreement that the selection of experts left a good deal to be desired, both as regards their technical qualifications and their personal aptitude for a task that required much more than technical expertise for its proper performance. . . . The real "expert" is a scarce, and an expensive, commodity. Those *rarae aves* who really deserve the term should be used sparingly and well. . . . Thus it would be foolish to claim that an Agency has met its commitments by supplying six experts needed for a project on time, if those experts were not qualified to carry out the work entrusted to them.

To announce, in fact, as the United Nations annually does, that so many thousand experts have gone to the field, that so many hundred projects have been launched or beached, is to tell us little: what is the caliber of this assistance, and what will be *all* of its apprehensible results, indirect as well as direct? A lack of Headquarters coordination with the activities of field workers is described by Jackson as a "major and increasing problem," exacerbated rather than diminished by the lightning stopovers at field offices of Headquarters officials intent on salesmanship.

It should be added that United States citizens comprise a large proportion of the tens of thousands of technicians recruited for fixed-term missions in the field by the United Nations since the inception of the development programs; and that these experts are also subject to United States security clearance before taking up their United Nations assignments.

"*The phenomenon of aging*"

It is sometimes said that the true service performed by multilateral development aid is to educate those who administer it. Accessibility to other-ness, however, is a matter of age and individual temperament, and of a long submission to other life, lore, and language, rather than simply of information and exposure.

Considerations of age — *which are of first importance in the entire United Nations administrative crisis* — and of what in some cases has been the lifelong conditioning of a national experience, have a crucial bearing on the nature of United Nations policies towards economic and social problems. In discussing what it calls "the phenomenon of aging in the Secretariat," the Joint Inspection Unit's Report on Personnel Problems has this to say:

The proportion of staff members under thirty years of age is extremely small. For the Secretariat as a whole it is only 4 per cent. . . . The proportion aged thirty to forty years is also very small . . . and negligible in the higher grades . . . 37 per cent of the staff are over fifty years old.

Correspondingly, the Federation of International Civil Servants Associations informs us that "the average age of recruitment to the Professional grades is about forty, and to the General Service grades thirty years."

On the same issue, the comments of the Jackson Study — of which some words have already been quoted — are as follows:

Today, the UN system seems to be a disproportionately old and bureaucratic organization. Many governments, steeped in much longer traditions, are far more progressive and ready to respond to modern conditions. One reason advanced for this is the lack of enlightened personnel policies; another is the uneven quality of staff management demanded by such a complex group of organizations. Whatever the reasons, a sense of urgency — which must be a vital factor in any development programme — is lacking in many parts of the system. The age of officials alone does not explain the situation. Some of the oldest are youngest in spirit; some of the youngest are most conservative and unadventurous.

The UN system has more than its fair share of "experts" in the art of describing how things cannot be done. There is some relationship between the impression of disproportionate age and this attitude of negativism. Certainly, both conditions undoubtedly exist and affect capacity adversely. They provide strong reasons for keeping a restructured United Nations Development Programme as free as possible of the bureaucratic undergrowth which now strangles action.

This intricate, incapacitating relation of age, negativism and bureaucracy may be retraced, strand by strand, to the repressive policies of the United Nations' early years, to the system of restrictive screening practices and the atmosphere they have created, to the discouragement of idealism and initiative, and to the consolidation of administrative authority in the conformist, the officious, and the geographically designated.

The upper ranks of United Nations development staff, like those of all UN departments, categorically exclude youth and contemporaneity both at Headquarters and in the field.* It need hardly be said that this is the area that would most profit from an intake of qualified younger persons; and in which youth, being most affected, has most claim to be heard. However, over the past decade, the age group of UN development leaders has climbed out of the fifties into the sixties, seventies, and even eighties.

Paul Hoffman, who retired as head of the UN development programs in 1971, at the age of eighty, was sixty-eight when he joined the United Nations, and came to the Organization from a long career in the automobile industry, the Marshall Plan, and American foundations. His successor, sixty-eight-year-old Rudolph Peterson, is a former businessman and president of the Bank of America. The appointment, to a position of high authority, of a younger person or team of younger per-

---

* The Jackson Study reports that the average age of United Nations Resident Representatives (that is, of the quasi-ambassadorial appointees heading UN aid missions in underdeveloped countries) is fifty-five; and that, of nearly one hundred such representatives, only seven are under forty-five. This average owes much to senior posts abroad having not infrequently been awarded as post-retirement favors to Headquarters personnel: the statutory UN retirement age was sixty, until this regulation was liberalized in 1971; and, although mandatory in the lower and intermediate grades, it was often deferred in the upper ones. This practice has of course greatly contributed to the exclusion of youth from all positions of authority in the Secretariat.

sons in touch with the ecological consciousness of the 1970's and less committed by experience to the economic and financial past, seems to be a virtual United Nations impossibility.

Along with the policy of confining leadership to this age group has come the hankering for a prestige that is expressed in top-heaviness — in a concentration of senior appointments, rather than in disseminated and simplified authority. (The recent United Nations proposal for "Restructuring the Department of Economic and Social Affairs" emphatically calls for the addition of a large group of new Assistant Secretaries-General and directors, but goes on to remark: "Beyond this, precise staffing requirements cannot be determined until the implementation programme is farther along." This is like putting the roof on before the walls are built.) It must be said that this tradition was established and consolidated by Hammarskjöld.

Age, as Sir Robert Jackson says, is no index of ability. Some of the wisest and most progressive thinking in this "new" field of development is being done by mature people. But there is little indication that it is being done at the United Nations, or that it could be successfully applied there to a truly cooperative venture. "The UN Development system *could* do a remarkable job in co-operating with the Third World," says Sir Robert Jackson. "But the prospects are not very promising unless the machine can be brought under control."

As a foreword to his Capacity Study, Sir Robert Jackson reproduced his own letter, written to a head of state who had asked him to comment on the experience of preparing the report. Some observations from this foreword have already been included in the preceding pages; and the present chapter may close by quoting briefly from the opening and closing remarks of the letter:

Here is the letter I promised.

We have diagnosed the patient's sickness and written a prescription. It remains to be seen whether he will take the medicine. . . . As you anticipated, by the time it was all over, I had had an extraordinary insight into the United Nations system. I wouldn't be human if I did not feel I had come full circle. I was at the centre of things at Lake Success about twenty years ago, and the roots of many of today's problems were apparent even then, but, significantly, governments were not prepared to deal with them effectively. . . .

However, the sheer force of political circumstances will compel governments to act sooner or later. The sooner they respond, the greater will be the prospects for a better world. The longer they delay, the greater will be the dangers. . . .

Never before has mankind destroyed so much of its inheritance so quickly. We still have time to do the most constructive job in the history of the world.

Eight.

"*A Body with a Different Structure*"

W̲e may believe," Dag Hammarskjöld said, "that the United Nations needs basic reforms. We may even share the view held by some that its task ultimately will have to be taken over by a body with a different structure. . . . Only those who do not want to see can deny that we are moving these days in the direction of a new community of nations. . . . Could it be otherwise, when no other road appears open out of the dangers a new era has created?"

No thinking person can doubt that the world's public would welcome any effective show of international initiatives in the alarms and uncertainties of the 1970's. The "decline of internationalism," of which much is currently heard, is in reality a failure of confidence not in internationalism itself but in its present impotent forms. That the first, and ultimate, responsibility for this failure rests with delinquent national governments is obvious to all. Yet the self-exonerating abuse heaped on the United Nations member states as sole culprits — in the post-retirement writings of U Thant, for example, or by other Secretariat leaders — does nothing to advance the Organization's prospects. An enterprising, active, and courageous Secretariat has a crucial role to play in any realization of internationalist aims: that obligation is embodied in the United Nations Charter, and it was recognized and fulfilled in the peacemaking efforts of Hammarskjöld.

In the early years of the United Nations it used to be said, by UN delegates and Secretariat officials alike, that this was "the first of many United Nations organizations." Growth and adaptation and, above all, the accumulation and use of experience were taken for granted as leading to a series of United Nations incarnations, each profiting from knowledge of the past. This process was no doubt benignly envisaged as

> slowly broadening down
> From precedent to precedent

— such suffering as was implied being absorbed in an amorphous, historic sense of proportion. What was not foreseen was that the original United Nations Organization would become so stultified in its early years, so antagonistic to self-knowledge, and so subservient to transient national demands, with expansion preeminently in volume over quality, and initiative turned inwards to officialism, that it could be propelled into its next, more fruitful phase only by an agonizing convulsion requiring the complete dismantling of the present body.

The current United Nations Organization is, for the present, in a more fortunate position than was the League of Nations in its last months and years: its dissolution in favor of an effective successor need not — and cannot possibly — await the outcome of a world war. Attribution of national and international responsibility for its failures need not be delayed for exhumation in tomes like those compiled after the League's demise — where the sequence of destruction, however obsessively refuted at the time by "those in the know," may be followed like a chart by any reader. Nor need correction be deferred awaiting evidence that is all too likely to be, in every sense, conclusive.

246

As with the catharsis of any long-festering human dilemma, there will be release and stimulation, as well as anguish, in confronting the issues at last. Nothing, moreover, of the current United Nations' experience need be wasted; or its central tragedies reenacted, as were those of the League. It serves as a highly instructive model of everything to be avoided by its successor, and its examples should be studied not in a bureaucratic sifting but with a public consciousness of their large outlines of cause and consequence. One is moved to propose that not one single person associated with the present body should be allowed near the future one — at least until some salutary period of rehabilitation has been passed in the invigorating air of reality.

Reformation — or opportunity for it — may be less remote than it appears. The Organization, both as a political forum and an administrative body, is nearing the end of its long-attenuated tether. Its leaders have themselves been declaring — for some years now — that it will be defunct in a decade if it is not radically reformed. With the admission of China, the United Nations played its last important card as a world assembly, and will now be more than ever challenged by events that it cannot evade or absorb.

Retouchings of the status quo cannot rekindle public interest. When U Thant retired it was — as was remarked of Mr. Asquith's fall from power — as if a pin had dropped. Mr. Waldheim's accession will not in all likelihood bring great change — unless he should reject the system he has been chosen to lead. Nor can any single outward event bring about a United Nations rebirth. But the present Organization is a veritable haystack of last straws, without resilience for the unexpected.

The existing United Nations has made less and less attempt to honor the confidence originally invested in it by humanity. Lacking the discipline of a continuous world attention to United Nations affairs, national leaders have ridden roughshod over the Organization's possibilities. To recall to Secretariat leaders, on the other hand, their sworn independence from national pressures has come to be like reminding heads of state: "Thou shalt not kill." The best case for a new and different United Nations is the existing one. The Organization as it now stands usurps the place of an authentic body of the kind, responsive to the terrible emergencies of the times and formidable complexities of the future, and animated by direct public involvement in its affairs. As to the present apparatus, Cromwell's words to the Long Parliament, tragically quoted to Neville Chamberlain in 1940, might be invoked to its assemblies: "You have sat too long here for any good you have been doing. In the name of God, go."

Mr. Barry Commoner has written, in his environmental study *The Closing Circle*, "In our progress-minded society, anyone who presumes to explain a serious problem is expected to offer to solve it as well." Nothing could be more indicative of our modern predicament than the simplistic call for "solutions" — a cry that derives more from advertising slogans and political campaigning than from an understanding of human affairs, and which is put forward to repel complexities, as if the contemplation of a difficulty played no part in its resolution. Grave and intricate maladies that have accreted over generations will not be disposed of in a set of glib recommendations, or in the reiteration of exhausted abstractions. It is in fact far easier to propose the eternal "concrete measures" than to reckon with the fluidity of time and events in which these must be usefully employed. All the "solutions" of standards — of quality and selection, of dimensions and emphasis, of thought, attitude, and practice, of adherence to stated principles and vigorous action in their application — put forward in this book are nothing more than a framework on which a true and eventual solution might be constructed over years in an alliance of intellect and intention with public vigilance.

Similarly, international security is not only a settling of separate conflicts, but an inexorably created context in which conflict will gradually become less likely to arise. "Peace is not an absence of war," said Spinoza, "it is a virtue, a state of mind, a disposition for benevolence, confidence, justice."

This book opened by paying tribute to the role of the public who, in requiring that the international concept be brought to life, took the world's emergency more seriously than did their leaders and expressed their faith in a human capacity for reason and goodwill. Everything now rests, as never before, with what Hammarskjöld called "the final, least tangible, but perhaps most important new factor in diplomacy: mass public opinion as a living force in international affairs"; with the public will to regard the United Nations as a world body that must be energetically and implacably held to its responsibilities and encouraged to fulfill its great promise, without mindless abuse or vitiating indulgence but with an unremitting pressure of high standards. *The United Nations is not a place of sacred worship whose rites need be comprehensible only to the initiated: it is an instrument for survival and civilization, conceived and financed by the peoples of the world, and answerable to them.*

The present United Nations example is a particularly painful one, because it is a human occasion that has not been risen to. Yet the occasion has only grown more momentous, and the need to meet it more compelling. "We do not think the United Nations is a failure," wrote Senator Fulbright in 1972; "we think it has never been tried." It is for the public, who understand the terrible stakes better than do their leaders, to press for inauguration of this trial by which humanity will be given some of its last chances.

Notes

Chapter One: The Tunnel of Love

Page

5 *Franklin Roosevelt's project*
J. William Fulbright, "In Thrall to Fear," *The New Yorker*, 8 January 1972, p. 41.

5 *I did my duty*
Dean Acheson, *Present at the Creation* (New York: Norton, 1969), p. 111.

5 *Senator Tom Connally*
Theodore J. Lowi, *The End of Liberalism* (New York: Norton, 1969), pp. 174–175; quoted from Bertram Gross, *The Legislative Struggle* (New York: McGraw-Hill, 1953), p. 368.

6 *bunk*
Quoted in obituary, New York *Times*, 13 October 1971.

6 *The report of the 1946 United Nations Headquarters Commission*
Report of the Headquarters Commission to the Second Part of the First Session of the General Assembly of the United Nations, Lake Success, N.Y., October 1946. UN document A/69.

7 *in his work Le Nouveau Cynée*
Eméric Crucé, *The New Cyneas* (Philadelphia: Allen, Lane and Scott, 1909).

7 *footnote*
John Maynard Keynes, *The Economic Consequences of the Peace* (London: Macmillan edition for the Royal Economic Society, 1971), pp. 164–165.

8 *was later to complain loudly*
Trygve Lie, *In the Cause of Peace* (New York: Macmillan, 1954), p. 387.

8 *had not entered my head*
Ibid., pp. 11, 17.

8 *footnote*
Ibid., p. 4. See also J. W. Wheeler-Bennett and A. Nicholls, *The Semblance of Peace* (London: Macmillan, 1972), pp. 528–553.

9 *I had fought the Communists*
Trygve Lie, *In the Cause of Peace*, p. 391.

12 *left a much higher salary*
Ibid., p. 51.

Chapter Two: "The Purgatory of the Investigations"

14 *it would be possible for the FBI*
Trygve Lie, *In the Cause of Peace* (New York: Macmillan, 1954), p. 389.

15 *contracted a secret agreement*
Activities of United States Citizens Employed by the United Nations: Hearings before the Subcommittee to Investigate the Administration of the Internal Security Act and Other Internal Security Laws of the Committee on the Judiciary, United States Senate, 82nd Congress, 2nd Session, October 13, 14, 15, 23, 24; November 11, 12; December 1, 2, 10, 11, 17, 1952, pp. 267–305 and 328–390; Appendices B, C, D, E, with particular reference to Appendix D, section 2 ("Arrangements with U.N. for the Provision of Information on U.S. Nationals" and "Outline of Recommended Procedure") pp. 415–416. (Hereinafter cited as McCarran Hearings.)

15 *confirmed by Hammarskjöld to the General Assembly*
Report of the Secretary-General on Personnel Policy. UN document A/2533, 2 November 1953, p. 39. See also Official Records, General Assembly, Seventh Session, 413th Meeting, 10 March 1953.

16 *I knew there was a secret arrangement*
McCarran Hearings, p. 352.

16 *cover plan*
Ibid., pp. 353–354.

16 *highly confidential*
Ibid., p. 412.

16 *orally*
Ibid., p. 338.

16 *would not be revealed*
Ibid., pp. 336–337.

16 *It was Byron Price*
Ibid., pp. 373, 417.

16 *a series of papers*
Ibid., Appendices B, C, D, E.

16 *The text of the provisions for secrecy*
"1. The full scope of the participation of the Department in arrangements with U.N. will be kept secret at all times.

"2. All contacts between the U.N. and the Department and within the Department between UNA [United Nations Affairs] and SY [Security], will be conducted by designated officers at a high executive level and will be a matter of strictest confidence.

(a) Papers pertaining to arrangements with U.N. will be classified 'secret.'

. . . . .

"4. . . . (a) All checks will be made in complete secrecy so far as the purpose of the check is concerned.

. . . . .

"7. . . . (a) Notification will be given U.N. through direct (not through the mission), informal, confidential, word-of-mouth channels."

Extract from document furnished to Senator Pat McCarran by the U.S. Department of State, 2 January 1953. (Full text in Appendix D.2 to McCarran Hearings as "Outline of Recommended Procedure — Provision of Information to the U.N. covering U.S. Citizens Employed by U.N. or considered for Employment.")

17 *On the basis of the report*
Statement by the Secretary-General, UN press release SG/43, 17 January 1950; Lie, statement to staff, UN document SCC/68, 19 January 1950.

17 *was no longer required by the Secretariat*
Frank J. Donner, Arthur Kinoy, Leonard B. Boudin, Morris J. Kaplan, In the United Nations Administrative Tribunal: Brief on Behalf of Nineteen Applicants [1953], pp. 202–203.

20 *It must therefore be stated emphatically*
Statement before the United Nations Administrative Tribunal on the Right of the Secretary-General to Terminate Temporary-Indefinite Contracts and His Right to Withhold Reasons for Such Termination, Respectfully Submitted for the Secretary-General, 9 August 1951, p. 22. See also UN press release ORG/201, 25 August 1951, p. 5.

21 *The case of the employees was upheld*
Judgement No. 4, Judgements of the United Nations Administrative Tribunal. UN document AT/DEC/1 to 70, pp. 8–23. See also UN press release SG/205, 7 September 1951.

21 *footnote*
Judgement No. 4, Judgements of the United Nations Administrative Tribunal. UN document AT/DEC/1 to 70, p. 19. See also UN press release ORG/201, 25 August 1951, pp. 12–13.

21 *the most elementary attributes*
Brief submitted in UN Joint Appeals Board by firm of Donner and Kinoy, August 1952, p. 4.

21 *The civilized legal order*
Brief on Behalf of Nineteen Applicants, p. 165.

22 *impressively documented account*
Ibid.

22 *The judgments of the Administrative Tribunal*
Lie, *In the Cause of Peace*, p. 390. See also UN press release SG/205, 7 September 1951, and UN Note to Correspondents No. 383, 7 September 1951.

22 *The reports and circulars*
UN document series SCC, 1950–1953.

23 *impairment of the international character*
UN document SCC/111, 19 March 1951, p. 2. See also SCC/152, 1 December 1952, and SCC/154, 16 February 1953.

23 *"Farewell to Lake Success"*
UN document SCC/111, 19 March 1951, p. 20.

23 *disloyalty and self-seeking*
Document, unsigned and undated (October 1950) handed to UN Staff Committee by Assistant Secretary-General for Administrative and Financial Services Byron Price. Text in UN document SCC/99, 16 November 1950.

23 *If you are really*
Written statement by the Secretary-General handed to staff representatives on 13 November 1950. Text in UN document SCC/99, 16 November 1950.

23 *footnote*
Of the seven members: Brief on Behalf of Nineteen Applicants, p. 24. *At a press conference:* Secretary-General's Press Conference No. 16 [? number unclear in original], Lake Success, New York, 16 February 1951, pp. 14–16.

24 *I would strongly advise*
Letter to Chairman of UN Staff Committee, 2 October 1950. See Brief on Behalf of Nineteen Applicants, p. 222.

24 *if any specific cases of disloyalty*
Administrative circular, 2 October 1950. See Brief on Behalf of Nineteen Applicants, pp. 222–223.

24 *footnote*
Statement unanimously adopted by UN Staff Council 14 November

1950: UN document SCC/99, 16 November 1950. See also UN document ORG/178, 16 February 1951.

24 *If the staff in New York*
Statement by the Secretary-General, 26 November 1951. See Brief on Behalf of Nineteen Applicants, p. 35; UN documents SCC/131 and 132, 3 January 1952; and SCC/152, 1 December 1952, p. 7.

24 *The question of the motive*
Judgements of the United Nations Administrative Tribunal, Numbers 1 to 70, 1950–1957. UN document AT/DEC/1 to 70, p. 48.

25 *The high qualities*
Judgements of the Administrative Tribunal, p. 53.

25 *If there was even one*
Lie, *In the Cause of Peace*, p. 388.

25 *Amendments to the Staff Regulations*
Official Records of the General Assembly, Sixth Session. Annexes, Agenda Item 45: Permanent Staff Regulations of the United Nations, with particular reference to Regulation 9.1(c). See also Secretary-General's bulletins to the staff ST/AFS/SGB/81/Rev. 6, 27 February 1952, and ST/AFS/SGB/94, 1 December 1952; and UN document SCC/147, 9 September 1952; Lie, *In the Cause of Peace*, p. 390.

25 *footnote*
Secretary-General's press conference, 6 June 1952. UN Note to Correspondents No. 464, 6 June 1952, pp. 10-c to y, 10-z.

25 *up to nine years*
UN press release ORG/201, 25 August 1951, p. 3. See also Judgements of the Administrative Tribunal, pp. 8–23.

26 *submitted no facts*
Lie, *In the Cause of Peace*, p. 394.

26 *On the one hand*
Ibid., p. 397.

26 *footnote*
Ibid., p. 400.

27 *I did not want them there*
Ibid., pp. 391, 400–401.

27 *it doesn't go quite that far*
McCarran Hearings, pp. 272–273.

27 *it must be borne in mind*
UN document A/2364, 30 January 1953, Report of the Secretary-General on Personnel Policy; Annex I, Statement by the Assistant Secretary-General for Administrative and Financial Services, 23 December 1952, p. 6.

27 *footnote*
Statement by Robert C. Alexander, assistant chief of the State Department Visa Division, testifying before Senate Judiciary Com-

mittee 20 July 1948, New York *Times*, 21 July 1948. On 21 July 1948, Secretary Marshall told a news conference that he did not know "of a single case of foreign espionage in the United Nations" (New York *Herald Tribune*, 22 July 1948). A three-man committee appointed by Marshall on 23 July 1948 to investigate the charges delivered its report on 1 September 1948, saying it was "shocked" at the "irresponsible" accusations (New York *Herald Tribune*, 2 September 1948). On 21 October 1948, Alexander was "formally reprimanded." Reporting this on 22 October 1948, the *Herald Tribune* quoted State Department spokesmen as saying that this was the mildest punishment that could have been imposed. See also Lie, *In the Cause of Peace*, pp. 394–395.

28   *A number of Western European nationals*
"U.N. Security Drive Ousts 4 Europeans," New York *Times*, 11 December 1952.

28   *redundancies*
Brief on Behalf of Nineteen Applicants, p. 35.

28   *allegation, by Whittaker Chambers*
McCarran Hearings, p. 153.

29   *go back where you came from*
Ibid., p. 219.

29   *suspicion is attached*
Ibid., p. 218.

29   *one witness is attacked*
Ibid., p. 19.

29   *footnote*
Report of the Special Committee on the Federal Loyalty-Security Program of the Association of the Bar of the City of New York (New York: Dodd, Mead, 1956).

30   *awful pressure*
Lie, *In the Cause of Peace*, p. 399.

30   *The situation lent itself*
Ibid., p. 392.

30   *an American Communist is not*
Ibid., p. 388.

30   *footnote*
Roy Cohn, *McCarthy* (New York: New American Library, 1968), pp. 8–10; *A Fool for a Client* (New York: Hawthorn Books, 1971), p. 166.

31   *forty thousand dollars*
Judgements of the Administrative Tribunal, p. 142.

31   *Mr. Feller and I*
Lie, *In the Cause of Peace*, p. 397.

31   *the unceremonious nature*
UN document SCC/152, 1 December 1952, p. 6.

32 *international committee of three jurists*
Opinion of the Commission of Jurists submitted to the United Nations Secretary-General, 29 November 1952; reproduced as UN press release ORG/231 of that date. The opinion also appears as Appendix A to the McCarran Hearings, and as Annex III to UN document A/2364, 30 January 1953. The objections of the staff are recorded in UN document SCC/172, 20 January 1954, p. 3.

32 *was conferring with Roy Cohn*
New York *Times*, 22 November 1952. The meeting took place on 21 November 1952, and included Robert Morris and senior Secretariat officials who are listed. The New York *Times*, 14 November 1952, quoted Robert Morris as having held previous conferences at United Nations Headquarters.

33 *Mr. Sourwine*
McCarran Hearings, p. 348.

33 *footnote*
Dean Acheson, *Present at the Creation* (New York: Norton, 1969), p. 698.

33 *when he objected*
Brief on Behalf of Nineteen Applicants, p. 202.

33 *about the identical political matters*
Ibid., p. 204.

34 *a minimum of 45*
New York *Times*, 23 October 1952.

34 *in exchange for their silence*
Brief on Behalf of Nineteen Applicants, p. 56. See also UN Note to Correspondents No. 464, 6 June 1952, pp. 10-c to y.

34 *economies*
Brief on Behalf of Nineteen Applicants, p. 35.

35 *In one such case*
Judgements of the Administrative Tribunal, pp. 251–259.

35 *This committee's records were immediately destroyed*
UN document A/2364, 30 January 1953, Annex II: The Work of the Selection Committee for the Review of Staff Members on Temporary Appointments, p. 5. See also Judgements of the Administrative Tribunal, pp. 220, 230, 235, and Note to Correspondents No. 464, 6 June 1952, p. 10-z.

36 *what the score sheet was*
McCarran Hearings, p. 353.

36 *I think they would go so far*
Ibid., p. 350.

37 *It was agreed*
Ibid., Appendix C, pp. 412–413.

38 *Numerous others may be examined*
Judgements of the Administrative Tribunal, pp. 74, 99, 127, 158, 167, 175, 183, 191, 201, 204, 208.

38 *The unquestioned capability*
Brief on Behalf of Nineteen Applicants, p. 107. See also UN Note to Correspondents No. 464, 6 June 1952, pp. 12–13 and 15–17.

38 *The Tribunal awards*
Judgements of the Administrative Tribunal, p. 142.

39 *does not dispose*
Dag Hammarskjöld, Introduction to the Annual Report 1959–1960, 31 August 1960. Reprinted in *Dag Hammarskjöld, Servant of Peace: A Selection of His Speeches and Statements,* edited by Wilder Foote (New York: Harper & Row, 1963), p. 300.

39 *In an election-eve appearance*
Daily Compass, 24 October 1952. See also New York *Times,* 4 January 1953.

39 *Trygve Lie, in a public statement*
New York *Times,* 7 January 1953.

39 *take real pride*
New York *Times,* 8 January 1953.

40 *arising from future publicity*
Brief on Behalf of Nineteen Applicants, pp. 7–8.

40 *negative evaluations*
Lie, *In the Cause of Peace,* p. 389.

40 *It is true*
McCarran Hearings, Appendix E, p. 417.

40 *I am proud*
New York *World-Telegram and Sun,* 12 November 1952.

41 * *footnote*
Nation, 20 September 1952, 11 October 1952, 22 November 1952, 13 December 1952, 20 December 1952, 7 February 1953; *New Republic,* 9 June 1952; *Saturday Evening Post,* 17 November 1951.

41 † *footnote*
UN transcript of international television program "United or Not," originating at the United Nations, October 1952.

41 *The UN has arrived*
Daily Compass, 1 November 1951, 22 May 1952; see also Edel in *Daily Compass,* 18 October 1951, 2 November 1951, 22 September 1952.

42 *the tool of the United States arm-twisters*
Lie, *In the Cause of Peace,* p. 384.

42 *footnote*
In the autumn of 1952: Lie, *In the Cause of Peace,* p. 398. *You longed to be able: The Memoirs of Lord Gladwyn* (London: Weidenfeld & Nicolson, 1972), p. 255.

42 NIXON BLAMES DEMOCRATS
New York *World-Telegram and Sun*, 16 October 1952.

42 *On 10 November 1952*
Lie, *In the Cause of Peace*, p. 406.

43 *The purgatory of the personnel investigations*
Ibid., p. 385.

43 *accumulated tension*
New York *Times*, 14 November 1952. See also UN press releases
SG/268, 13 November 1952, and PM/2435 and 2436, 16 November
1952.

43 *the strain of defending American employees*
New York *Times*, 14 November 1952; UN press release SG/268,
13 November 1952.

43 *Abe Feller was a victim*
Lie, *In the Cause of Peace*, p. 399.

43 *Under the impact*
New York *Times*, 19 November 1952, reported that the federal grand
jury had invited Lie by telegram to appear before it; 21 November
1952, that he had declined the request and had not intended offense
to the grand jury.

43 *the atmosphere of Greek tragedy*
Lie, *In the Cause of Peace*, p. 398.

44 *American pressures*
New York *Times*, 14 November 1952.

44 *I should like to thank*
McCarran Hearings, p. 126 (15 October 1952).

45 *members of the Secretariat*
New York *Times*, 14 November 1952.

45 *The press abroad*
E.g., *Economist*, 12 July 1952; *Gazette de Lausanne*, 13 August 1952;
Journal de Genève, 14 August 1952; *Manchester Guardian*, 3 December 1952, 1 January 1953; *Le Monde*, 22 November 1952; *New Statesman and Nation*, 30 August 1952, 18 October 1952; *L'Observateur*, 6 November 1952; *The Times*, 2 December 1952.

45 *Many Americans*
"Beaucoup d'Américains seront choqués de semblables propos: les
uns par réalisme, qui ne voudront pas voir abandonner l'immense
et dérisoire building construit à grands frais pour l'Organisation:
les autres par réaction sentimentale et méfiance. Peut-on leur demander de réfléchir posément à ceci: si l'O.N.U. siégeait à Leningrad, si l'U.R.S.S. couvrait ses frais à concurrence de 40%, si les
journalistes et les observateurs étrangers (non diplomates) éprouvaient des difficultés pour obtenir leur visa, si une 'commission
Beria' enquêtait sur les fonctionnaires internationaux accusés de
sympathie américaine, si le chef des services juridiques renouvelait

— comme Feller — le dernier geste de Jan Masaryk à Prague, quelle serait la réaction des Etats-Unis? Ne penseraient-ils pas que l'indépendance de l'Organisation exige le transfert de son siège sur un territoire moins 'engagé'? Et n'auraient-ils pas raison de le penser?" *Le Monde*, 22 November 1952.

45 *an official security review*
Executive Order of the President of the United States 10422 (18 F.R. 239), 9 January 1953 (appears as Annex V to UN document A/2364, 30 January 1953); as later amended by Executive Order 10459, 2 June 1953 (appears as the Appendix to Annex I of UN document A/2533, 2 November 1953). See also the Appendix to this book.

45 *That this review*
New York *Times*, 11 January 1953.

46 *Mr. Lodge said the investigation*
New York *Times*, 27 January 1953.

46 *reasonable ground for believing*
New York *Times*, 5 February 1953.

46 *I welcomed it*
Lie, *In the Cause of Peace*, pp. 402–403. See also SCC/154, 16 February 1953.

49 *It was Lie's belief*
Lie, *In the Cause of Peace*, p. 413.

49 *She was informed*
Judgements of the Administrative Tribunal, pp. 193–199, 205–207.

50 *Lie presented a report*
Report of the Secretary-General on Personnel Policy. UN document A/2364, 30 January 1953.

50 *A statement by Byron Price*
Ibid., Annex I, Statement by the Assistant Secretary-General for Administrative and Financial Services, 23 December 1952.

51 *No organization dedicated*
Ibid., Annex I, p. 9.

51 *The report was acrimoniously debated*
Official Records of the General Assembly, Seventh Session, 413th–422nd Meetings, March–April 1953. See also UN document A/2367, 2 March 1953, and General Assembly Resolution 708 (VII), 1 April 1953.

Chapter Three: "Subversion"

52 *If the Secretariat is regarded*
Address to the staff in the UN General Assembly Hall, 8 September 1961, in *Dag Hammarskjöld, Servant of Peace: A Selection of His*

Speeches and Statements, edited by Wilder Foote (New York: Harper & Row, 1963), p. 376.

52 *footnote*
Louis Halasz, in Rome *Daily American,* 21 September 1971.

53 *In a circular of 20 January 1954*
UN document SCC/172, 20 January 1954, p. 5. See also Conor Cruise O'Brien, *Writers and Politics* (New York: Vintage Books, 1967), pp. 210–211.

53 *A reading of the judgments*
Judgements of the United Nations Administrative Tribunal, Numbers 1 to 70, 1950–1957: UN document AT/DEC/1 to 70, pp. 193, 199, 202, 205, 208.

55 *The 1954 report*
Report on Standards of Conduct in the International Civil Service, 1954. UN document COORD/CIVIL SERVICE/5.

55 *The staff expressed*
UN document SCC/201, 31 May 1955, p. 3.

55 *a short nightmare*
Joseph P. Lash, *Dag Hammarskjold, Custodian of the Brushfire Peace* (New York: Doubleday, 1961), pp. 49–50.

55 *Once an allegation*
Statement to the General Assembly, 3 October 1960, in Foote, *Hammarskjöld,* p. 317.

56 *the Secretary-General and the Organization*
"The International Civil Servant in Law and in Fact," lecture delivered to Congregation at Oxford University, 30 May 1961, in Foote, *Hammarskjöld,* p. 340.

56 *Hammarskjöld's most detailed public statement* and subsequent discussion
Ibid., pp. 339–340. See also UN Note to Correspondents No. 657, 12 May 1953.

59 *an advisory opinion*
International Court of Justice: Reports of Judgements, Advisory Opinions and Orders, 1954, pp. 47–63. See also General Assembly Resolutions 785 (VIII), 9 December 1953 and 888 (IX), 17 December 1954; and UN document SCC/181, 19 July 1954.

59 *footnote*
International Court of Justice Advisory Opinion, 11 April 1949, I.C.J. Reports 144A, pp. 174, 179.

60 *an error which has to be corrected*
Dag Hammarskjöld, *Markings,* translated from the Swedish *Vägmärken* by Leif Sjöberg and W. H. Auden, with a Foreword by W. H. Auden (New York: Knopf, 1964), p. 114.

60   *The United Nations faces the choice*
Report of the Headquarters Commission to the Second Part of the First Session of the General Assembly of the United Nations, October 1946. UN document A/69, p. 23.

61   *footnote*
Dean Acheson, *Present at the Creation* (New York: Norton, 1969), pp. 698, 714.

61   *The reason, as I understand it*
Activities of United States Citizens Employed by the United Nations: Hearings before the Subcommittee to Investigate the Administration of the Internal Security Act and Other Internal Security Laws of the Committee on the Judiciary, United States Senate, 82nd Congress, 2nd Session, October 13, 14, 15, 23, 24; November 11, 12; December 1, 2, 10, 11, 17, 1952, pp. 348–349, 367.

63   *footnote*
United States Executive Order 10459, 2 June 1953 (appears as Appendix to Annex I, UN document A/2533, 2 November 1953).

63   *The very qualities*
Egon F. Ranshofen-Wertheimer, *The International Secretariat* (Washington: Carnegie Endowment for International Peace, 1945), p. 251.

64   *The Governments of the Member States*
F. P. Walters, *A History of the League of Nations* (New York: Oxford University Press, 1952), Vol. I, p. 419.

64   *In answer to this question*
UN document 1155, I/2/74(2), 22 June 1945, UNCIO, p. 394.

64   *Of a punitive bill*
Bill Introduced in the United States Senate, 7 January 1953. Reprinted as Annex IV to UN document A/2364, 30 January 1953.

64   *To my dismay*
Trygve Lie, *In the Cause of Peace* (New York: Macmillan, 1954), p. 401.

66   *Report on Personnel Problems*
Personnel Questions: Report of the Joint Inspection Unit on personnel problems in the United Nations. UN document A/8454 (Parts I and II), 5 October 1971, pp. 141–142. (Hereinafter cited as JIU, Personnel Problems.)

66   *The further considerations*
Ibid.

66   *The fact is*
Ibid., Part II, p. 285.

67   *the international service is only now*
Thomas M. Franck, *The Structure of Impartiality* (New York: Macmillan, 1968), p. 288.

68   *footnote*
JIU, Personnel Problems, Part I, pp. 172, 185.

Chapter Four: Effects, Ill Effects, and Aftereffects

70 *The issue in this case*
Frank J. Donner, Arthur Kinoy, Leonard B. Boudin, Morris J. Kaplan, In the United Nations Administrative Tribunal: Brief on Behalf of Nineteen Applicants [1953], p. 65.

71 *Having controlled the United Nations*
J. William Fulbright, "In Thrall to Fear," *The New Yorker*, 8 January 1972, p. 60.

72 *The United States weakened*
Le Monde, 22 November 1952.

72 *The financial contribution*
Hearings before a Subcommittee of the Committee on Foreign Relations, United States Senate, 81st Congress, 1st Session, 1950, pp. 112–113.

73 *Senator Alexander Wiley*
New York *Times*, 12 December 1952.

73 *However, any move*
New York *Post*, 12 December 1952.

72 *never know the full considerations*
New York *Times*, 30 October 1971.

76 *I find many men*
Bertrand Russell, *Portraits from Memory* (New York: Simon and Schuster, 1956), pp. 55–56.

76 *WHITE HOUSE DENIES*
New York *Times*, 10 January 1972.

77 *Thus when Mr. Kurt Waldheim*
National Broadcasting Company television program *Meet the Press*, 9 January 1972.

77 *As far as the United States is concerned*
Fulbright, "In Thrall to Fear," p. 61.

77 *more in the realm*
The United Nations: The Next Twenty-five Years. The Twentieth Report of the Commission to Study the Organization of Peace (New York: Oceana Publications, 1970), p. 41.

78 *There is, I believe*
Stuart N. Hampshire, "So Little Is Worth Trying," Op-Ed page article, New York *Times*, 8 December 1971.

79 *people caught up*
New York *Times*, 10 November 1971.

80 *When the United Nations was created*
"The Development of a Constitutional Framework for International Cooperation," address at the University of Chicago Law School, 1

May 1960, in *Dag Hammarskjöld, Servant of Peace: A Selection of His Speeches and Statements,* edited by Wilder Foote (New York: Harper & Row, 1963), p. 255.

81   *the main and probably inescapable*
The International Secretariat of the Future: Lessons from Experience by a Group of Former Officials of the League of Nations (The Royal Institute of International Affairs; Oxford University Press, 1944), p. 47. (Known as the "London Report.")

81   *the United Nations should be so situated*
UN document PC/EX/113/Rev. 1, 12 November 1945, p. 116.

81   *should not be located*
Yearbook of the United Nations, 1946–1947, p. 41. (Department of Public Information, United Nations, Lake Success, New York, 1947.)

82   *footnote*
Trygve Lie, *In the Cause of Peace* (New York: Macmillan, 1954), p. 57; Dean Acheson, *Present at the Creation* (New York: Norton, 1969), p. 698.

83   *some drastic staff reduction*
"The Crisis of Our Environment and the Quality of Life," address delivered by Maurice F. Strong, Secretary-General, United Nations Conference on the Human Environment, to the National Foreign Trade Convention, Waldorf-Astoria Hotel, New York, 17 November 1971. United Nations Centre for Economic and Social Information document CESI/NOTE 62, 17 November 1971, pp. 16–17.

84   *The United Nations is*
Lie, *In the Cause of Peace,* p. 423.

86   *The present assault*
John G. Stoessinger, "It Takes Money to Run a U.N.," Op-Ed page article, New York *Times,* 24 November 1971.

86   *Although there has been pressure*
New York *Times,* 22 November 1971.

87   *The paramount consideration*
Charter of the United Nations, Article 101.3.

88   *a subject of criticism*
Report of the Fifth Committee on Personnel Questions to the 26th Session of the General Assembly. UN document A/8604, 15 December 1971, pp. 4, 5, 10.

89   *The Secretariat*
Joseph P. Lash, *Dag Hammarskjold: Custodian of the Brushfire Peace* (New York: Doubleday, 1961), p. 286. See also Foote, *Hammarskjöld,* pp. 336–337.

89   *is now well established*
UN document ORG/696, 1 June 1971, p. 5. See also UN document A/7359, 27 November 1968, pp. 35–37.

89   *as far as is known*
New York *Times,* 31 December 1971.

89   *an official United Nations handbook*
    Everyman's United Nations (New York: United Nations, 8th edition, 1968), p. 480.

89   *The political interests*
    Brief on Behalf of Nineteen Applicants, p. 107.

90   *Increased interventions*
    Staff Committee Bulletin, United Nations Staff Union. UN document SCB/267, 22 July 1971, p. 12. (Hereinafter cited as FICSA Report.)

90   *integrity, conviction, courage*
    C. Wilfred Jenks, "Some Problems of an International Civil Service," *Public Administration Review*, vol. 93 (1943), p. 98.

90   *But, alas, it is patent*
    Andrew A. Stark, "The Secretariat — Twenty-five Years After," *UN Monthly Chronicle*, vol. VII, no. 8 (August–September 1970), p. 106.

91   *what governments will or will not*
    FICSA Report, p. 11.

92   *devastating two-volume official report*
    Personnel Questions: Report of the Joint Inspection Unit on personnel problems in the United Nations. UN document A/8454 (Parts I and II), 5 October 1971. (Hereinafter cited as JIU, Personnel Problems.)

92   *the final proof*
    Guardian, 7 November 1967.

93   *In 1970 a confidential report*
    New York *Times*, 22 March 1970, 21 June 1970.

93   *We have known*
    Bulletin of the Atomic Scientists, February 1971, p. 43.

93   *There is a sense of malaise*
    New York *Times*, 2 December 1968.

95   *the suggestion did not seriously arise*
    UN documents ST/AI/207, 23 December 1971, and ST/ADM/SER.A /1578, 20 January 1972.

95   *the General Service provides*
    FICSA Report, p. 7.

95   † *footnote*
    JIU, Personnel Problems, pp. 51–53.

97   † *footnote*
    Ibid., p. 185.

99   *footnote*
    "My Daughter Tricia," interview with Paul F. Healey, *Ladies' Home Journal*, June 1970.

100 *In this connection, the texts*
    UN document series A/AC.150/R, 1971–1972. See also UN document A/8428, 1 June–24 August 1971, and press releases SG/SM/ 1489 and ORG/696, 1 June 1971.

100 *proposal by the government of Japan*
UN document A/AC.150/R.1/Add.1, 31 January 1972.

101 *There is a keen desire*
JIU, Personnel Problems, p. 17.

102 *It is hardly necessary*
Ibid., p. 27.

102 *U Thant's last statements*
UN document A/C.5/1376, 6 October 1971, p. 1.

103 *the officials responsible*
JIU, Personnel Problems, p. 125.

103 *footnote*
When one engaged: UN document SCB/265, 14 July 1971.

103 *that the relative importance*
UN document A/8604, 15 December 1971, p. 5.

104 *Of the total*
JIU, Personnel Problems, pp. 41, 42, 43.

105 *Lack of job satisfaction*
FICSA Report, p. 6.

106 *has supposedly been modified*
Conversations with the author.

106 *We have a privileged class*
Correspondence with the author.

106 *the present serious anomalies*
UN document SCB/258, 19 May 1971.

106 *the system of two categories*
FICSA Report, p. 14.

107 *the efficiency of a modern civil service*
JIU, Personnel Problems, p. 327.

107 *the report favors discontinuance of promotion*
Ibid., pp. 286–323. See also A/7359, 27 November 1968, Report of
the Committee on Reorganization of the Secretariat, p. 47.

107 *footnote*
FICSA Report, p. 15.

107 *an artificial "solution"*
A Special Service Category: Paper submitted by Mr. Georges
Palthey. UN document A/AC.150/R.7, 14 December 1971.

108 *Whatever the structure*
FICSA Report, pp. 14–15.

109 *The dimensions of the tragic deterioration*
Hugh L. Keenleyside, "What's Wrong at the United Nations,"
Saturday Review, 19 June 1971, pp. 11–13 and 29–30.

111 *Clogging of work programme*
JIU, Personnel Problems, pp. 17–18.

112 *the outstanding problems*
UN document SCC/111, 19 March 1951, pp. 2–21.

112 *the general conception of administrative methods*
JIU, Personnel Problems, p. 20.

112 *Professional staff lacking in motivation*
UN document A/C.5/SR.1433, 9 November 1971.

112 *Yet the question remains*
"The Crisis of Our Environment and the Quality of Life," pp. 16–17.

113 *Few would dispute*
View of the Federation of International Civil Servants Associations, 21 December 1971. UN document A/AC.150/R.4, p. 23.

114 *digestion-challenging round*
New York *Times*, 8 October 1968.

115 *anyone eating in the Cafeteria*
UN document SCB/260, 11 June 1971.

115 *The irresponsibility*
Keenleyside, "What's Wrong at the United Nations," p. 12.

115 *We're in the process*
The New Yorker, 16 October 1971, p. 33.

115 *It was a rewarding experience*
Conversation with the author.

115 *Dopo le sedute*
Alberto Giovanetti, *Il Palazzo è di Vetro* (Rome: Coines Edizioni, 1971), p. 112.

115 *footnote*
Egon F. Ranshofen-Wertheimer, *Victory Is Not Enough* (New York: Norton, 1942), p. 293.

116 *three of four cocktail parties*
Giovanetti, *Il Palazzo è di Vetro*, p. 112.

116 *footnote*
New York *Times*, 21 March 1971.

117 *a spirit of luxury*
Report of the Headquarters Commission to the Second Part of the First Session of the General Assembly of the United Nations, October 1946. UN document A/69, pp. 28–29.

117 *not become 'great'*
Ibid., p. 27.

118 *In 1971 the Secretary-General secured*
UN documents SCB/261, 1 July 1971; SCB/262, 1 July 1971, pp. 3–4; SCB/265, 14 July 1971; SCB/268, 22 July 1971; Secretary-General's

letter of 26 July 1971 to Chairman of Staff Committee, reproduced as staff circular; UN documents SCB/276, 1 October 1971; ST/ADM/SER.P/27, 28 October 1971.

118 *In 1972, the Secretariat staff*
UN document SCB/303, 14 July 1972.

less than that of the Fire Department
Address by the Secretary-General of the United Nations, Mr. Kurt Waldheim, at the "American Business and Labor Visit the United Nations" dinner, Hilton Hotel, New York City, 25 May 1972. Full text reproduced in *The Delegates World Bulletin*, vol. 2, no. 13, 5 June 1972, p. 360.

118 *INITIAL BUDGET ESTIMATES*
UN press release GA/4395, 16 August 1971, pp. 1, 4.

119 *While little enough of the actual total*
Ibid., p. 6. See also UN documents A/8406 and addenda, A/8408 and corrigenda, and A/8531 and addenda (Official Records of the General Assembly, Twenty-sixth Session).

119 *will hopefully allow*
Commitment: United Nations Development Programme Service Bulletin, DSIS/UNDP, vol. I, no. 1 (1971).

120 *I'd be satisfied*
Conversation with the author.

121 *the sum recenty paid*
New York *Times*, 6 December 1970.

122 *A shocking aspect*
Daily Compass, 1 November 1951.

122 *If, indeed, Mr. Lie*
Letter to the Editor, New York *Times*, 16 November 1952.

125 *pronounce them "vindicated"*
Meeting of the Senate Foreign Relations Committee, 21 July 1971, reported in New York *Times*, 22 July 1971. See also New York *Times* 16 June 1972; "Profiles" (John Service, by E. J. Kahn, Jr.), *The New Yorker*, 8 April 1972, p. 91; and letter from Professor Henry Steele Commager in New York *Times*, 6 March 1972.

126 *vicious and distorted*
Lie, *In the Cause of Peace*, pp. 391, 397.

126 * *footnote*
Ibid., p. 395.

126 † *footnote*
The Memoirs of Lord Gladwyn (London: Weidenfeld & Nicolson, 1972), pp. 257–258.

128 *Lie actually sent to Washington*
Brief on Behalf of Nineteen Applicants, p. 224. See also Activities of United States Citizens Employed by the United Nations: Hearings

before the Subcommittee to Investigate the Administration of the Internal Security Act and Other Internal Security Laws of the Committee on the Judiciary, United States Senate, October 13, 14, 15, 23, 24; November 11, 12; December 1, 2, 10, 11, 17, 1952, pp. 386–390.

132 *Only a dozen were dismissed*
Conversation with the author.

132 *The International Civil Service Advisory Board opinion*
Report on Standards of Conduct in the International Civil Service, 1954. UN document COORD/CIVIL SERVICE/5.

133 *The international civil servant*
"The International Civil Servant in Law and in Fact," lecture delivered to Congregation at Oxford University, 30 May 1961, in Foote, *Hammarskjöld*, p. 348.

133 *What sort of creature*
Conor Cruise O'Brien, *To Katanga and Back: A UN Case History* (New York: Simon and Schuster, 1962), p. 55.

134 *While recognizing*
UN Note to Correspondents No. 1840, 9 July 1958.

135 *aberrant*
UN press release SG/651, 15 January 1958.

136 *Today, the UN system*
A Study of the Capacity of the United Nations Development System. Vols. I and II combined, UN document DP/5 (Geneva, 1969; UN Publication Sales No. E.70.I.10), p. 49.

136 *Another official survey*
A Study of the Feasibility of the Establishment of a Staff College to meet the needs of the Agencies of the United Nations System. Unnumbered draft report prepared by Mr. Richard Symonds at the request of the Executive Director of the United Nations Institute for Training and Research (Geneva, July 1970), pp. 1, 9. [Final version not available at time of this writing.] See also UN document A/7359, 27 November 1968, pp. 41–43.

137 *We're still in the embryonic stage*
Interview with Brian Urquhart, *The New Yorker*, 17 June 1972, p. 24.

138 *a monster, created*
New York *Times*, 15 February 1970.

139 † *footnote*
See UN documents SCC/121, 8 August 1951; SCC/148, 12 September 1952; SCC/152, 1 December 1952.

143 *There are five hundred*
UN Press Feature No. 213/Rev. 7, February 1971, p. 18.

144 *has dropped all pretense*
New York *Daily News*, 27 October 1971.

144 *the incident of the Taiwanese newsmen*
New York *Times*, 18, 22 December 1971; 7, 8 January 1972; 11, 24, 25 February 1972.

145 *who after reproaching Strong*
Delegates World Bulletin, vol. I, no. 8, 1 December 1971, p. 1.

145 *Bureaucracy*
Karl Marx, "Critique of Hegel's Philosophy of the State" (1843). *Writings of the Young Marx on Philosophy and Society*, edited and translated by Loyd D. Easton and Kurt H. Guddat (New York: Doubleday, 1967), p. 185.

146 *In 1960, Cuba was prevented*
Official Records of the Security Council, XV, 874th Meeting, 18 July 1960, p. 27. See also Thomas M. Franck, *Word Politics* (New York: Oxford, 1971), p. 60.

146 *far older than this one*
Official Records of the Security Council, XVII, 1022nd Meeting, 23 October 1962, p. 12.

146 *undoubtedly the most important*
New York *Times*, 13 December 1970.

146 *an instrument for negotiation*
Foote, *Hammarskjöld*, p. 122.

Chapter Five: "The World of Action"

147 *They didn't like me*
Joseph P. Lash, *Dag Hammarskjold: Custodian of the Brushfire Peace* (New York: Doubleday, 1961), p. 9.

147 *Amused but not interested*
Trygve Lie, *In the Cause of Peace* (New York: Macmillan, 1954), p. 416; Lash, *Hammarskjold*, p. 12.

148 *it is recorded by various biographical writers*
Sten Söderberg, *Hammarskjöld: A Pictorial Biography* (New York: Viking, 1962), pp. 6–7; Lash, *Hammarskjold*, pp. 7–8.

148 *His posthumously published "journal"*
Dag Hammarskjöld, *Markings*, translated from the Swedish *Vägmärken* by Leif Sjöberg and W. H. Auden, with a Foreword by W. H. Auden (New York: Knopf, 1964).

148 *Hammarskjöld did not say*
Gustaf Aulén, *Dag Hammarskjöld's White Book: The Meaning of Markings* (Philadelphia: Fortress Press, 1969), p. 128.

149 *an elegiac essay*
Castle Hill, publication of the Dag Hammarskjöld Foundation (Uppsala, 1971).

149   *a massive Småland block of granite*
      Sven Stolpe, *Dag Hammarskjöld: A Spiritual Portrait* (New York:
      Scribner's, 1966), p. 17.

149   *an oedipal culmination*
      See Inaugural Address to the Swedish Academy, 20 December 1954,
      in *Dag Hammarskjöld, Servant of Peace: A Selection of His
      Speeches and Statements*, edited by Wilder Foote (New York:
      Harper & Row, 1963), pp. 63–79.

149   *reserve and isolation*
      Stolpe, *Hammarskjöld*, p. 17.

149   *a perpetual conflict*
      Letter to Bo Beskow, in Bo Beskow, *Dag Hammarskjöld: Strictly
      Personal* (New York: Doubleday, 1969), p. 33.

149   *something to live for*
      Markings, p. 85.

149   *How well I understand*
      Ibid., p. 82.

150   *The years before his appointment*
      Stolpe, *Hammarskjöld*, p. 113.

150   *an intricate pattern*
      Söderberg, *Hammarskjöld*.

150   *We knew him*
      Conversation with the author.

150   *it is difficult to appreciate*
      Brian Urquhart, "Books: The Point of Rest," *The New Yorker*, 31
      October 1964, p. 244.

150   *That we all — every one*
      Markings, p. 13.

151   *the alienation of great pride*
      Ibid., p. 64.

151   *My salvation*
      Letter to Bo Beskow, 24 November 1954, in Beskow, *Hammarskjöld*,
      p. 32.

151   *I felt as if I were walking*
      Winston S. Churchill, *The Second World War*: Vol. I, *The Gathering
      Storm* (Boston: Houghton Mifflin, 1948), chap. 17, p. 667.

151   *You are dedicated*
      Markings, p. 110.

151   *Success — for the glory*
      Ibid., p. 150.

151   *A fable*
      Ibid., p. 64.

152 *a sort of white book*
Markings, undated prefatory letter to Leif Belfrage, p. v.

153 *To me it is a completely absurd thought*
Quoted in Henry P. Van Dusen, *Dag Hammarskjöld: The Statesman and His Faith*, pp. 221–222.

153 *These entries provide*
Markings, prefatory letter, p. v.

153 *no man can draw*
Ibid., p. ix.

154 *I should say . . . such criticisms are unjust*
Ibid., pp. xii–xiii.

154 *arose from his feelings of loneliness*
Urquhart, *The New Yorker*, 31 October 1964, p. 233.

154 *Strange that Hammarskjöld*
Eyvind Bartels, "Dag Hammarskjöld og Hans Gud," *Kristeligt Dagblads Forlag* (Copenhagen), 1964; excerpts translated in Stolpe, *Hammarskjöld*, pp. 103–112.

155 *You ask yourself*
Markings, p. 144.

155 *relentless earnestness*
Ibid., p. xviii.

155 *The fun*
Ibid., p. 201.

157 *Those who knew Dag Hammarskjöld*
Quoted in Stolpe, *Hammarskjöld*, p. 41.

157 *There was nothing formidable*
Quoted in Emery Kelen, *Hammarskjöld* (New York: Putnam, 1966), p. 89.

157 *august aloofness*
Urquhart, *The New Yorker*, 31 October 1964, pp. 232, 233–234.

158 *Intimacy with him*
André Malraux, *Felled Oaks: Conversation with de Gaulle* (New York: Holt, Rhinehart & Winston, 1972), p. 22.

158 *In my constant dialogue*
Quoted in Van Dusen, *Hammarskjöld*, p. 111.

158 *with a few friends and aides*
Lash, *Hammarskjold*, p. 220.

158 *He could smile*
Kelen, *Hammarskjöld*, p. 127.

158 *apart from any value*
Markings, p. 166.

159 *You listen badly*
Ibid., p. 108.

159 *In life*
Urquhart, *The New Yorker*, 31 October 1964, p. 244.

159 *Mr. Urquhart's own study*
Brian Urquhart, *Hammarskjöld* (New York: Knopf, 1972).

160 *What distinguishes the "elite"*
Markings, p. 173.

160 *In our era*
Ibid., p. 122.

161 *The Secretary-General*
Urquhart, *The New Yorker*, 31 October 1964, p. 239.

162 *It has rightly been said*
Foote, *Hammarskjöld*, pp. 93–94.

163 *develop as an instrument*
Ibid., pp. 376, 222, 239.

163 *I spoke before . . . instrument directly*
Ibid., pp. 208, 150, 336.

164 *Hammarskjöld's view*
Lash, *Hammarskjöld*, p. 143.

164 *exceeded his authorization*
Conversation with the author.

164 *For the Secretary-General*
"The International Civil Servant in Law and in Fact," lecture delivered to Congregation at Oxford University, 30 May 1961, in Foote, *Hammarskjöld*, p. 345.

165 *The UN exists*
Reproduced as editorial in *International Herald Tribune*, 22 September 1971.

167 *Dumb, my naked body*
Markings, p. 207.

168 *I knew only too well*
Transcript of extemporaneous remarks to the staff, 10 April 1958, in Foote, *Hammarskjöld*, p. 167.

169 *His concern for the staff*
United Nations *Secretariat News*, vol. XV, Edition 16, 29 September 1961.

169 *Hammarskjöld's first reports and proposals*
UN documents A/2533, 2 November 1953, Report of the Secretary-General on Personnel Policy; A/2554, 12 November 1953, Report of the Secretary-General on the Organization of the Secretariat; A/2731, 21 September 1954, Report of the Secretary-General (incorporating Report of the Secretary-General's Survey Group on Reorganization).

170 *a single supervisory level*
UN document A/2731, 21 September 1954, p. 2.

170 *in order to bring more closely*
Ibid., p. 2.

170 *A set of generally grim recommendations*
UN document A/2533, 2 November 1953; General Assembly resolution 782 (VIII) A, B, and C, 9 December 1953.

170 *a press release by the Secretary-General*
UN press release SG/353, 18 November 1953. See also New York *Times*, 4 and 14 November 1953.

171 *From the beginning*
UN document series SCC, 1953–1955; with particular reference to SCC/172, 20 January 1954; SCC/191, 26 January 1955, pp. 5–7; and SCC/207, 22 September 1955, pp. 1–3.

171 *My personal experience*
UN press release SG/728, 9 October 1958, p. 11.

173 *on a sort of steeplechase*
Lash, *Hammarskjöld*, p. 6.

174 *Let me mention also*
Statement on His Re-Election to a Second Term, before the General Assembly, 26 September 1957, in Foote, *Hammarskjöld*, p. 149.

174 *There is only one answer*
Last Words to the Staff, 8 September 1961, in Foote, *Hammarskjöld*, pp. 376–377.

175 *he had a tendency*
Stolpe, *Hammarskjöld*, p. 69.

175 *consciousness of superiority*
Urquhart, *The New Yorker*, 31 October 1964, p. 233.

175 *serve gladly for the value of serving*
"Addresses given by the Secretary-General, Mr. Dag Hammarskjöld, and by Mr. R. V. Klein, Chairman of the Staff Committee, on the occasion of Staff Day, General Assembly Hall, 8 September 1961, 4:30 P.M." Unnumbered UN document circulated to UN staff September 1961, p. 5.

175 *In our era*
Markings, p. 122.

176 *Live your individuality*
Ibid., p. 53.

176 *Forward! Whatever distance*
Ibid., p. 145.

176 *Only he who at every moment*
Ibid., p. 96.

176 *the 'great' commitment*
Ibid., p. 131.

176 *ordinary everyday*
Ibid., p. 133.

178 *not only tolerated*
Van Dusen, *Hammarskjöld*, p. 111.

179 *It was difficult*
UN *Secretariat News*, 29 September 1961.

179 *he quickly brought together*
Lash, *Hammarskjöld*, p. 42.

179 *between a youngish headmaster*
Conor Cruise O'Brien, *To Katanga and Back: A UN Case History* (New York: Simon and Schuster, 1962), p. 51.

179 *"One-Man Job"*
Lash, *Hammarskjöld*, pp. 281–292.

179 *What was legally stipulated*
Ibid.

181 *a full stop*
Eyvind Bartels, "Dag Hammarskjöld og Hans Gud," as cited in Stolpe, *Hammarskjöld*, pp. 103–112.

181 *The first duty*
Transcript of extemporaneous remarks to the staff, 10 April 1958, in Foote, *Hammarskjöld*, p. 167.

181 *The UN organizations*
Statement by the President of the Federation of International Civil Servants Associations before the Salary Review Committee, 22 July 1971, in Staff Committee Bulletin (FICSA Report). UN document SCB/267, 22 July 1971, p. 6.

181 *It must be said, however*
Personnel Questions: Report of the Joint Inspection Unit on personnel problems in the United Nations. UN document A/8454 (Parts I and II), 5 October 1971, pp. 29, 186, 188.

182 *Naturally, however, the experiences*
Introduction to the Annual Report, 1959–1960, 31 August 1960, in Foote, *Hammarskjöld*, p. 300.

182 *The full text*
"Addresses given by the Secretary-General, Mr. Dag Hammarskjöld, and by Mr. R. V. Klein, Chairman of the Staff Committee, on the occasion of Staff Day, General Assembly Hall, 8 September 1961, 4:30 P.M." Unnumbered UN document circulated to UN staff, September 1961.

184 *no unauthorized access*
UN Note to Correspondents No. 1701, 16 December 1957, p. 9.

184 *Bang-Jensen was suspended*
UN Note to Correspondents No. 1701, 16 December 1957; UN press release SG/645, 21 December 1957.

185 *the disputed papers were burned*
UN press release SG/654, 24 January 1958.

185 *The investigating committee censured Bang-Jensen*
UN press release SG/651, 15 January 1958. See also UN press release SG/652, 18 January 1958; UN Note to Correspondents No. 1714, 21 January 1958, pp. 14–16, 18, 21; Note to Correspondents No. 1727, 6 February 1958, pp. 11–15; Note to Correspondents No. 1736, 19 February 1958.

186 *The finding of this disciplinary committee*
Excerpts from Joint Disciplinary Committee Report dated 5 June 1958, appended to UN Note to Correspondents No. 1840, 9 July 1958.

186 *terminated his association*
UN press release SG/700, 3 July 1958.

186 *completely unbalanced*
Conversation with the author.

186 *Representative extracts from Hammarskjöld's letter*
". . . I am forced to the conclusion that you have been guilty of behaviour even more reprehensible than that reviewed by the Joint Disciplinary Committee. . . . The Rapporteur [of the Special Committee on Hungary states] that he regards your behaviour 'to say the least, as unbecoming a member of the Secretariat,' that he is of the opinion that you did considerable harm and that your allegations were largely childish and without foundation, and that he reserved the necessity of raising the situation 'at a higher level so that proper disciplinary action may be taken to see that it stops.' . . .

"While it is not necessary to my decision . . . I wish nevertheless to lay particular stress on my conclusion that the charges . . . are borne out by the evidence. I need hardly emphasize that your behaviour towards the Rapporteur by itself constitutes sufficient grounds for dismissal for misconduct by any member of the Secretariat. It is unthinkable . . . and cannot be countenanced. . . .

"With respect to your refusal . . . to deliver the papers in your possession for safekeeping . . . [this] revealed a most serious and indeed dangerous lack of judgment. . . . It is further my view that any moral reservations which might have prevented you from obeying my instructions do not ameliorate the impropriety of your conduct as a member of the Secretariat in refusing an order by the Secretary-General relative to official papers. It is my view that if you considered your clear official duty to acknowledge my authority in Secretariat matters to be in conflict with your private moral convictions arising from an unauthorized assumption of authority, it was your duty to resign from the service.

"I endorse the Joint Disciplinary Committee's opinion that the general charge against you of grave misconduct could be regarded as amply justified on the sole basis of [part of the charges alone]. In addition, as I have stated above, I consider that your conduct with respect to the [officials named] was in itself particularly reprehensible and unbecoming an official of the United Nations and constituted grave misconduct. Your conduct as dealt with [in the charges] indicate [sic] so serious a lapse of judgment and a lack of understanding of the responsibility of a United Nations official as to indicate that your continued employment by the United Nations would be inconsistent with the maintenance of a high level of efficient service. I fully concur with the Joint Disciplinary Committee's conclusion that 'the evidence as a whole reveals on the part of Mr. Bang-Jensen a pattern of behaviour incompatible with membership in the Secretariat of the United Nations.' " Letter of 3 July 1958 from United Nations Secretary-General Dag Hammarskjöld to Mr. Povl Bang-Jensen. Full text appended to UN Note to Correspondents No. 1840, 9 July 1958.

186 *was rejected by the Administrative Tribunal*
Judgements of the United Nations Administrative Tribunal, Numbers 71 to 86, 1958–1962: UN document AT/DEC/71 to 86, pp. 15–28, Judgement No. 74. See also unnumbered UN press releases of 22 December 1959 and 1 January 1960.

187 *Challenged on this point*
UN Note to Correspondents No. 1714, 21 January 1958, p. 16.

187 *a staff representative*
UN Note to Correspondents No. 1727, 6 February 1958, p. 11.

187 *the committee was not a formal group*
Ibid., p. 11.

187 *insulting a Danish reporter*
UN Note to Correspondents No. 1701, 16 December 1957, p. 8.

188 *formally requested by a member state*
UN Note to Correspondents No. 1840, 9 July 1958; covering statement.

190 *laid end to end*
UN Press Feature No. 213/Rev. 7, February 1971, p. 17.

190 *drowning in its own words*
New York *Times*, 26 May 1970.

190 *a more substantial investment*
New York *Times*, 15 November 1970.

191 *footnote*
Publications and Documentation of the United Nations: Report on Recurrent Publications, by Robert M. Macy, Joint Inspection Unit, p. 16. UN document A/8362, 20 August 1971.

191 *A refreshingly frank treatment*
Ibid.

192 *a 219-page report*
Report of the Special Committee on the Rationalization of the Procedures and Organization of the General Assembly. UN docu-

ment A/8426: Official Records, Twenty-sixth Session, Supplement No. 26, 1971.

192   *The report takes the bull*
New York *Times*, 4 November 1971.

192   *In one sequence*
New York *Times*, 2 December 1969.

193   *the 1971 FICSA summary*
See Chapter Four of the present work.

193   *Sir Robert Jackson's 1969 Study*
See Chapter Seven of the present work.

193   *Language is not only*
Sunday *Times* (London), 10 October 1971.

194   *simpler and smoother methods*
Transcript of press conference, 5 February 1959, in Foote, *Hammarskjöld*, p. 263.

Chapter Six: " 'Collapse' Would Be Better"

197   *I may not be getting anywhere*
Life, 8 May 1970, p. 48.

198   *Mr. Thant, undramatic*
New York *Times*, 25 October 1970.

198   *Considering how much*
Sunday *Times* (London), 6 August 1967.

198   *About this débâcle*
Ibid.

199   *I can tolerate*
Ibid.

199   *a safety valve*
The *Times* (London), 22 October 1970.

199   *the best thing*
Louis Halasz, "Signs of UN Maturity," Rome *Daily American*, 3–4 January 1971.

200   *a long-time member*
New York *Times*, 10 June 1972.

200   *United Nations, whatever else it does*
New York *Times*, 17 September 1969.

200   *While the generals*
New York *Times*, 12 August 1970.

201   *footnote*
Official Records of the Security Council, XIX, 1141st Meeting, 7 August 1964, pp. 9–10.

201   *Undoubtedly Viet Nam*
      The Times (London), 22 October 1970.

202   *an instrument for negotiation*
      Dag Hammarskjöld, *Servant of Peace: A Selection of His Speeches and Statements,* edited by Wilder Foote (New York: Harper & Row, 1963), p. 122.

202   *what has been lost*
      "The Linnaeus Tradition and Our Time," Presidential Address at the Swedish Academy, 20 December 1957, in Foote, *Hammarskjöld,* p. 158.

202   *exceptional diligence and devotion*
      New York *Times,* 29 December 1971.

202   *One of the criticisms*
      New York *Times,* 31 December 1971.

202   *the Secretary-General has*
      New York *Times,* 26 December 1971.

203   *Dag Hammarskjöld was*
      The Times (London), 23 December 1971.

204   *Even the frustrations*
      The New Yorker, 29 July 1967, p. 23.

204   *Lord Gladwyn comments*
      The Memoirs of Lord Gladwyn (London: Weidenfeld & Nicolson, 1972), p. 250.

205   *persistent illusion*
      UN press release SG/SM/1531, 16 September 1971.

205   *you can't have a strong Secretary-General*
      "Profiles" (Francis T. P. Plimpton, by Geoffrey T. Hellman), *The New Yorker,* 4 December 1971, p. 120.

205   *one of the few solid U.N. accomplishments*
      Ibid., p. 116.

205   *feels the need*
      General Assembly records A/PV.1865, 14 October 1970.

206   *If a mountain wall*
      Statement on his Re-Election to a Second Term, before the General Assembly, 26 September 1957, in Foote, *Hammarskjöld,* p. 149.

207   *It is not for me*
      Trygve Lie, *In the Cause of Peace* (New York: Macmillan, 1954), p. 404. Original text of Lie's statement in Official Records of the General Assembly, Seventh Session, 413th Meeting, 10 March 1953.

207   *In 1971, Gunnar Jarring*
      New York *Times,* 24, 31 December 1971; *Time,* 13 September 1971.

207   *his own strong views*
      New York *Times,* 25 April 1971.

207 *footnote*
when H. L. Keenleyside. See New York *Times,* 16 October 1951. *A recent administrative circular:* UN document ST/ADM/SER.A/1303, 24 January 1969.

208 *a negative neutrality*
Address before the Students Association, Copenhagen, 2 May 1959, in Foote, *Hammarskjöld,* p. 209. See also UN Note to Correspondents No. 2347, 12 June 1961, pp. 6–31.

209 *Thus, if the office*
Statement of Reply to Attacks upon his Office and Conduct of Operations in the Congo, before the General Assembly, 26 September 1960, in Foote, *Hammarskjöld,* p. 316.

210 *the United Nations has only*
New York *Times,* 26 May 1970.

211 *Criticisms of the United Nations' weaknesses*
New York *Times,* 16 September 1970.

211 *It often happens*
Emilio Arenales of Guatemala, to the General Assembly. UN document A/PV.1752, 21 December 1968.

211 *The parochialism and the lack*
Miss Angie E. Brooks of Liberia, to the General Assembly. UN document A/PV.1839, 15 September 1970.

211 *It is like entering*
Press conference at the New York Hilton, 21 October 1970.

211 *We are in a beleaguered fortress*
New York *Times,* 18 October 1970.

212 *Their jargon*
New York *Times,* 21 June 1970; *Time,* 27 July 1970.

212 *I'm happy I was able*
New York *Times,* 16 October 1970.

212 *the house of illusion*
Boston *Globe,* 20 October 1971.

212 *Do go to some meeting*
New York *Times,* 18 October 1970.

212 *We are no Vatican*
Transcript of extemporaneous remarks to the staff, 10 April 1958, in Foote, *Hammarskjöld,* p. 168.

212 *"The United Nations," said Hammarskjöld*
Address to the American Jewish Committee, New York, 10 April 1957, in Foote, *Hammarskjöld,* p. 128.

213 *this kind of war*
New York *Times,* 15 September 1965.

213 *confident that substantial relief*
The *Times* (London), 7 June 1971.

214 *initially found Government representatives*
New York *Times,* 23 January 1972.

215 *was said to have no intention*
New York *Times,* 25 November 1971.

215 *a chief executive officer*
"The International Civil Servant in Law and in Fact," lecture delivered to Congregation at Oxford University, 30 May 1961, in Foote, *Hammarskjöld,* p. 336.

215 *has unrivalled possibilities*
Brian Urquhart, "Books: The Point of Rest," *The New Yorker,* 31 October 1964, p. 239.

215 *has a great deal of power*
New York *Times,* 26 December 1971.

216 *large and latent assets*
Ernest A. Gross, "Memo to the Secretary-General," Op-Ed page article, New York *Times,* 3 February 1972.

216 *Such a pledge*
Ibid.

216 *What voice has been raised*
Letter to the Editor, New York *Times,* 16 November 1952.

Chapter Seven: The Whole of Life

217 *the vast and remarkable report*
A Study of the Capacity of the United Nations Development System. Vols. I and II combined, UN document DP/5 (Geneva, 1969; UN sales no. E.70.I.10). (Hereinafter cited as Jackson Study.)

218 *For many years*
Ibid., p. 13.

218 *Sir Robert's report*
V. Duckworth-Barker, *Breakthrough to Tomorrow* (UN Centre for Economic and Social Information; UN sales no. E.71.5).

219 *In its efforts*
Jackson Study, p. 16.

220 *Objectively regarded*
Ibid., p. 147.

220 *At the headquarters level*
Ibid., p. iii.

221 *there is a tendency*
Gunnar Myrdal, *The Challenge of World Poverty* (New York: Pantheon, 1970), p. 3.

221 *From the point of view*
Ibid., p. 44.

222   *The UN development system*
Editorial, *Life*, 8 May 1970, p. 48.

223   *The first one is positive*
Jackson Study, p. ii.

224   *a still unborn United Nations*
Lewis Mumford, "The Megamachine — III," *The New Yorker*, 24 October 1970, p. 96.

225   *are, or should be, world authorities*
Jackson Study, p. 65.

226   *an expenditure of roughly*
Ibid., p. 10.

226   *in the category of non-worthwhile*
Ibid., p. 73.

226   *exceeded — sometimes by a considerable*
Ibid., p. 88.

227   *A questionable amount*
Budget Estimates for the Financial Year 1972: Restructuring the Department of Economic and Social Affairs: A Response to the Second Development Decade. Report of the Secretary-General. UN document A/C.5/1380, 11 October 1971, p. 7.

227   *footnote*
Letter to the Editor, New York *Times*, 29 March 1970.

228   *learnt to resist change*
Jackson Study, p. v.

228   *Twenty years on*
Ibid., p. 120.

229   *I do not imply*
Ibid., p. iv.

229   *In reality*
Myrdal, *The Challenge of World Poverty*, p. 13.

229   *many experts continue*
Denis Goulet, *The Cruel Choice: A New Concept in the Theory of Development* (New York: Atheneum, 1971), p. 16.

230   *there are very few*
Jackson Study, p. 49.

230   *Superstition or poor hygiene*
Goulet, *The Cruel Choice*, pp. 49–50.

230   *one basic reason*
Criteria and Methods of Evaluation: Problems and Approaches. UN document UNITAR 1, 1969, p. 55. See also M. T. Farvar, J. P. Milton, *The Careless Technology* (New York: Natural History Press, 1972).

231   *From the standpoint*
V. L. Urquidi, "The So-Called Social Aspects of Economic Develop-

ment," *Developing the Underdeveloped Countries*, edited by Alan B. Mountjoy (London: Macmillan, 1971), p. 80.

231 *The economist foresees*
Ibid., p. 81.

231 *Does the economy exist*
Hyman G. Rickover, "Technology and the Citizen," address at the Publishers' Lunch Club, 7 January 1965. (Privately circulated document, in possession of present author.)

232 *Notwithstanding impressive mastery*
Goulet, *The Cruel Choice*, p. 16.

232 *the wisdom of the world*
Sebastian de Grazia, *Of Time, Work, and Leisure* (New York: Twentieth Century Fund, 1962), p. 5.

232 *Every human society*
Goulet, *The Cruel Choice*, p. 239.

233 *"The fish," wrote Horace*
Odes, Book III, i.

233 *an International Environmental Agency*
George F. Kennan, "To Prevent a World Wasteland: A Proposal," *Foreign Affairs*, April 1970, p. 408.

235 *Now a stage is being reached*
Address by Mr. A. Malik, President of the 26th United Nations General Assembly, 21 September 1971. UN document A/PV.1934, 21 September 1971.

235 *At the age of 80*
Time, 17 January 1972.

237 *The question of mandates*
World Population: A Challenge to the United Nations and Its System of Agencies. A Report of a National Policy Panel established by the United Nations Association of the United States of America. New York, May 1969, pp. 22, 24, 40.

237 *Unless the United Nations*
New York *Times*, 8 June 1969.

238 *With the exception of work*
Hugh L. Keenleyside, *International Aid: A Summary* (Toronto: McClelland and Stewart, 1966), p. 75.

238 *There is widespread criticism*
Jackson Study, p. 9.

239 *a Professional staff member*
Personnel Questions: Report of the Joint Inspection Unit on personnel problems in the United Nations. UN document A/8454 (Parts I and II), 5 October 1971, pp. 21–22, 149. (Hereinafter cited as JIU, Personnel Problems.)

239 *footnote*
A Study of the Feasibility of the Establishment of a Staff College

to meet the needs of the Agencies of the United Nations System.
Unnumbered draft report prepared by Mr. Richard Symonds at the
request of the Executive Director of the United Nations Institute
for Training and Research (Geneva, July 1970), p. 12. [Final version
not available at time of this writing.]

240 *As far as the quality*
Jackson Study, pp. 79, 119.

241 *The proportion of staff members*
JIU, Personnel Problems, pp. 47–48, 53.

241 *the average age of recruitment*
UN document A/AC.150/R.4, 21 December 1971, p. 24 *note.*

241 *Today, the UN system*
Jackson Study, p. 49.

242 *footnote*
Ibid., p. 41; UN document ST/ADM/SER.A/1578, 20 January 1972
(pending revision of ST/AI/161).

243 *Beyond this, precise staffing*
Budget Estimates FY 1972, A/C.5/1380, 11 October 1971, pp. 24–25.

243 *The UN Development system*
Jackson Study, p. vi.

243 *Here is the letter*
Ibid., pp. i, xi.

Chapter Eight: "A Body with a Different Structure"

245 *We may believe*
Statement on his Re-Election to a Second Term, before the General
Assembly, 26 September 1957, in *Dag Hammarskjöld, Servant of
Peace: A Selection of His Speeches and Statements,* edited by Wilder
Foote (New York: Harper & Row, 1963), p. 149.

245 *Only those who*
"The Linnaeus Tradition and Our Time," Presidential Address at
the Swedish Academy, 20 December 1957, in ibid., pp. 157–158.

245 *the post-retirement writings of U Thant*
U Thant, "Reflections of a Mediator," *World,* 4 July 1972, pp. 38–41.

248 *In our progress-minded society*
Barry Commoner, *The Closing Circle* (New York: Knopf, 1971),
p. 300.

249 *the final, least tangible*
"New Diplomatic Techniques in a New World," Address to the
Foreign Policy Association, New York, 21 October 1953, in Foote,
Hammarskjöld, p. 51.

249 *We do not think*
J. William Fulbright, "In Thrall to Fear," *The New Yorker,* 8
January 1972, p. 58.

Appendix

National clearance procedures for United States citizens who are applicants for positions in the United Nations international Secretariat: extract from United States Executive Order 10422 of 9 January 1953, as amended by Executive Order 10459 of 2 June 1953 (paragraphs 3.7 and 4)

The preliminary investigation conducted by the Civil Service Commission shall be a full background investigation conforming to the investigative standards of the Civil Service Commission, and shall include reference to the following:

(a) Federal Bureau of Investigation files.
(b) Civil Service Commission files.
(c) Military and naval intelligence files as appropriate.
(d) The files of any other appropriate Government investigative or intelligence agency.
(e) The files of appropriate committees of the Congress.
(f) Local law-enforcement files at the place of residence and employment of the person, including municipal, county, and State law-enforcement files.
(g) Schools and colleges attended by the person.
(h) Former employers of the person.
(i) References given by the person.
(j) Any other appropriate source.

However, in the case of short-term employees whose employment does not exceed ninety days, such investigation need not include reference to sub-paragraphs (f) through (j) of this paragraph.

Whenever information disclosed with respect to any person being investigated is derogatory, within the standard set forth in Part II of this order, the United States Civil Service Commission shall forward such information to the Federal Bureau of Investigation, and the Bureau shall conduct a full field investigation of such person: *Provided*, that in all cases involving a United States citizen employed or being considered for employment on the internationally recruited staff of the United Nations for a period exceeding ninety days, the investigation required by this Part shall be a full field investigation conducted by the Federal Bureau of Investigation.

The full text of Executive Order 10459 appears as the Appendix to Annex I of UN document A/2533, 2 November 1953.